A BEGINNER'S GUIDE TO QUALITY IN MANUFACTURING

Also available from Quality Press

A TQM Approach to Achieving Manufacturing Excellence
A. Richard Shores

Statistical Quality Control Methods
Irving W. Burr

SPC Tools for Operators
John T. Burr

Statistical Process Control Methods—For Long and Short Runs
Gary K. Griffith

The Self-Instructional Route to Statistical Process Control and Just-in-Time Manufacturing
I. Louis Bare and Bebe Bare

SPC for Practitioners: Special Cases and Continuous Processes
Gary Fellers, PhD

Quantitative Methods for Quality and Productivity Improvement
Marilyn K. Hart and Robert F. Hart

Statistical Process Control in Manufacturing
J. Bert Keats and Douglas C. Montgomery

Glossary and Tables for Statistical Control, Second Edition
ASQC Statistics Division

To request a complimentary 80-page catalog of publications, call 800-952-6587.

A BEGINNER'S GUIDE TO QUALITY IN MANUFACTURING

Michael Tedaldi
Fred Scaglione
Vincent Russotti

ASQC Quality Press
Milwaukee, Wisconsin

A BEGINNER'S GUIDE TO QUALITY IN MANUFACTURING

Michael Tedaldi, Fred Scaglione, and Vincent Russotti

Library of Congress Cataloging-in-Publication Data

Tedaldi, Michael
   A beginner's guide to quality in manufacturing/Michael Tedaldi,
Fred Scaglione, Vincent Russotti.
      p. cm.
   Includes bibliographical references and index.
   ISBN (invalid) 0-87389-186-6
    1. Quality control.   2. Production management—Quality control.
   I. Scaglione, Fred.   II. Russotti, Vincent.   III. Title.
   TS156.T425   1992
   658.5'62—dc20   92-3731
                                                             CIP

© 1992 by ASQC Quality Press
All rights reserved. No part of this book may be reproduced in any form or by any means, electronic, mechanical, photocopying, recording, or otherwise, without the prior written permission of the publisher.

10 9 8 7 6 5 4 3 2 1

ISBN 0-87389-186-6

Acquisitions Editor: Jeanine L. Lau
Production Editor: Mary Beth Nilles
Marketing Administrator: Susan Westergard
Set in 11-point Bookman by Patricia L. Coogan.
Cover design by Laura Bober.
Printed and bound by BookCrafters.

For a free copy of the ASQC Quality Press Publications Catalog, including ASQC membership information, call 800-952-6587.

Printed in the United States of America

 Printed on recycled paper

 ASQC
Quality Press
611 East Wisconsin Avenue
Milwaukee, Wisconsin 53202

CONTENTS

Preface ix

Chapter 1 **The Product**

    1.1   Introduction.. 1
    1.2   Product Specifications and Requirements.............. 2
    1.3   Production Costs, Selling Price, and Company Profits... 7

Chapter 2 **The Process of Making the Product**

    2.1   Introduction.. 21
    2.2   Manufacturing Processes 21
    2.3   Basic Steps in the Manufacturing Process........... 22
    2.4   Planning the Manufacturing Process 23
    2.5   Flowcharting the Process 31

Chapter 3 **The Facility**

    3.1   Introduction.. 43
    3.2   Components of the Facility.................................. 43
    3.3   Guidelines for Arranging the Facility 44
    3.4   Facility Layout 47

Chapter 4 **Quality Control**

    4.1   Introduction.. 59
    4.2   Inspection and the Quality Product 59
    4.3   Inspection Points and the Manufacturing Process 62
    4.4   Basic Resources for a Quality Control Program ... 74

Chapter 5 **Incoming Inspection**

    5.1   Introduction.. 81
    5.2   Measuring Quality 82

	5.3	Acceptable Quality Level	86
	5.4	Measuring Quality Through Sample Inspections	88
	5.5	Normal, Tightened, and Reduced Inspection	95
	5.6	Single, Double, and Multiple Sampling Plans	102
	5.7	Classes of Defects	109
	5.8	100 Percent Inspection	111
	5.9	Rejects	112
	5.10	Inspection Records and Average Quality Level	112
	5.11	Supplier Certification	114

Chapter 6   Statistical Quality Control

6.1	Introduction	125
6.2	Process Control Sites	125
6.3	Variations in the Manufacturing Process	128
6.4	Measuring Process Capabilities	129
6.5	Process AQLs	133
6.6	Normal Distribution Curves and Measures of Central Tendency	133
6.7	Measuring Quality Level by Attribute	153
6.8	Controlling the Variation	155
6.9	Control Charts	156
6.10	First Piece Inspection	168

Chapter 7   The Mathematics of Quality Control

7.1	Introduction	177
7.2	True Quality Level vs. Measured Quality Level	177
7.3	Probability and Expectation	178
7.4	The Binomial Distribution	182
7.5	Cumulative Probability	184
7.6	Levels of Confidence	184
7.7	Operating Characteristic Curves	187
7.8	Tightened Inspection	190

Chapter 8   Final Inspection

8.1	Introduction	199
8.2	Need for Final Inspection	199
8.3	Final Inspection and Testing at the Closet Door Manufacturer	204
8.4	Final Inspection and Testing at the Bakery	205
8.5	The "Fitness for Use" Decision	206

Chapter 9   Quality Control and Field Data

9.1	Introduction	213
9.2	Reasons for Field Returns	213

9.3	Field Returns and Customer Complaints	215
9.4	Reaching Out to the Customer	219
9.5	Publications and Independent Market Research Organizations	221
9.6	Competitive Analysis	222
9.7	The Bottom Line	222

Chapter 10 The Quality Improvement Loop

10.1	Introduction	227
10.2	Observation	227
10.3	Analysis	228
10.4	Action	236
10.5	Repeating the Cycle	237

Chapter 11 Test Procedures, Reports, Equipment, and Calibration

11.1	Introduction	243
11.2	Test Procedures	243
11.3	Test Reports	247
11.4	Test Equipment	248
11.5	Calibration	250

Chapter 12 A Brief History of the Quality Movement

12.1	Introduction	257
12.2	Quality During the Industrial Revolution	258
12.3	Bell Laboratories and the Statistics of Quality Control	258
12.4	Quality Control Goes to War	259
12.5	Quality Spreads to Japan	260
12.6	International Competition Based on Quality	263
12.7	The United States Responds	263
12.8	An Introduction to Quality Assurance	264
12.9	Management's Role	270
12.10	Continuous Improvement and Zero Defects	271

Chapter 13 People of Quality

13.1	Introduction	277
13.2	The Evolution of the Quality Professional	278
13.3	Quality Is Everybody's Job	279
13.4	Management's Role	280
13.5	Enlisting the Troops	284
13.6	Quality Means People	286

Index 291

PREFACE

This book teaches the fundamental principles of quality control as they apply to the manufacturing process. It is aimed at the high school or college student studying the manufacturing process in either a technical high school or college, as part of a vocational education or industrial engineering curriculum. It is also applicable to the business student interested in gaining insight into the manufacturing process and quality control. Finally, this book can provide a basis for training programs at manufacturing facilities.

The book prepares the student to understand quality control principles by first teaching the basics of the manufacturing process. The text uses three products as vehicles to teach the concepts of efficient manufacturing and quality control practices. The student starts by learning how to specify products and manufacture them. Quality control concepts are then applied to the products and the associated manufacturing processes.

Throughout, the book focuses on the purpose of the quality control process: to increase both profit and productivity. The three products used to illustrate the concepts of manufacturing and quality control will also demonstrate how quality control practices create higher yields while reducing material and labor costs.

This book presents the total quality picture in an understandable step-by-step manner. It provides a model for a complete quality control program in a modern manufacturing environment.

Every chapter concludes with questions aimed at reinforcing the concepts presented in that chapter. As an additional feature, each chapter recommends an appropriate project. Students specify their own products, set up manufacturing facilities and apply the proper quality control techniques. These combined end-of-chapter exercises will not only reinforce the concepts, they will also integrate them.

The idea of achieving quality in all facets of commercial endeavor has become popular, and with good reason. Competition for markets is at an all-time high. This book presents a rational approach for ensuring a place in the market. It enables the student to learn and prosper.

CHAPTER 1

THE PRODUCT

1.1 Introduction

The goal of most companies is to earn a profit—to make money, pure and simple. For manufacturing firms, this primary aim leads to several secondary but equally important goals.

Manufacturers must make a product that satisfies the needs of their customers. People who buy a manufacturer's product require it to perform specific functions. Cars must run. Watches must tell time. Chairs must support the people who sit on them. Clothes must fit and provide warmth. If a car starts but has no power, or if it cannot hold the road in rainy weather, the customer will not be satisfied. If a manufacturer's watches do not always tell time accurately, consumers will quickly lose confidence in the brand name. Eventually, such manufacturers will have trouble finding customers to buy their products; and if they cannot sell, they cannot make money.

Manufacturers must be able to make a profit on the items they produce. They must be able to sell their products at a price which allows them to compete with similar items of equal quality. At the same time, they must be able to manufacture the products at a cost which is far enough below the selling price to give them a reasonable return for their labors.

This chapter will explore the ways in which these two goals—satisfying a customer's needs and making a profit—are connected. We will examine the things customers look for in the products they buy and the ways in which manufacturers satisfy these needs. We will also analyze the costs involved in manufacturing a product. Finally, we will see how using quality control (QC) techniques will not only satisfy the customer's needs but actually reduce production costs and increase profits.

1.2 Product Specifications and Requirements

In this section we will learn about customers' specifications and how manufacturers characterize the product to give customers what they want.

Customers' Specifications

Manufacturers satisfy customers by giving them what they want. The things a customer wants from a product are called the customer's *specifications*. Customers will judge the quality of a product according to how well it conforms to their specifications. The manufacturer's first step in making a satisfactory product is to learn what the customer is looking for from the item. Here are some examples.

A loaf of bread: The customer's expectations here are quite simple. The customer expects the bread to taste good, be nutritious, look appealing, and be fresh.

A closet door: Here again, the expectations are understandable. The door must fit the closet opening, be easy to install, and look nice.

An AM radio: The customer wants the radio to sound good, receive all available stations, and look nice in its setting.

Manufacturer's Specifications

It's fairly easy to see what the customer expects from a product because we have had experience in being customers. Manufacturers, however, must go further. Once they have identified the customer's specifications, they must translate them into a useful series of measures. These measures will guide the production process and tell when the customer is satisfied. Manufacturers must develop their own specifications which are more specific than those of the customer. The bread manufacturer, for example, must understand in detail what makes bread tasty, nutritious, and fresh. For each of these three examples, here is what the manufacturers must do to specify the product.

Bread: The loaf must weigh 1 pound. It must be 10" long, 4" wide, and 5" high. A chemical analysis must reveal a predetermined content of vitamins and nutrients. The color is important to create the proper look. The bread must pass a master baker's taste test. The ingredients must also be fresh to ensure proper taste.

The closet door: The door must be 6'8" high, 2'6" wide, and 1 3/8" thick. It must have the proper cut-outs for hinges and doorknobs. The appearance must be monitored. Outer surfaces should not have any knots or scratches. The door must be free from warping (all surfaces must be flat).

AM radio specifications: The radio must tune to all the channels in the AM band. It must receive stations from far away (sensitivity) and should receive only one station at a time (selectivity). Its power output should be able to create a loud sound which contains all the high and low tones (harmonic distortion). The radio must run on battery power. It should conform to specifications for width, height, depth, color, and weight.

Compare the customer's specifications to the manufacturer's specifications. Customers normally state their expectations in qualitative terms. Qualitative terms describe characteristics: the bread tastes good; the door looks nice; the radio sounds good. In contrast, manufacturers must describe or specify their products in quantitative terms. Manufacturers must assign number values to their specifications: the bread must weigh 1 pound; the door must be 2'6" wide; the radio must tune within the AM band range (540 to 1650 kilohertz). Manufacturers use quantitative specifications because they are measurable. We define quality as the product's conformance to the specifications and requirements. By making the specifications and requirements measurable, we have a way to monitor quality. Therefore, the first principle in defining product specifications and requirements is to make them quantitative.

Functional Specifications

Sometimes specifications go beyond a physical description of product. Functional specifications describe in detail what an item will do. They are particularly common with more complicated products that are expected to do more than one thing, such as a telephone answering machine. Here are some functions we might expect from an answering machine:

1. Begin operating after either two or four rings.
2. Record personalized answer messages.
3. Record caller messages for 30 seconds.
4. Record up to 25 caller messages.

Product Requirements

The specifications we have discussed thus far have been set by manufacturers so that the product will be acceptable to the customer. As we have seen, the customer's requirements are qualitative and general. They are not precise. It is also important to note that, in most cases, the customer's specifications are informal. The manufacturer learns about them through experience or marketing surveys.

In some cases, however, customer specifications become much more precise and formal, or outside agencies make rules and regulations which manufacturers must follow. These rules and regulations are called product *requirements*.

In many industries, certain product specifications become so widely accepted that they become requirements for the manufacturer. In the construction industry, for example, there are certain standard door sizes. Architects draw their building plans for only those sizes. Carpenters make the door openings for the standard size doors. Therefore, if our door manufacturer wants to sell a door, the door must be a standard size.

Another example of an industry standard is the grading of wood used to manufacture the door. The lumber industry has established an elaborate series of specifications to grade and label wood of various types and qualities. These specifications and grading systems let buyers and sellers know the material they are trading. This avoids the need for inspection and negotiation with each purchase.

Certain industries have established formal testing laboratories to ensure that products conform to accepted standards. One outside agency which services a broad range of industries is Underwriters Laboratories (UL). UL is a not-for-profit organization that tests various products to determine whether they are safe to use. Products that meet the requirements of UL may display the UL trademark. Manufacturers want their products to be "listed" with UL because customers know and trust the UL trademark. Also, manufacturers will pay lower insurance premiums for products that have passed these safety tests.

A radio receiver is a good example of a product that could be UL listed. The manufacturer would contact UL and request the listing. UL would test the product for any electrical or fire hazards. If UL found the device acceptable, the manufacturer could use the UL trademark on the receiver. UL would write a test report and describe the product. Thereafter, UL would visit the factory and check the radio receiver to make sure it conforms to its description. The manufacturer must report any changes in the radio receiver to UL for re-evaluation.

As we've seen, individual customers' specifications can be imprecise and informal. Industry associations and testing laboratories such as UL are ways in which private sector customers formalize their specifications and establish requirements for products. Government also plays a major role in setting rules and regulations for manufacturers.

THE PRODUCT

Many organizations within the federal government are empowered by Congress to ensure that manufactured products are safe and effective. The Federal Communications Commission (FCC) is one such government agency. The FCC makes sure that commercial radio communications are maintained. We expect to turn on our television sets and receive a picture and sound. We only want to hear sound from the program we are watching, not interference from some other station. Police and fire stations communicate with radios; their channels must be free from other communications. Navigation channels for airplanes and ships must be open for safe travel. The FCC's rules and regulations ensure that the channels are kept free for their assigned tasks. The radio receiver is subject to these rules and regulations. It must be tested to determine whether it complies. The FCC must be notified that it complies, and the radio must display an FCC identification number.

Individual state and local governments also have their own laws affecting various products, and manufacturers must ensure that their products comply with these laws as well. These governments create administrative agencies, just as the federal government does, to enforce their laws. One example is a state's Department of Health, which establishes regulations for the production and handling of food. These codes must be obeyed when making the loaf of bread. The laws protect the bread from contamination such as food poisoning. Health department workers will visit the bakery and make inspections.

Specifications and Tolerances

Even when manufacturers set precise specifications, the finished product may not always match their expectations. The care and attention with which employees carry out their tasks can vary over the course of the workday. Saw blades warp, and equipment settings loosen. Raw materials and pre-purchased components can vary in size, shape, and quality.

Let's look at one morning's output in our closet door factory. As we have already seen, the manufacturer has set detailed specifications for the door's outer dimensions. The height will be 6'8", the width 2'6", and the thickness 1 3/8". The factory has made 10 doors with the dimensions shown in Table 1.1.

The manufacturer has quite a problem. Only two doors (numbers 4 and 8) precisely meet all the specifications. Should the manufacturer sell only the two precisely-made doors and throw away the other eight? We can answer this question by taking a closer look at the customer's needs.

A BEGINNER'S GUIDE TO QUALITY IN MANUFACTURING

Door Number	Height	Width	Thickness
1	6'8"	2'6"	1 1/2"
2	6'7"	2'6"	1 3/8"
3	6'8"	2'5"	1 1/4"
4	6'8"	2'6"	1 3/8"
5	6'9"	2'7"	1 3/8"
6	6'8"	2'6"	1 1/2"
7	6'9"	2'6"	1 3/8"
8	6'8"	2'6"	1 3/8"
9	6'8"	2'6"	1 1/4"
10	6'7"	2'5"	1 5/8"

Table 1.1: Measurements of 10 Doors

Does the width of the door have to be exactly 2'6"? If it's wider, the door will not close; if it's narrower, the door will not span the entire opening. Therefore, the width of the door must be very near to the 2'6" dimension. We will let it vary by only 1/8".

The door must be close to 6'8" high. If it is 1/2" smaller, we will consider it acceptable. It can be a little higher because the installer can always cut the door down to size. If the door is no more than 2" higher than the specification, we will accept it.

The door needs to be close to 1 3/8" thickness. We will let this dimension vary by only 1/8".

The amount by which we allow the specification to vary is called the *tolerance*. Table 1.2 redefines the specifications by adding tolerances. Also included are the maximum and minimum dimensions we will accept. We determine the maximum dimension by adding the positive tolerance value to the stated specification. For instance, we calculate the maximum dimension for the height of the door by adding 2" to the stated specification of 6'8". We determine the minimum dimension by subtracting the magnitude of the negative tolerance from the stated specification. For the height of the door, this involves subtracting 1/2" from the stated specification of 6'8".

Dimension	Specification	Tolerance		Maximum	Minimum
Height	6'8"	+2"	−1/2"	6'10"	6'7 1/2"
Width	2'6"	+1/8"	−1/8"	2'6 1/8"	2'5 7/8"
Thickness	1 3/8"	+1/8"	−1/8"	1'1/2"	1'1/4"

Table 1.2: Exterior Door Specifications

THE PRODUCT

We will now re-evaluate the 10 doors described in Table 1.1.

Door 1 has the correct height and width, and the thickness is within our tolerance. Therefore, door 1 is acceptable.

Door 2 is too short. It must be rejected.

Door 3 is too narrow. It must be rejected.

Door 4 is correct in all dimensions.

Door 5 is too wide. It must be rejected.

Doors 6, 7, 8, and 9 all fall within tolerance and can be accepted.

Door 10 is too short, too narrow, and too thick. Door 10 must be rejected.

Based on our newly defined specifications, six doors are acceptable to send to the customer. That's quite an improvement over the two we thought we could sell previously. Unfortunately, four doors do not meet our specifications and must be rejected.

To properly specify a product, the manufacturer must assign all the characteristics of the product a stated value. In addition, a tolerance normally accompanies this value. The manufacturer aims to make each product perfect. Each characteristic should measure its stated value. In this way, rejects are kept to a minimum. We will be learning techniques for maintaining product characteristics. We will learn how to alter the manufacturing process when products move toward these minimum or maximum specified limits. The goal is no rejects. Certainly, if the door manufacturer does not correct his 40 percent reject rate, he will not be in business long. But we will visit him again and find ways to improve his performance.

1.3 Production Costs, Selling Price, and Company Profits

As we've already noted, manufacturers must do more than simply satisfy their customers to succeed as a business. They must also be able to sell finished products for a profit.

Here, again, manufacturers are faced with several different questions. First, they must identify their own expenses in manufacturing a product. Second, they must determine a selling price that is affordable to the customer and competitive with other products on the market. Third, they must calculate whether this target selling price exceeds production costs enough to provide a profit worthy of the effort.

Let's analyze the effects of quality control techniques on production costs, selling price, and profits.

Production Costs

Manufacturers face many different expenses when they attempt to produce an item. For our purposes, we will divide these into two major categories: variable costs and fixed costs.

==Variable costs== are expenses tied directly to the individual unit of production. They increase as the total level of production increases. When total production drops, variable costs also fall.

Variable costs include the supplies and raw materials that eventually become part of the finished product. They also can include the costs of labor required to manufacture the product. Variable costs can even include the costs of utilities such as gas or electricity, which may rise or fall with varying levels of output.

To simplify this presentation, we will consider only the variable costs of supplies and materials going into the finished product. For the loaf of bread, these are the costs of the ingredients and the packaging material. For the door, we need to include the costs of framing wood, exterior wood surface, the glue, and packaging material. For the AM radio, material costs include electrical components, the casework, the user's manual, and packaging.

We calculate material costs for each product using a ==bill of materials.== This document lists: (1) each of the raw materials or component parts used in manufacturing the product, (2) the amount of each material and/or number of components required to produce a single unit of the product, and sometimes (3) the cost of the raw material or component to make one unit. These individual material prices are then added to determine the total material cost per unit of production. Tables 1.3, 1.4, and 1.5 summarize the cost breakdowns for the loaf of bread, the closet door, and the AM radio.

Ingredients	Amount/Loaf	Cost/Loaf
Milk	0.17 pints	$0.0371
Sugar	1.0 ounce	$0.0826
Salt	0.2 ounces	$0.0021
Butter	0.3 pounds	$0.0987
Water	0.5 pints	$0.0001
Flour	0.9 pounds	$0.2324
Yeast	0.2 ounces	$0.1540
Poly bag	1 bag	$0.0700
Total Material Cost		$0.6770/Loaf

Table 1.3: Bill of Materials—Loaf of Bread

Quantity	Material	Cost/Door
2	Vertical framing wood (1" × 6" × 6'8")	$3.70
5	Horizontal framing wood (1" × 6" × 1'6")	$2.10
2	Exterior panel (3/16" × 2'6" × 6'8")	$3.15
1	Glue (8 ounces)	$0.20
32	Staples	$0.14
1	Packaging	$3.00
	Total Material Cost	$12.29/Door

Table 1.4: Bill of Materials—Closet Door

Quantity	Material	Cost/Component	Cost/Radio
1	Antenna	$0.30	$0.30
1	Tuner capacitor	$0.20	$0.20
4	Transformers (tunable)	$0.15	$0.60
7	Transistors	$0.08	$0.56
22	Resistors (fixed)	$0.005	$0.11
1	Resistor (variable)	$0.12	$0.12
17	Capacitors (fixed)	$0.0058	$0.10
2	Capacitors (variable)	$0.13	$0.26
2	Diodes	$0.01	$0.02
1	Speaker	$0.35	$0.35
1	Earphone jack	$0.18	$0.18
1	Switch/volume control	$0.16	$0.16
1	Printed circuit board	$0.40	$0.40
1	Case	$0.68	$0.68
1	User's manual	$0.01	$0.01
1	Packaging	$0.38	$0.38
	Total Material Cost		$4.43/Radio

Table 1.5: Bill of Materials—AM Radio

Finding the best prices for each component is the responsibility of the Purchasing Department. This department must buy materials and components that comply with the product's specifications. Well-written component specifications ensure that the Purchasing Department buys the correct parts.

The costs of raw materials and components, however, are not a manufacturer's only expense.

Fixed costs are all other costs that are not directly tied to the individual unit of production and do not vary directly with changes in level of output. For example, the baker must buy or rent space. The baker must pay these space costs whether monthly production is 20,000 loaves or only 10,000. Similarly, the baker's administrative and supervisory costs will not vary with minor changes in output. Costs for sales and distribution also will not vary directly with swings in production. The baker must still hire a route sales representative and lease a delivery truck regardless of the number of loaves each customer buys.

In some cases, even direct labor costs can be "fixed" for certain ranges of production. The baker must have a certain number of employees to operate equipment when the bakery produces 15,000–25,000 loaves per month.

Once again, we will simplify our analysis by considering all of the baker's salary expenses as fixed costs.

Table 1.6 lists the fixed costs for the bakery. These costs are averaged for each month of the year.

Cost	Amount
Rent	$ 1,200
Electricity	70
Gas	210
Telephone	50
Office supplies	30
Maintenance	85
Salaries (including benefits)	9,000
Vehicle leasing	450
Vehicle gas and oil	750
Total Monthly Fixed Costs	$11,845

Table 1.6: Monthly Fixed Costs for Bakery

To determine the fixed cost for each loaf of bread, we simply divide the total monthly fixed costs by the number of loaves sold per month. Our bakery makes and distributes about 20,000 loaves of bread per month. Therefore, the fixed cost per loaf is $0.60.

$$\text{Fixed Cost/Unit} = \frac{\text{Total Fixed Cost}}{\text{Total Production}} = \frac{\$11,845}{20,000} = \$0.60$$

Now that we know the fixed cost, we are ready to determine overall costs for each product.

Total cost per unit equals the fixed costs per unit plus the variable costs per unit.

Let's look at the bakery first. The total cost for a loaf of bread equals the fixed costs ($0.60) plus the variable costs ($0.68). It costs the bakery $1.28 to bake and deliver a loaf of bread.

    Total Costs = Fixed Costs + Variable Costs
      $1.28   = $0.60   + $0.68

The closet door manufacturer has done a similar analysis. Monthly fixed costs amount to approximately $33,000. The door manufacturer makes and sells approximately 3,300 doors per month. Therefore, fixed costs are $10 per door. By adding this fixed cost to the variable costs ($12.29/door), we arrive at a total cost of $22.29 each.

The radio manufacturer has also determined her costs. She has calculated that total monthly fixed costs for the AM radio are approximately $237,336. The manufacturer makes and sells approximately 26,400 radios per month. Therefore, the fixed costs are $8.99 per radio ($237,336 ÷ 26,400 radios). By adding the variable costs of $4.43 to the fixed costs of $8.99, she arrives at a total cost of $13.42 per radio.

Quality Control and Production Costs

Now we are almost ready to look at how improved quality control can reduce these production expenses. Before we do, however, let's re-examine our cost structure from a "quality" viewpoint and make sure we didn't miss anything.

In the initial analysis of costs, our door manufacturer neglected to look at the effect which his reject rate had on his material costs. The company rejected four doors out of every 10 it made. Therefore, the manufacturer was losing $12.29 in materials for each rejected door. These losses in raw material and components used in rejected products are called ==scrap costs.==

Scrap costs add significantly to the production cost of each door sold. For each 10 doors manufactured, total scrap costs equal $49.16 ($12.29 for each of the four doors rejected).

Total Scrap Costs = Material Costs/Unit × Number of Rejected Units

Total Scrap Costs = $12.29 × 4 = $49.16

This additional material cost must be absorbed by the six remaining doors which were acceptable for sale. As a result, the actual material cost for each of these six doors was increased by $8.19.

Additional Material Costs =
                Total Scrap Costs/Number of Acceptable Units

Additional Material Costs = $49.16 ÷ 6 = $8.19

Lack of quality control has added a whole new cost element—scrap costs—to our calculation of total cost per unit. The new formula is:

$$\text{Total Cost} = \text{Variable Cost} + \text{Fixed Cost} + \text{Scrap Costs}$$

For the door manufacturer, this increases the total cost per acceptable door to $30.48. This is the total of $12.29 in variable costs plus $10 in fixed costs plus $8.19 in scrap costs.

By eliminating rejects, the manufacturer can immediately save $8.19 per door in scrap costs. This is a 27 percent savings in total unit cost and brings production costs back down to the previous estimate of $22.29.

However, the manufacturer's savings from implementing quality control techniques go even further. Let's take another look at fixed costs.

As we've noted, a company's *total* fixed costs don't change as total production increases or decreases. For instance, salaries stay about the same, and so does rent.

However, our formula tells us that fixed costs *per unit* do change as total production varies. If total production falls, fixed cost per unit increases; if total production rises, fixed cost per unit drops. Therefore, a manufacturer can decrease cost per unit by increasing the number of units produced in a month.

Quality control can help us accomplish this goal by increasing the number of finished products that meet specifications. By decreasing the number of rejects, we are actually increasing total production.

To see how this works, we will re-examine the door manufacturer's fixed costs per unit product. We have determined that fixed costs per month are $33,000. Each month the manufacturer produces 3,300 doors which meet specifications and are acceptable for sale. Thus, fixed costs per unit are

$$\text{Fixed Costs per Unit} = \frac{\text{Fixed Costs per Month}}{\text{Units Made per Month}} = \frac{\$33,000}{3,300}$$

$$\text{Fixed Costs per Unit} = \$10.00$$

However, we also said that the door manufacturer actually produces many more doors than the 3,300 that are acceptable for sale. The company has a 40 percent reject rate. For every 10 doors made, four cannot be sold; only six are acceptable for sale. Therefore, the manufacturer has an *acceptance rate* of 60 percent.

$$\text{Acceptance Rate} = \frac{\text{Number of Acceptable Units}}{\text{Total Number of Units Produced}} \times 100\%$$

$$\text{Acceptance Rate} = \frac{6}{10} \times 100\% = 60\%$$

THE PRODUCT

If our manufacturer's quality control program was completely successful, there would be no rejects. All units produced would be acceptable, and the acceptance rate would be 100 percent.

Now let's calculate what the manufacturer's fixed costs would be with a 100 percent acceptance rate. First we compute the number of units the manufacturer is actually producing. Since we know both the door manufacturer's current monthly production of acceptable products and the current acceptance rate, we can easily calculate his improved monthly production if he eliminated all rejects. Let's go back to our formula.

$$\text{Acceptance Rate} = \frac{\text{Total Number of Acceptable Units}}{\text{Total Number of Units Produced}} \times 100\%$$

$$60\% = \frac{3{,}300}{\text{Total Number of Units}} \times 100\%$$

Let X be the total number of units. Now we will solve for X.

$$60\% = \frac{3{,}300}{X} \times 100\%$$

$$X = 3{,}300 \times \frac{100\%}{60\%} = 5{,}500$$

$$\text{Total Number of Units} = 5{,}500$$

By achieving a zero defect rate, the door manufacturer can increase total monthly production from 3,300 doors to 5,500 doors. That's a two-thirds jump in total output.

What effect does this increase in production have on fixed costs per unit? Let's take a look.

$$\text{Fixed Costs per Unit} = \frac{\text{Fixed Costs per Month}}{\text{Units Made per Month}} = \frac{\$33{,}000}{5{,}500}$$

$$\text{Fixed Costs per Unit} = \$6.00$$

The manufacturer has been able to reduce fixed costs per door from $10.00 to $6.00 by eliminating rejects and increasing total production of acceptable units. When we add this fixed cost per unit to the variable cost per unit ($12.29), we calculate the manufacturer's new total cost of $18.29 for each door. This figure is 18 percent lower than the latest total cost estimate of $22.29 per door.

$$\frac{(\$22.29 - \$18.29)}{\$22.29} = 18\%$$

The combined reduction in scrap costs and fixed costs has reduced the total unit cost by 40 percent—from $30.48 to $18.29.

$$\frac{(\$30.48 - \$18.29)}{\$30.48} = 40\%$$

Table 1.7 compares costs at the 0 percent and 40 percent reject rates.

Selling Price and Profit

The manufacturer must sell his product for more than it costs to produce. The difference between this selling price and the total cost is profit. If the selling price doesn't cover production costs, the manufacturer is operating at a loss.

The bakery, has set its selling price at $1.50 for a loaf of bread. Recall that total costs per loaf were $1.28. The bakery is earning a profit of $0.22 per loaf.

$$\begin{aligned} \text{Profit} &= \text{Selling Price} - \text{Total Cost} \\ \text{Profit} &= \$1.50 - \$1.28 \\ \text{Profit} &= \$0.22 \end{aligned}$$

The bakery sells 20,000 loaves of bread per month, 240,000 loaves per year. Multiplying the number of loaves per year times the profit for one loaf equals an annual profit of $52,800.

The door manufacturer, on the other hand, originally calculated total cost per door at $22.29, forgetting to count the scrap cost. Based on this estimate, the company set the selling price of the door at $24.00. We have seen that scrap costs increased the actual total cost per door to $30.48. Our manufacturer is losing money on every door produced.

$$\begin{aligned} \text{Loss} &= \text{Total Cost} - \text{Selling Price} \\ \text{Loss} &= \$30.48 - \$24.00 \\ \text{Loss} &= \$6.48 \end{aligned}$$

It's easy to see that this closet door company will be going out of business very soon unless it improves its performance.

The remedy, as we've already seen, is to implement quality control techniques and reduce costs. By reducing the reject rate to zero, the door company brings its total cost per door down to $18.29—less than the selling price of $24.00. The result is a profit of $5.71 per door. Quality control has taken a losing proposition and made it profitable.

Unfortunately for most manufacturers, selling price cannot be based on production costs alone. The market in which a product is sold also affects the selling price. If the manufacturer has no competition and the customer needs the product, then the manufacturer can sell at a high price and make a large profit. However, this is usually not the case.

THE PRODUCT

Most markets have many suppliers competing for customers. The manufacturer wants to set the selling price as low as necessary to attract more customers and increase sales.

Quality control offers a competitive advantage, because if the manufacturer is producing efficiently, with no rejects, the costs per unit go down. The manufacturer can then sell at a lower price and still make a profit.

Let's take a look at our door manufacturer's competitive position. Based on the original inaccurate estimate of costs, he set a selling price of $24.00 per door. This error was also influenced by pressures from competitors who were selling their doors for $23.00 each.

By implementing quality control techniques, the manufacturer has reduced cost per unit to $18.29. This has made production profitable at the $24.00 selling price. Unfortunately, the manufacturer is still having trouble attracting customers because of competition.

The manufacturer's cost savings from reduced reject rates have been so great, however, that he can now reduce the selling price to $22.00 per door—the lowest price on the market—and still turn an acceptable profit.

$$\text{Profit} = \text{Selling Price} - \text{Total Cost}$$
$$\text{Profit} = \$22.00 - \$18.29$$
$$\text{Profit} = \$3.71$$

Based on its improved competitive position, the company is able to sell all 5,500 of the doors which it manufactures to specifications each month. This translates into a monthly profit of $20,405.

Table 1.7 details the cost savings after implementing quality control techniques. This improvement saved the closet door manufacturer from probable bankruptcy and turned it into a profitable competitor.

Item	40% Reject Rate	0% Reject Rate
Monthly Production	3,300	5,500
Variable Costs/Unit	$12.29	$12.29
Fixed Costs/Unit	$10.00	$ 6.00
Scrap Costs/Unit	$ 8.19	$ 0.00
Total Costs/Unit	$30.48	$18.29
Selling Price	$24.00	$22.00
Unit Profit/(Loss)	($ 6.48)	$ 3.71
Monthly Profit/(Loss)	($21,384.00)	$20,405.00
Annual Profit/(Loss)	($256,608.00)	$244,860.00

Table 1.7: Cost Comparison Between 40% and 0% Reject Rate for the Closet Door

Chapter Summary

1. To earn a profit, a manufacturer must satisfy the customers and sell the product for more than it costs to produce.

2. A customer's specifications define what the customer wants from the product.

3. Manufacturers must set specifications that are more precise than those set by the customer. While customers' specifications are generally qualitative, manufacturers' specifications should be quantitative so that they can be measured. Specifications can also include functions which the product must perform. Tolerances define the limits within which actual finished products can vary from the stated specification.

4. Manufacturers must also ensure that their products conform to requirements set by industry associations and governmental agencies.

5. The total cost of a product includes both variable costs and fixed costs. Variable costs are those directly tied to the individual unit of production, such as the expense of raw material and component parts. Fixed costs are the manufacturer's other costs that do not vary directly with the level of production. Examples include administrative salaries and rent for facilities.

6. Scrap costs increase the total cost of a product. Scrap costs are the costs of materials wasted in rejected products.

7. Quality control can reduce expenditures by eliminating scrap costs.

8. Quality control can reduce fixed costs per unit by eliminating rejects and increasing the number of acceptable products.

9. Quality control can lower production costs which, in turn, results in larger profits and an improved competitive position.

THE PRODUCT

Questions for Chapter 1

Refer to Table 1.8 to answer questions 1, 2, and 3. A company wishes to manufacture a closet door. The detailed specifications for the door's outer dimensions are as follows: height, 7'1"; width, 2'6"; and thickness, 1 5/8". The company makes 10 doors with the following dimensions:

Door Number	Height	Width	Thickness
1	7'1"	2'6"	1 1/2"
2	7'1"	2'6"	1 5/8"
3	7'2"	2'6"	1 5/8"
4	7'2"	2'5"	1 3/4"
5	7'2"	2'6"	1 3/4"
6	7'1"	2'6"	1 5/8"
7	7'2"	2'6"	1 3/8"
8	7'1"	2'6"	1 3/4"
9	7'2"	2'6"	1 1/4"
10	7'1"	2'6"	1 5/8"

Table 1.8: Door Dimensions

1. How many of the doors satisfy the specifications? List the doors that are acceptable.

2. The door manufacturer has decided to accept a door whose height is up to 1" larger or 1/2" smaller than 7'1"; width may vary by 1/8"; and thickness may vary by 1/8". Construct a table similar to Table 1.2 showing the tolerances and the maximum and minimum dimensions.

17

3. Using the table constructed in question 2, re-evaluate the 10 doors. How many are acceptable? List them.

Use the following information for questions 4 through 10. The door manufacturer finds that 7 of every 10 doors produced meets specifications. The variable cost for each door produced is $13.25. Fixed costs per month are $53,900, and each month the company produces 4,900 doors that meet specifications.

4. What is the acceptance rate?

5. Compute the fixed costs per unit.

6. (a) Compute the scrap costs for each group of 10 doors produced. (b) How much do the scrap costs add to the cost of each of the seven doors that meet specifications?

7. What is the total cost of each door?

8. Using the formula for acceptance rate, compute the total number of units produced.

9. If there is a zero defect rate: (a) What would be the fixed costs per unit? (b) What will be the total costs per unit? (c) By what percentage will total costs have dropped?

10. If the manufacturer sells each door for $25.00, compute the unit, monthly, and annual profit (loss) at (a) the 30 percent reject rate and (b) the zero percent reject rate.

Use the following example to answer questions 11 through 17. A radio manufacturer finds that 8 of every 50 radios produced cannot receive all stations on the AM band due to defective components. The factory produces 3,780 acceptable radios each month. The fixed costs are $18,900 per month; variable costs are $4.43 per radio.

11. What is the acceptance rate?

12. For each unit, compute the fixed costs.

13. Compute the scrap costs for each group of 50 radios produced, and determine how much this adds to the cost of each acceptable radio.

14. Compute the total cost.

15. What is the total number of radios produced each month?

16. If there are zero defects, what would be the fixed costs per radio? What would be the total costs per radio?

17. The manufacturer wishes to make a 20 percent profit. What should the selling price be if (a) defects are not eliminated; (b) there is successful quality control with a zero defect rate?

Chapter 1 Project

Choose a product that you would like to make. Answer the following questions about your product:

1. Who will buy your product, and why?

2. How will you specify your product to ensure that the buyer will be satisfied with it? Remember that your specifications should include stated specifications, tolerances (with minimum and maximum values), and functional descriptions.

3. Create a bill of materials for the product. Remember to include all the components and raw materials for the product, as well as quantity, cost/component, and cost/unit product. Use Tables 1.3, 1.4, and 1.5 as a guide. Calculate the total material cost for one product.

THE PROCESS OF MAKING THE PRODUCT

2.1 Introduction

Manufacturing is a process. Raw materials and component parts are transformed into finished products. The process generally consists of several different steps required to bring about this transformation. Procedures for each step in the process must be carefully planned and well documented. The steps must be arranged in the most appropriate sequence, and this sequence must also be carefully documented. The way a manufacturer plans the production process will profoundly affect the company's efficiency and the quality of the final product.

2.2 Manufacturing Processes

Manufacturing is a process by which raw materials are transformed into usable products. Industrial engineers generally divide these processing functions into two major categories: primary processing and secondary processing.

Primary processing takes raw materials in their most basic form and changes them into usable, yet still very basic, products.

Raw timber, for example, is cut and milled into lumber of various types and sizes. Food processors transform harvested wheat into flour. The textile industry processes raw cotton and spins it into yarn.

Secondary processing takes the products produced by primary processors and transforms them further into products which can be used by the ultimate consumer. Each of the three manufacturers we've been studying are secondary processors. The door manufacturer buys lumber and alters it until it becomes a usable closet door. The baker takes flour and mixes it with other ingredients to bake bread. The radio manufacturer puts together a variety of equipment to make a radio.

2.3 Basic Steps in the Manufacturing Process

The manufacturing process consists of several basic steps: receiving, processing, subassembly, final assembly, packaging, and shipping.

Receiving, the first step in the production process, occurs when a manufacturer's suppliers deliver the raw materials and component parts needed to make the product. As we've already seen, the closet door manufacturer buys boards, panels, and glue. The baker needs milk, flour, and other ingredients. The radio manufacturer purchases a wide variety of electronic components.

During the receiving step, all these materials and components must be unloaded from the truck, container, or railroad car and brought to the manufacturer's facility. This is also the point at which most manufacturers check that they have actually received the materials or component parts they ordered. We will talk in detail about the role and techniques of incoming inspections in a later chapter.

In some facilities, raw materials and component parts are stored in inventory until they are needed. Other manufacturers use them immediately. In these facilities, the raw materials and components are brought directly to the factory floor, where they go into production.

Processing is a step where a raw material or component is changed so that it can be used in the final product. The closet door manufacturer buys long pieces of framing wood, then cuts these boards into shorter pieces with specified dimensions to make components of the door frame. The manufacturer also buys large sheets of plywood and cuts them for use as face panels on the door.

The baker, too, must go through several processing steps to produce a loaf of bread. The ingredients must be mixed to make dough. The dough, in turn, must be fermented, punched, shaped, and baked.

Subassembly is a step in which product components are brought together to form a part of the final product. They make the task of final assembly easier. The AM radio manufacturer attaches electrical components (resistors, capacitors, chokes, etc.) to a Printed Circuit Board (PCB) which connects them electrically. This forms a subassembly which will later be joined to other parts to form the AM radio.

In a similar fashion, after cutting long boards into smaller pieces, the closet door manufacturer assembles them into a door frame.

Final assembly is the step in which all the raw materials, components, and subassemblies are put together to make the finished product. The AM radio manufacturer joins the circuit board to the case and attaches the tuning and volume knobs to make the final product. Similarly, the door manufacturer glues the exterior panels onto the door frame.

Additional processing may be necessary after final assembly. For example, after gluing on the exterior door panels, the door manufacturer must plane and sand the door, and cut holes and mortises for the doorknobs and hinges.

Packaging is the final step in preparing the product for the customer. The package must protect the product during storage and transport. The baker seals the bread in a plastic bag using a specialized piece of automated equipment. Employees at the closet door company place the finished doors in heavy plastic wrapping using corrugated cardboard frames to separate them.

During the packaging step, all necessary paperwork must be included with the product. For the radio, this would include a user's manual and a warranty card.

Shipping is the last step in the manufacturing process. In some facilities, the packaged product goes to a storage area to wait for someone to purchase it. Other facilities ship the product to the customer immediately.

2.4 Planning the Manufacturing Process

The objective in planning a manufacturing process is to produce a high-quality product for the least possible cost. To achieve this goal, a manufacturer must identify and specify precisely the processing steps needed to transform materials or components into the planned finished product. The manufacturer must lay out these production steps in the most appropriate order, eliminating any duplication of labor or unnecessary handling of materials or components. The plan must also ensure a steady, even flow of products through the process. Materials, subassemblies, and assemblies should not pile up between steps; nor should workers be kept waiting for any of these items. Many companies now strive to eliminate incoming and finished goods inventory entirely to increase efficiency and decrease costs. These ideas are part of the "Just-in-Time" (JIT) philosophy. When planning a production process, it's important to be flexible. Changes in the process should be considered whenever efficiency can be improved.

Specifying the Steps

To better understand how the manufacturing process is organized, let's discuss some of the steps needed to start a production line.

Having identified and specified the finished product, the manufacturer must plan the production process by developing a series of *pre-production drawings*. These drawings should show the precise appearance, measurements, and tolerances of the finished product, all subassemblies, and each component which the manufacturer will either purchase or create from raw material.

The closet door manufacturer, for example, should have drawings showing the finished closet door, exterior door panels, the assembled door frame, and each frame component to be cut from the purchased lumber. The AM radio manufacturer should have drawings of component parts, the printed circuit board (PCB) before and after assembly, the case, and the fully assembled radio. Drawings are less appropriate for the bakery. In this case, precise descriptions of the size, shape, and composition of the dough at each stage of the mixing, fermenting, and baking process would suffice.

These pre-production drawings should be reviewed by the manufacturing engineers for *manufacturing feasibility*. That is, the company should be sure that it can produce the components or assemble the finished product as outlined in the drawings. The AM radio manufacturer, for example, may find that there is not sufficient room between electrical components to allow for actual assembly onto the circuit board. The closet door manufacturer may find that lumber is not available in the specified sizes or that existing equipment will not hold or cut it at the cited measurements and tolerances.

The manufacturing department must agree that the pre-production drawings are acceptable. Normally, manufacturing feasibility is tested during the first production run, called the "pilot run." Once all the problems are corrected and the product is considered manufacturable, the pre-production drawings are accepted by the manufacturer and become the production drawings.

The manufacturer should also consider the *make vs. buy* decision. In some cases, it may be cost effective for a company to buy a given component rather than manufacture it from raw materials.

The AM radio manufacturer, for example, purchases the molded plastic case in which the actual receiver is placed. Buying this component is clearly less expensive than establishing an entire plastics forming operation just to meet her own limited needs. Similarly, she purchases the speaker and all of the electronic components which go into the radio itself. These purchases are also cost effective. In fact, the AM radio manufacturer does no processing of raw materials whatsoever. She simply assembles pre-purchased component parts to create the finished radio.

The closet door manufacturer, on the other hand, has decided that it is less expensive to cut the components of the door frame from standard lengths of 1" × 6" lumber than to purchase the components already cut to size.

After confirming the manufacturing feasibility of all components to be produced in-house, the manufacturer must carefully document each production process. Among the items which this documentation should include are:

1. The operation number which the process has been assigned in the overall production plan

2. A description of actual processing to occur during the step, including the machinery to be used and any gauge settings required

3. The finalized production drawing showing the component or assembly following completion of each process step

4. Identification of the raw material or components which the process will involve

5. A part number assigned to the completed component or assembly

Laying Out the Overall Process

Once the manufacturer has identified individual processing steps, it is critical to arrange them in the proper order. Determining the proper order will depend on a number of considerations, including the relationship between individual processing steps, the company's equipment resources, and the layout of the manufacturing facility.

In considering these issues, it is important to point out a basic distinction between two types of manufacturing facilities.

Job shops are factories that produce a variety of different products using the same pieces of equipment. Each product goes through a different series of processing steps, and the individual steps are arranged in varying patterns. One example would be a carpentry shop which produces wooden tables, shelving, and cabinets all using the same saws, drill presses, routers, and sanders. Another example is a bakery which uses a single mixer, fermentation room, and oven to produce a variety of breads, cakes, and pastries depending on the orders it has received.

In job shops, equipment is not purchased or arranged according to the manufacturing requirements of a single product. For this reason, manufacturers may have to arrange the sequence of their processing steps according to equipment location and availability.

Production line manufacturers, on the other hand, produce only one product or a limited series of products, all of which go through approximately the same processing steps in approximately the same order. These manufacturers normally produce large quantities of products.

Production line manufacturers purchase and arrange equipment to meet the processing requirements of their specific products. In production line companies, therefore, the processing steps are arranged in a fixed pattern with the goal of maximizing total output relative to costs and anticipated sales requirements. Individual raw materials and components may follow separate processing paths on their way to the final product. However, the production routings will always be geared toward producing the maximum amount of final product with the minimum amount of time, labor, and materials.

Each of the companies we examined so far—the closet door company, the bakery, and the AM radio producer—are production line manufacturers. In this book, we will consider only this type of manufacturing facility.

The Sequence of Processing Steps

When arranging the overall process, it is important to assure that operations are not repeated. For example, the AM radio should be tuned before it is assembled in its case. If the opposite were true, the radio manufacturer would assemble the case, take it apart to tune the radio, and then reassemble it. To avoid duplication of steps, it is advisable to process any components and raw materials early in the manufacturing process before any assembly is done. Similarly, manufacturers should make subassemblies early in the process so that operations can be performed on the subassembly and final assembly can be done quickly.

Sometimes steps may even be added to save time or material costs or to improve quality. Before making the final dough, the baker makes a "sponge," i.e., a mixture of water, yeast, and part of the flour. The sponge shortens the final fermentation period, increases flavor, and decreases the amount of yeast needed for the bread. By adding this step, the baker has decreased the time for final fermentation, increased quality, and saved money on material costs.

Balancing the Production Line

To ensure maximum efficiency, it is important that products flow evenly through the various steps in the production process. Raw materials, components, subassemblies, and finished goods should move from one manufacturing step to another without stopping. If

THE PROCESS OF MAKING THE PRODUCT

a product cannot move from one step to another, it must be stored until it can proceed down the production line. Storing the product, even if we keep it close to the production line, wastes time and labor. Someone must first store the product and then retrieve it when it can proceed to the next step. Moreover, these unnecessary extra steps create additional opportunities for parts or materials to be damaged during handling. Having things pile up is one problem that manufacturers must strive to eliminate.

It is equally important to ensure that workers do not lose time waiting for products delayed in earlier steps in the production process. In this case, it's easy to see that time wasted equals higher production costs.

The only way to avoid problems with product flow is to balance product movement throughout the manufacturing process. The manufacturer should analyze each step in the production process to determine its precise requirements in both employee and equipment time. The manufacturer must then allocate these resources to ensure that each manufacturing step has a relative allotment equal to its required output for a unit of finished product.

The closet door company, for example, wishes to assemble 165 doors per day. To do this, it must set up cutting stations for both door frame components and exterior panels. How many pieces of equipment should be devoted to each of these two tasks?

The following equation allows a manufacturer to identify the equipment needs at a given stage in production based on machine capabilities and a stated production target.

$$N = \frac{t}{60} \times \frac{p}{h \times u}$$

where N is the desired number of machines needed

t is the standard time in minutes required to process one unit

p is the total production of units required per day

h is the standard number of hours available per day per machine

u is the acceptance rate of pieces produced in the process

The closet door company needs to cut 1,155 door frame components daily to meet its production goal of 165 completed doors. Time studies show that it takes 45 seconds (0.75 minutes) to cut each frame component. Let us also assume that each machine is available eight hours per day and that 95 percent of the cut components meet specification. We can now calculate our equipment requirements to meet the production goals.

$$N = \frac{t}{60} \times \frac{p}{h \times u}$$

$$N = \frac{0.75}{60} \times \frac{1{,}155}{8 \times .95}$$

$$N = 2 \text{ saws}$$

On the other hand, the company needs 330 exterior panels to go on the 165 door frames. It takes two minutes to cut each of the panels on a panel saw. Once again, the saw is available eight hours per day, and there is a 95 percent acceptance rate on finished panels. Let's see how many panel saws we need to meet the production goals.

$$N = \frac{t}{60} \times \frac{p}{h \times u}$$

$$N = \frac{2}{60} \times \frac{330}{8 \times .95}$$

$$N = 1.45$$

In light of the cost of buying an additional panel saw and space limitations in the facility, the manufacturer decides to round this calculation down and set up only one panel saw station relative to the two framing saw stations. The line will be approximately balanced, although production of exterior panels will fall slightly below the target needed for 165 finished doors per day. One method of making up for this shortfall would be to run a panel saw on overtime.

This formula can also determine equipment and staff needs and thereby balance product flow at every step in the production process. Beginning with the daily production target for finished product, a manufacturer can identify the daily requirement for processed component parts at each production step. By applying the formula discussed above, the manufacturer can identify relative equipment and staff needs for each processing step. Applying this equation all the way through the production process will allow for balanced output at each manufacturing step. Components and assemblies will not pile up between steps, nor will staff be idle waiting for work to come to their stations.

Minimizing Incoming and Finished Goods Inventories

Incoming and finished goods inventories should be eliminated wherever possible. It is costly in time, labor, space, and financing to store incoming components and raw materials. Moreover, the additional handling associated with moving materials into and out of inventory storage increases the possibility for damage and thereby increases scrap costs.

THE PROCESS OF MAKING THE PRODUCT

If possible, incoming raw materials and components should go directly to the factory floor for use in making the product. This requires a great deal of cooperation on the part of the supplier, so that incoming goods, raw materials, and components are received when they are needed. This purchasing system follows the "Just-in-Time" philosophy; the materials and component parts must arrive "just in time" to go into production.

A Just-in-Time system also requires a high degree of confidence in the quality of a suppliers' materials or component parts. Ways of ensuring supplier quality will be discussed in chapter 5.

By eliminating the need for inventory storage of incoming supplies and materials, manufacturers avoid an unnecessary step in the production process. They no longer need to devote valuable employee time toward putting materials into inventory, monitoring inventory levels, and removing the same materials from storage to put them into production. Similarly, the storage space saved through eliminating this step can lead to substantial benefits in the form of reduced facility costs.

Similar savings are available through eliminating, or at least minimizing, the finished goods inventory. A company's ability to do this will depend on the nature of the market it serves, its relationship with its customers, and its ability to accurately predict sales volume.

Implementing the Process

As we've indicated, flexibility is extremely important in planning the production process. Manufacturers should initially consider a wide variety of options when planning individual production steps and their sequence in the overall process. Companies must also be prepared to modify their manufacturing process as problems crop up during actual production. The pilot run (first production run) should be monitored by a process engineer who ensures that process steps are carried out exactly as planned and notes any unforeseen problems which may arise. Any proposed modification in processing plans should be reviewed thoroughly. Long-term savings to be achieved through changes should be compared to the costs of retooling, retraining, lost production, and so on.

Following final implementation of the production process, manufacturers should continue to remain alert for new ideas that reduce costs, save time or space, increase quality, and enhance the consumer's perception of the product. Again, they must weigh these possibilities for improvement against the relative costs of making the change.

Cost-saving ideas and solutions to problems can come from a variety of sources. A company's most valuable source of information is its own employees. As we've indicated, a manufacturer should gather the opinions of personnel at all levels—from product designers and engineering staff to front-line production workers—when planning or modifying the production process. These are the people who must implement the plan and who will be, or already are, experiencing problems firsthand. In a later chapter, we will discuss ways in which a manufacturer can involve employees in the production process to ensure the quality of the finished product.

The Bakery's Production Process

Let's examine the operation of the bakery to see how the various steps are arranged in the bread-making process.

First, the baker receives raw materials. Some ingredients, like milk and butter, must be stored in the refrigerator.

Then the baker starts making bread by measuring out water, yeast, and flour and mixing them to create the sponge. Next, he allows the sponge to ferment.

After fermentation, the rest of the ingredients are added, mixed, and punched with machines. This forces carbon dioxide out, redistributes the yeasts, and equalizes the temperature throughout the dough. The resulting mixture, called the dough, is left to ferment again.

Following the second fermentation, the dough is punched again. The dough is then rolled and cut to size. The cut dough is placed in a pan and allowed to ferment again.

Finally, the fermented dough is baked, cooled, and packaged, ready to be delivered.

The bakery illustrates the importance of carefully planning the production process. Each of the production steps must be carried out precisely as planned and in exactly the proper order to ensure the eventual production of an edible loaf of bread. The ingredients must be mixed correctly, fermented for the proper amount of time, and baked at the right temperature. The dough must be placed in the pan before final fermentation and cooled before wrapping. Any variation from the process will spell culinary and business disaster.

Similarly, the flow of products through the process is of special importance because of the time-limited nature of the baking process. Any "piling up" at the fermentation or baking steps can completely ruin the final product.

Also, the bakery can experience serious problems with its inventories of incoming ingredients and finished products. Milk, butter, and even flour can all go bad while waiting for their turn in the mixing room. Similarly, baked bread has a limited shelf life which can expire before reaching the bakery's loading dock. For this reason, the baker identifies customers in advance and bakes bread to fill predetermined orders. The baker's potential problems with incoming and finished product inventories, however, merely underline the problems which all manufacturers can experience in these areas.

The Closet Door Manufacturing Process

Let's also analyze the process of the closet door manufacturer.

After receiving raw materials (exterior panels and long pieces of framing wood), the manufacturer stores them in inventory. Unfortunately, the supplier will not make deliveries small enough to be brought directly to the factory floor.

Once put into production, the raw materials are cut down to their proper size. One sawing station cuts the framing wood. Another cuts the exterior panels. This is an example of component processing early in the manufacturing process.

The cut framing material is joined together to form the door frame. This is a subassembly.

The cut exterior panel is then glued to the frame. This is a final assembly.

To ensure that the exterior panel fits properly on the frame, the manufacturer puts the assembled door into a machine which presses the panels firmly into place. The excess glue which leaks out the sides must be cleaned, and the glue holding the panels in place must dry. To save time, the manufacturer dries the glue in an oven. This also keeps the doors moving evenly through the manufacturing process.

Holes and mortises must be cut into the door for doorknobs and hinges. The door is cleaned and smoothed during the planing and sanding operation.

Finally, the door is packaged and shipped. Like the baker, the door manufacturer knows where to send the product and thus avoids losing time, labor, and space storing the completed doors.

2.5 Flowcharting the Process

An easy way to understand the manufacturing process is to see a picture of it. A diagram that shows how materials move through the various processing steps can help us understand the activity that occurs at each step and the relationships between the stages of production. Since these diagrams show the sequence of manufacturing operations and the flow of a product through the process, they are called "flowcharts."

Flowcharting has been widely used in the information processing field. In fact, flowcharting is so common in the data processing industry that the American National Standards Institute (ANSI) has formally defined the symbols used to represent different types of data processing operations. We can use these symbols, with some modifications, to represent the operations in the manufacturing process.

Process symbol: The symbol below represents any kind of processing function. That is, it represents a step where materials or component parts are changed in any way. For our purposes, this symbol will represent a processing function that is not labor-intensive, i.e., a step where the processing is done by machine. Baking bread, for example, is not labor-intensive; the oven does the work.

Manual operation: For our purposes, this symbol will represent a processing function that is labor-intensive. For example, receiving raw materials and components is labor-intensive, as it requires a considerable amount of human activity.

Decision symbol: The symbol shown below represents a decision or switching type of operation that determines which of a number of paths is to be followed. This symbol will become important when we introduce quality control measures to the manufacturing process.

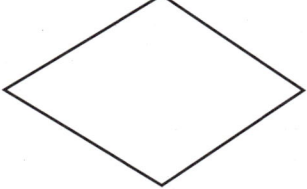

Flowline symbol: These symbols show the relationships between different steps in the production process. Arrows indicate the flow of materials or component parts from one production step to the next. Crossed lines have no interrelation except when a dot appears at the intersection. The relation of the dotted crossed lines will be made clear with arrows near the intersection. T-intersections are always interrelated, and arrows will show the interrelation.

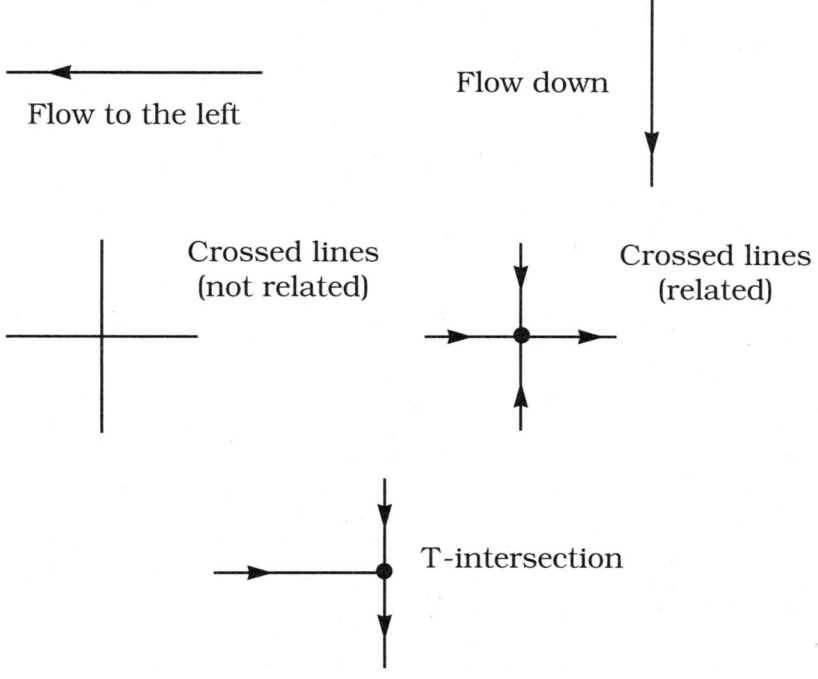

Now that we have defined our symbols, we will use them for diagramming the closet door manufacturing process. On page 31, we described the steps of the process. Table 2.1 provides a list of those steps and includes the type of symbol that will appear in our diagram.

Processing Step	Flowchart Symbol
Receive parts	Manual operation
Cut panels	Process
Cut framing sections	Process
Make door frame	Process
Glue panel to frame	Process
Press and clean door assembly	Process
Dry glue in oven	Process
Cut holes for doorknobs and mortises for hinges	Process
Plane edges of door	Process
Sand outer surfaces	Process
Package door	Manual operation
Ship door	Manual operation

Table 2.1: Closet Door Manufacturing Steps

Receiving, packaging, and shipping the doors are considered manual operations because handling the bulky doors involves extensive labor. All the other operations rely heavily on machines to do the work and are designated by process symbols. The cutting operations rely on saws. The door frames are made by special machines that hold the wood and insert staples. Pressing machines squeeze the exterior panels to the frame. Planing and sanding machines finish the surface of the door.

Now that we have identified all the process steps, we can arrange them in a diagram. Figure 2.1 is the diagram of how the raw materials, components, subassemblies, and final assemblies move through the manufacturing process to make the closet door.

Earlier in this chapter we discussed the bread-making process. Table 2.2 lists the various steps and identifies the type of symbol.

Processing Steps	Flowchart Symbols
Receive ingredients	Manual operation
Store ingredients	Manual operation
Measure and mix sponge	Process
Ferment sponge	Process
Measure, mix, and punch dough	Process
Ferment dough	Process
Punch dough	Process
Roll and cut dough	Process
Shape and pan dough	Manual operation
Ferment bread dough	Process
Bake bread	Process
Cool bread	Process
Package bread	Process
Distribute bread	Manual operation

Table 2.2: The Bread-Making Process

Receiving, storing, shaping, and distributing are all labor-intensive operations. The other operations involve either machines for mixing, cutting, packaging, and punching or ovens for fermenting and baking. Cooling is not labor-intensive. The flowchart for the process appears in Figure 2.2.

The flowchart is a visual presentation of the process. It allows us to see the process flow and makes it easier to analyze. In the next chapter we will use the flowchart to help us arrange the facility. Understanding the process flow more fully will enable us to make better decisions on how to arrange the physical layout of the plant.

THE PROCESS OF MAKING THE PRODUCT

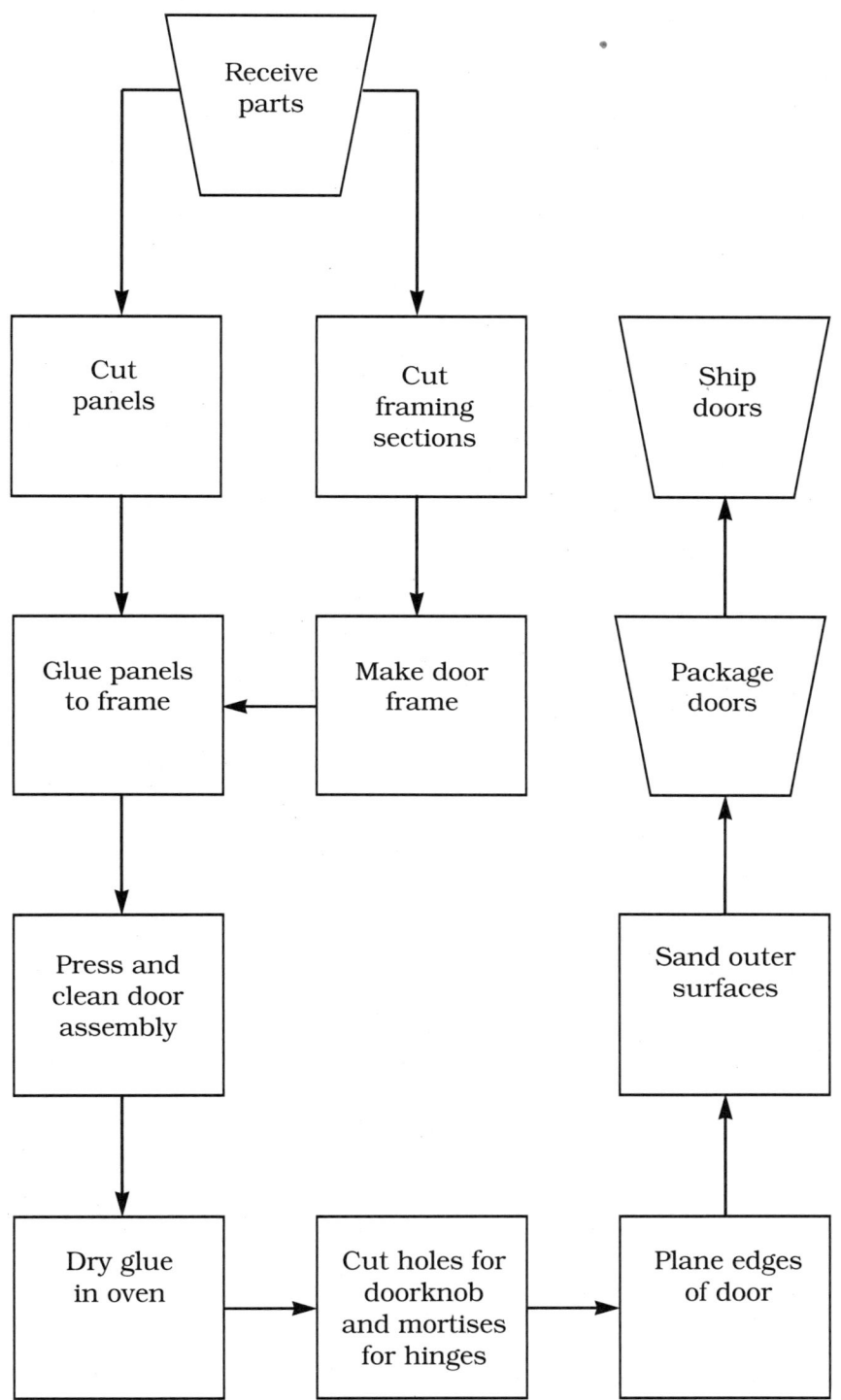

Figure 2.1: Flowchart of Closet Door Manufacturing Process

A BEGINNER'S GUIDE TO QUALITY IN MANUFACTURING

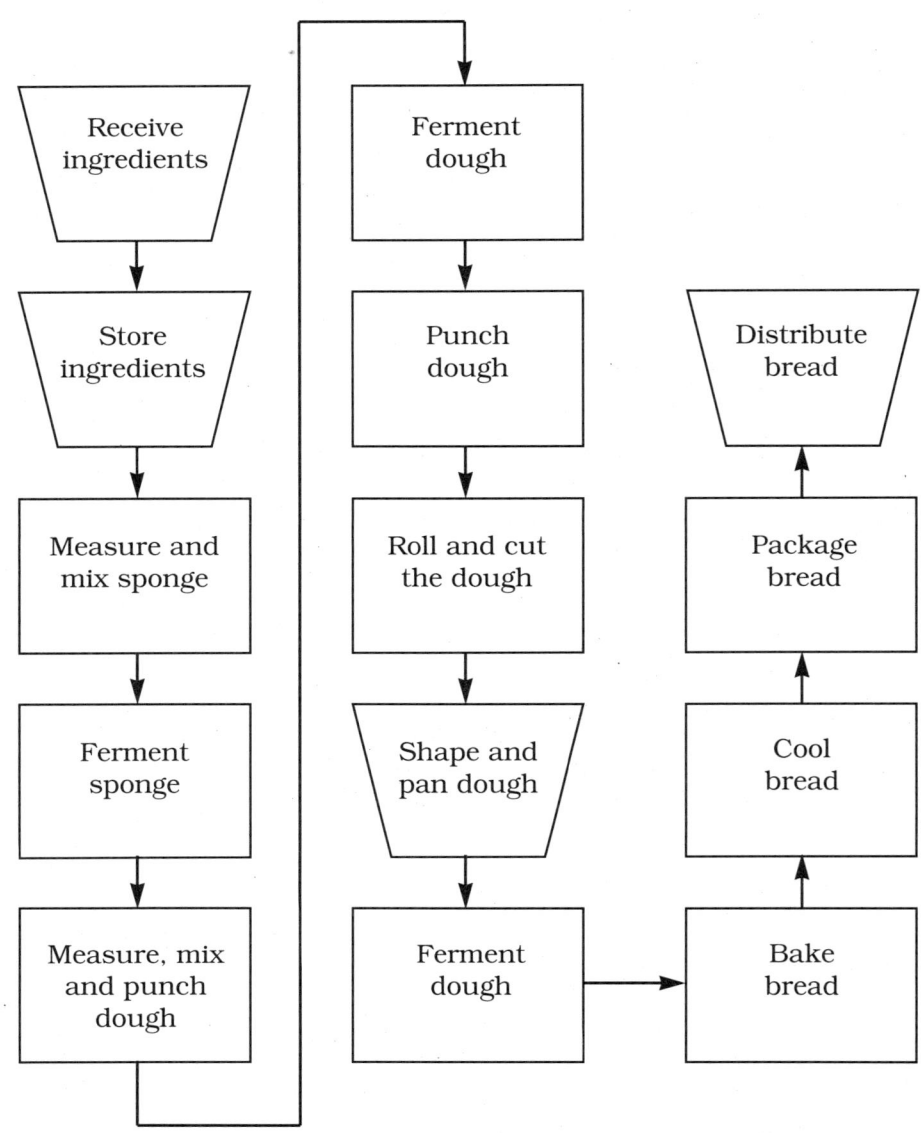

Figure 2.2: Flowchart of the Bread-Making Process

THE PROCESS OF MAKING THE PRODUCT

Chapter Summary

1. Manufacturing is a process that transforms raw materials and components into finished products.

2. The manufacturing process can be divided into basic steps: receiving, subassembly, final assembly, processing, packaging, and shipping.

3. Individual processes needed to create components, subassemblies, and finished products should be carefully specified and reviewed for manufacturing feasibility.

4. Manufacturers should evaluate the relative merits of making or buying individual components.

5. It is important to arrange the steps so that operations are done in their proper order. This will depend on the nature of the individual process as well as the availability, capabilities, and arrangement of machinery.

6. Products should flow evenly along the production process. Components processed in one step should not pile up waiting to be processed at the next step. Even flow of products results from balancing equipment and staff resources.

7. Incoming inventories are places where raw materials and components are stored. It is cost-efficient to eliminate these inventories, whenever possible, and send the received goods directly to the factory floor for immediate use.

8. Finished goods inventories are places where the packaged product is stored before they are sent to the customer. It is cost-efficient to eliminate these inventories, whenever possible, and send the product directly to the customer.

9. Change is an important part of the manufacturing process. Manufacturers should remain alert to possibilities to gain improved output or quality through changes in the production process. The potential savings from these changes should be weighed against the costs of lost production, retooling, and retraining associated with making the change.

10. Flowcharting is a graphic representation of how raw materials and components move through processing steps in the manufacturing process. Flowcharting uses symbols to represent steps in the process. It allows us to see where changes could improve the process, aids in planning for an even product flow, and enables us to make better decisions on how to arrange the physical layout of the plant.

Questions for Chapter 2

In this chapter, we have provided flowcharts for the closet door manufacturing process and the bread making process. Now, you will draw a flowchart for the AM radio manufacturing process.

1. For each of the processing steps, identify the correct flowchart symbol (either manual operation or process).

Processing Steps	Flowchart Symbols
Receive parts	
Send parts to factory floor	
Auto-insert components on PCB	
Solder components to PCB	
Hand-insert remaining components	
Tune radio	
Assemble radio in case	
Package radio	
Ship radio	

2. In the preceding exercise, you should have identified "auto-insert components on PCB" and "solder components to PCB" as "process" and the rest as "manual operation." Using a correct list, draw a flowchart for the AM radio manufacturing process, using the process, manual operation, and flowline symbols.

THE PROCESS OF MAKING THE PRODUCT

The following questions relate to the manufacture of a framed picture ready to hang on a wall. Another manufacturer will paint the picture or compose the print. We will receive the raw materials, make the frame, frame the picture, package it, and send it to the marketplace.

3. List the parts necessary to construct the wood frame. Remember to include the parts necessary to construct the hanging harness.

4. Describe the steps in the subassembly that processes the wood into a simple frame.

5. To this simple frame, we will attach four clips that will keep the picture in place. Describe the steps of a simple process to attach these clips.

6. Describe the steps required in the subassembly of the harness used for hanging the picture and the steps for attaching this harness to the frame.

7. Describe the packaging into which you will insert the finished product.

A BEGINNER'S GUIDE TO QUALITY IN MANUFACTURING

8. In answering questions 3–7, you outlined the steps necessary to manufacture a framed picture. Using these answers, make a list similar to that in Table 2.1 for the picture frame manufacturing process. Identify the steps as either manual operation or process.

9. Draw a flowchart, similar to the one in Figure 2.1, that will show the framed picture manufacturing process from receiving the parts to the final step of shipping the finished product. Check to make sure your steps are done in the proper order.

THE PROCESS OF MAKING THE PRODUCT

Chapter 2 Project

In chapter 1, you chose a product that you would like to make. You have already created a bill of materials; now you will identify the manufacturing processes and draw a flowchart.

1. Describe the assemblies and subassemblies necessary to produce your product.

2. Arrange these assemblies and subassemblies in the proper order, checking that operations are not repeated.

3. Prepare a list similar to Table 2.1 or Table 2.2, identifying each step as a manual operation or a process.

4. Using this list, draw a flowchart for the manufacturing of your product similar to Figure 2.1 or Figure 2.2.

CHAPTER 3

THE FACILITY

3.1 Introduction

Once we have carefully planned the process and defined the manufacturing steps, we must arrange our factory for the efficient production of high-quality products. To do so, we must consider a number of factors. First, the plant must be divided into general areas. We must consider where to place equipment and personnel, depending on our mix of products and their various processing requirements. Our goal is to make the product as fast as possible, while maintaining a high degree of quality.

3.2 Components of the Facility

The manufacturing plant can be divided into four basic areas: receiving, product processing, packaging, and shipping.

Receiving is the area where all raw materials and product components are brought into the plant from suppliers. Space must be provided for trucks that deliver the raw materials and components. The supplies must be checked to ensure that they are what was ordered. A record of what was received must be sent to the purchasing department so that suppliers can be paid. Space must be provided for all this checking and record-keeping. If the manufacturer stores supplies, there must be a storage area large enough to accommodate them. If the manufacturer stores a large number of raw materials and components, records must be kept on where each item is stored to help us find them quickly when we need them. If the manufacturer sends supplies directly to the factory floor, this area and the record-keeping can be eliminated. Since packaging from the supplies must be removed, an area must be provided for the storage of used packaging before it is discarded or recycled.

Product processing (manufacturing area) is the area where raw materials and components are transformed into the finished product. This is the area where the process steps take place, subassemblies are made, and the product is assembled. Accomplishing these tasks usually involves equipment. Space must be provided for the equipment. Additional space is usually required so workers can control, adjust, fix, and maintain the equipment. There are process steps that require a manual function. Space must be provided for the worker and, if needed, for tools, machines, equipment, or components. Raw materials, components, subassemblies, and final assemblies need enough space to move quickly from one step to another. Space must be provided for equipment that moves products along the manufacturing path, such as conveyer belts, hand trucks, or forklifts. Finally, workers and supervisors must have easy access to all areas on the manufacturing floor to perform their jobs. Pathways must allow them to move freely from one place to another.

Packaging is the area where the finished product is prepared for shipment. Usually the individual product is packed first, then the packaged units are bulk-packed for shipment. Space is required to store the packaging material. This is also the area where user's manuals, warranty information, promotional material, product surveys, installation materials, and the like are included in the packaging. Space must be provided for these items also. Some packaging areas require special equipment to close packages and bind them for shipment. This equipment and the workers doing the packaging all require the necessary space to perform their functions.

Shipping is the final area in the process. Some manufacturers store the packaged finished goods before sending them to the customer. These storage areas require space. Other manufacturers ship the packaged product directly to the customer, eliminating the need for finished goods storage. Space is needed to record what is being sent when filling the company's orders. Space is also needed to bring the packaged goods to the delivery trucks.

3.3 Guidelines for Arranging the Facility

The main object in arranging equipment and manual workstations is to minimize the handling and movement of raw materials, components, subassemblies, and final assemblies. Handling can be hazardous to the product. The more the product is handled, the greater its chances of being dropped and damaged. If it is a large product, this could also damage the facility or harm personnel.

THE FACILITY

Just as importantly, handling takes time. If you can arrange the factory so that you do not have to move the product frequently between workstations, you can use that wasted time and labor to make more products.

Types of Facility Layouts

There are three classic approaches to laying out the equipment and processing functions within a manufacturing facility.

Fixed position facilities come closest to meeting our goal of moving the product as little as possible as it undergoes production processing. In these facilities, the product occupies a constant fixed position in the center of the manufacturing area. Rather than physically moving the product through different processing points, the workers and equipment necessary for manufacturing steps are brought to the product. A good example of a fixed position manufacturing layout is a shipyard, where the ship under construction occupies a fixed position in the drydock. Certain aerospace industries also operate with fixed position manufacturing arrangements.

Process layouts are those in which equipment and workstations are arranged according to the type of process they perform. Saws would be in one part of the manufacturing area; drill presses would be in another; welding stations would be in a third; and paint booths would be in a fourth area. Process layouts are used primarily in job shops, where the facility produces a variety of different products and each requires a different series of processing steps to be performed in a different sequence.

Process layouts require the most movement of products from workstation to workstation since the equipment is arranged without regard to the processing needs of any one product. Job shops can attempt to reduce this unnecessary handling, however, by assessing movement between various workstations for each product. They can then determine the total number of product movements between workstations for all of their products and arrange the different process areas to reduce the total number of product movements.

Process layouts do have the advantage, however, of maximizing the efficiency of machinery usage. All products requiring drilling, for example, are moved to the same drill press. Therefore the total number of drill presses required is kept to a minimum.

Product layouts, on the other hand, are geared to production line operations which manufacture only one product or a limited series of products which undergo approximately the same processing steps in approximately the same sequence. In these cases, equipment and manual workstations are arranged to mirror the required flow of these specified products through the steps in the manufacturing process. If the first production process following reception of incoming raw material is cutting boards into door frame components, the first piece of equipment located adjacent to the receiving dock will be a saw. If the next process step is to assemble these components into a door frame, then adjacent to the first cutting station will be a frame assembly area.

While product layouts do require handling of products from step to step in the manufacturing process, they minimize the unnecessary movement of products between related steps by ensuring their close proximity.

Unlike process layouts, however, product layouts maximize the need for expenditures on equipment. Studies have shown that savings in process efficiency far outweigh these additional machine costs. If cutting stations are required at several steps along the processing route, product layouts would require purchasing separate saws for each step to allow the uninterrupted flow of work along the line.

Relationships Other Than Process Flow

The flow of product along the manufacturing process may not be the only factor in arranging workstations and support functions in the facility, however. Some processes have relationships to other processes and/or support functions which are unrelated to the flow of work. Certain pieces of equipment may require frequent emergency repair and should be located close to the maintenance shop. Other pieces of equipment may require special ventilation or lubrication.

Sometimes the relationships between two processing steps can actually be negative, making close proximity undesirable. For example, a sanding operation may immediately precede the finishing of a product with a sprayed coat of lacquer. The sanding generates large amounts of airborne dust, which can interfere with the spraying process.

When incompatibilities exist between steps, additional processing, such as cleaning steps, can be added. Additional equipment, like special exhaust fans, may also alleviate some of the problem. In general, all possibilities should be explored to ensure that movement of products is kept to a minimum.

Manufacturers can take these non-flow relationships into account using relationship charts which indicate the needs and reasons for closeness between all the processing steps and support functions.

Working with the Physical Plant

The physical size and shape of the facility—its walls, doors, windows, and plumbing—are also factors to take into account when planning a factory layout. These constraints will determine, in part, the path of our production line. Sometimes this path will be straight. Sometimes it will be circular, leading to and from the same loading dock that accommodates both incoming and shipping functions. In other cases, the production line may snake its way through the facility, around existing walls and partitions.

The receiving and incoming storage areas should be near a garage door or loading dock. This reduces the handling needed to bring raw materials and components into the plant. The shipping area should also be near a garage door so finished goods can be moved out easily.

As far as possible, manufacturers should plan the production line around the existing physical plant. However, if this leads to an inefficient production plan, it may be appropriate to make major changes to the physical plant. Once again, the firm will have to weigh the possibilities for savings from improved manufacturing efficiency against the costs of moving walls, making new garage doors, or expanding the factory.

When laying out individual work areas, the physical size of the equipment must be taken into consideration. There must be room for materials to move from one workstation to another. The door manufacturer, for example, has assembly machines for making the door frames. Workers must have enough room to go around the machine to place the framing wood into it and remove the finished frame.

Additionally, there must be enough space for workers to control the equipment, maintain it when necessary, and fix it when it breaks down. In the door manufacturing plant, sanding machines smooth the surfaces of the door. Periodically, worn sanding belts must be replaced. Room must be provided for this routine maintenance function. With adequate physical space, workers can change the belts quickly, and the machine can go back to the business of making the product (and the profit).

3.4 Facility Layout

The closet door manufacturer, the bakery, and the AM radio manufacturer are all production line operations and, therefore, will arrange their facilities in a product layout.

Let's look at how the bakery has arranged its physical plant. The layout drawing for the bakery appears in Figure 3.1. In chapter 2, we made a flowchart of the bread-making process

(Figure 2.2). By comparing this flowchart with the plant drawing, we can see how the bakery's layout relates to its product flow.

To begin with, the receiving area is located right next to the loading dock. This makes it easy to unload the ingredients. The flowchart indicates that the next step in the process is storing the ingredients. As we would hope, the baker has placed the storage areas right next to the receiving area. Notice the dry storage and cold storage areas in the layout. Cold storage is required for the milk and butter. Flour is kept in the dry storage area; it doesn't have to be refrigerated, but it should be kept cool and dry. Temperature is sometimes an important consideration in laying out the plant. For example, the cold storage area should not be located adjacent to the ovens, which can give off substantial heat.

The storage step is followed by the measuring and mixing process. Therefore, the storage area should be near the measuring and mixing equipment. Again, the bakery has used the flowchart to arrange the layout of the factory so that products take the shortest path through the process.

Once the ingredients are mixed into the sponge, they must be fermented. The fermentation chamber is located next to the mixing area. Movement of the product is kept to a minimum. The punching machines are also near the fermentation chamber, since this step occurs before and after fermentation.

After the final punching step, the dough is rolled and cut. The rolling and cutting area is next to the punching machine. The bread is then panned, and the panning area is next to the rolling and cutting area.

After panning, the bread is again fermented. The panning area is near the fermenting chamber. Because the bread must be fermented a number of times, the mixing, punching, rolling, cutting, and panning areas have all been arranged around the fermenting chamber. The chamber has been selected because it has sufficient capacity to handle the simultaneous fermenting of bread at each stage in the process. This allows the bakery to maintain a continuous flow of products. Notice, as well, that the fermenting chamber has two doors. This allows the bakers to put bread in from one side as it begins the fermentation process and take it out the other after the process is completed.

After the final fermentation, the bread goes to the ovens for baking. The baking ovens are near the fermentation chamber. After baking, the bread is taken to the cooling racks.

The cooling racks are near the baking ovens but in a different room. This is because the fermentation chamber and ovens give off heat and must be insulated from the cooling area.

Once the bread is cooled, it is packed and shipped. The packaging area is next to the cooling racks and near the shipping area. Finally, the shipping area is next to the garage door, so loaves of bread can be easily loaded onto delivery trucks.

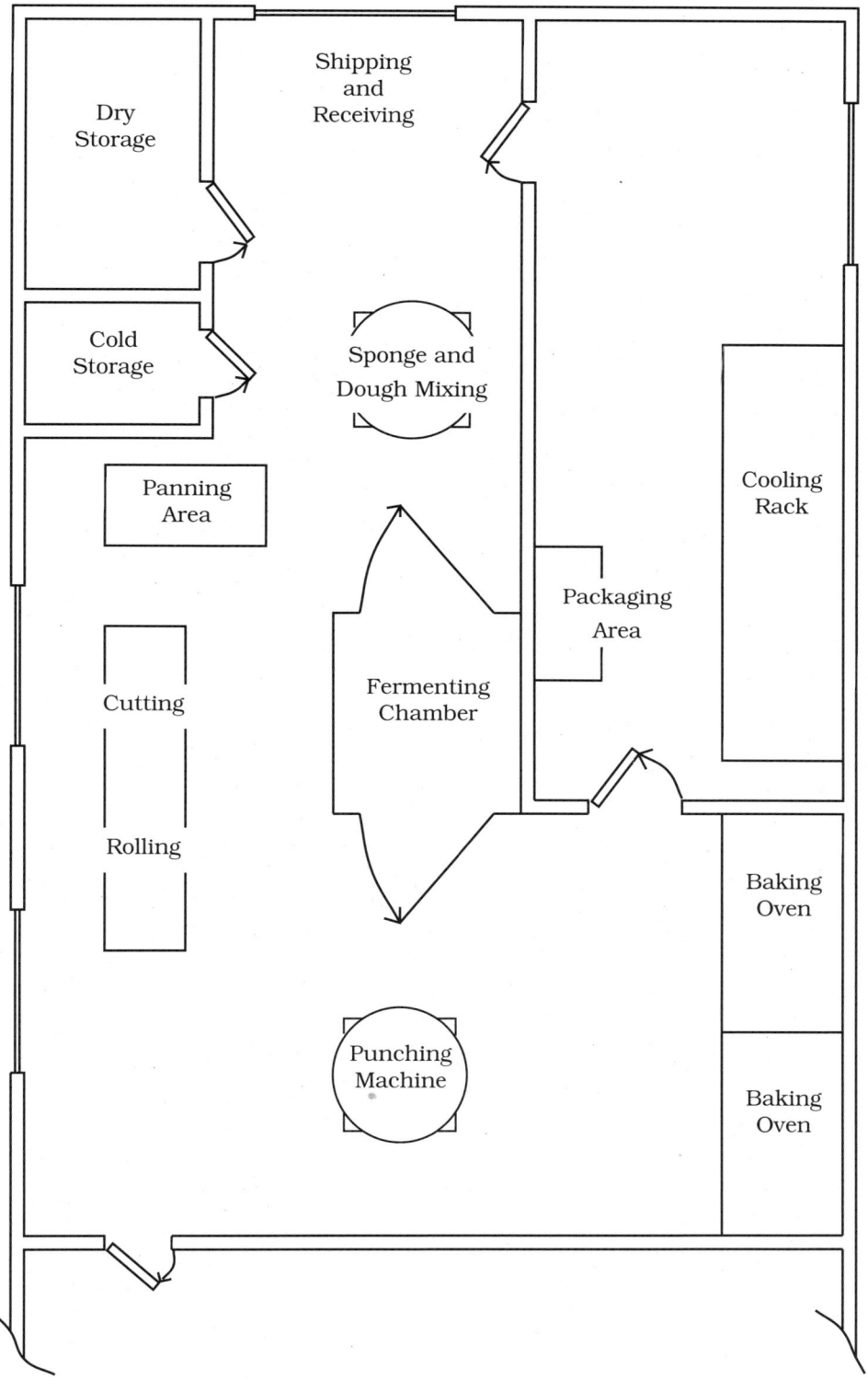

Figure 3.1: Layout of the Bakery

The bakery is a good example of a properly organized plant. As the product moves from one step to another, the physical areas where these steps are accomplished are near each other. Of the 14 steps in the bread-making process, five involve mixing, fermenting, and punching; and they follow one another in the flowchart drawing. Because these processes repeat, the baker has arranged the machines in a straight line, allowing the bread to move along this path quickly.

The baker has also left enough space around the machines so that workers can make necessary adjustments to the machines. The temperature of the fermentation chamber and ovens must be set properly. Adjustments to the rolling and cutting machines must be made so that the bread is the proper size. Enough room has been left for the workers to do the panning and packing. The baker has used the physical plant to best advantage. By reducing the time it takes to move the bread between steps, the baker can produce more bread.

Now let's look at the door manufacturer's plant. The flowchart appeared in Figure 2.1 of chapter 2. The factory layout appears in Figure 3.2. Compare the flowchart with the layout. Did the door manufacturer keep the receiving and shipping areas near garage doors? Are the process areas near those steps that precede them? Did the door manufacturer keep things moving in a straight line? Is there enough room around equipment for workers to control, maintain, and adjust machines?

From the layout drawing, it appears that the door manufacturer did locate the receiving and shipping area near garage doors. There also appears to be enough room around the machines for the workers to perform their jobs. But there are serious problems in the location of some of the machines.

According to the flowchart, after the framing material is received, it must be cut. The layout drawing shows that the receiving and storage area for the framing material is on the other side of the factory from the frame cutting equipment. This means time is wasted transporting uncut framing material all the way across the factory floor.

The door panels also present a problem during the early phases of production. They are received and stored in an area that is far away from the panel cutting saws. Once cut, they have to be moved all the way across the factory floor to the final assembly area. Again, time is wasted moving the panels from one place to another. It would be better if the pressing machine, drying ovens, cutting machines, planing machine, and sanding machines could be in a straight line so conveyer belts could easily move the doors from one process to another.

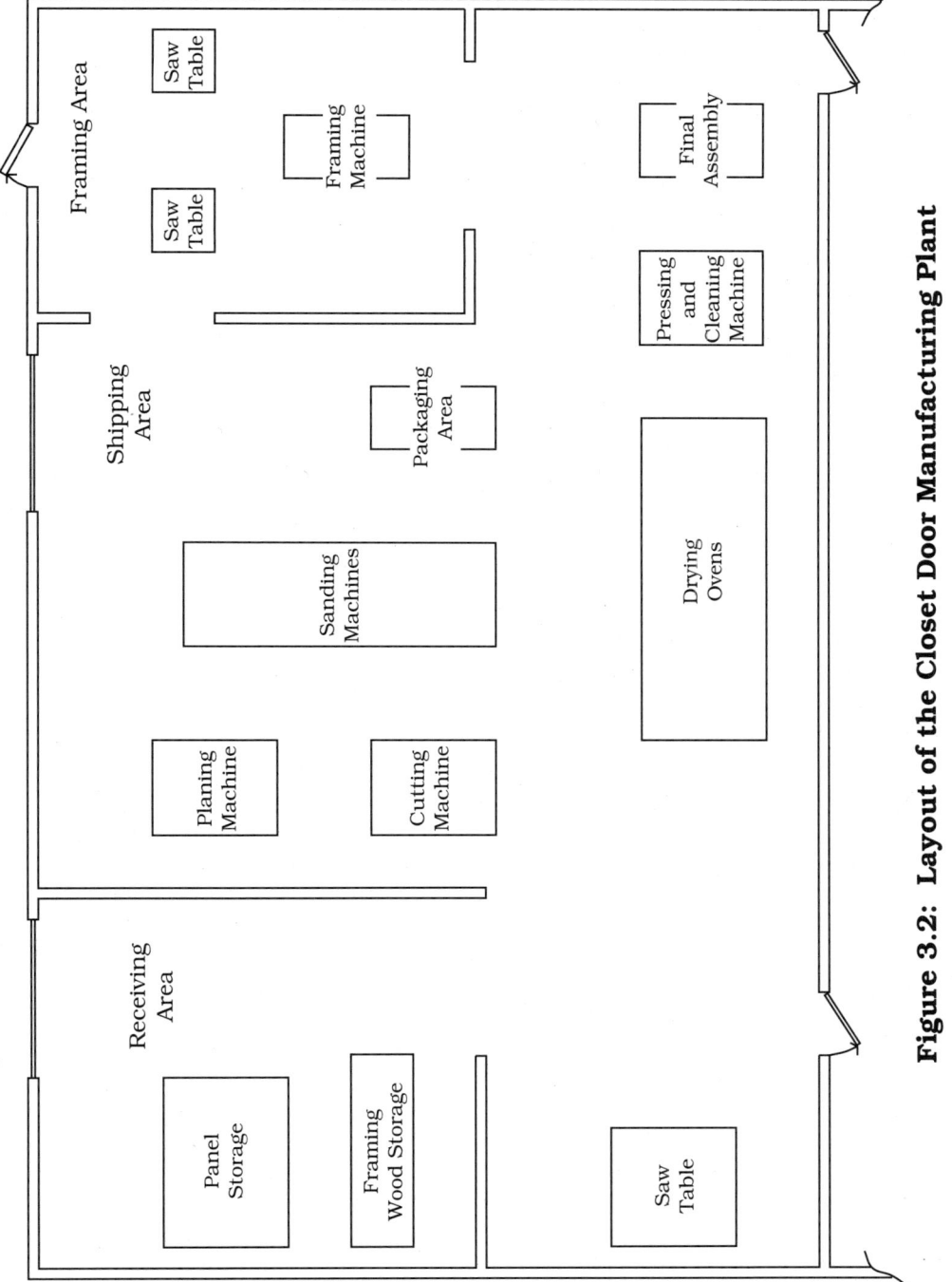

Figure 3.2: Layout of the Closet Door Manufacturing Plant

Figure 3.3 diagrams the movement of the door through various stages of production. As soon as we draw product movement lines on the layout diagram, it becomes apparent that the product is moving long distances between some manufacturing steps. It is also apparent that the product makes too many turns through the process.

What are some of the things that we can do to improve the situation? The first thing we might try is eliminating the interior walls on the factory floor. If they're not structural walls, we may be able to do this quite easily. We can add partitions where we need them.

The framing area must be moved closer to the receiving area. Let's store the framing wood between the receiving area and the framing area. Let's also move the panel cutting saw closer to the panel storage area. Then we'll locate the final assembly area near both the panel saws and the framing machine. Notice that we are closely following the flowchart for the door-making process.

Next, let's arrange the pressing and cleaning machine, drying oven, cutting machine, and planing machine along the long wall. We will use conveyer belts to move the door along this path. The sanding step comes next. Use the sanding machine to bring the door up to the shipping area. The packaging machine will separate the sanding machine from the shipping area.

All the processes are now included in our plan. The equipment follows the flowchart. Now we must be careful to leave enough room for workers to do their jobs, and our plan will be ready for final review. Remember, before any walls or equipment are moved, this plan must be drawn on paper. The plant and equipment must be drawn to scale. We must be sure everything will fit in the space we have provided and that there is enough room to work.

Plans for the new factory layout appear in Figure 3.4. Lines are used to show the product movement.

Compare Figure 3.3 with Figure 3.4. The first thing that you notice is that lines showing product movement are much shorter in Figure 3.4. By relocating the equipment, we have greatly reduced the distance needed to move the product through the factory. In fact, if you add up all the lines in Figure 3.3 and compare that total with the sum of all the lines in Figure 3.4, you will find that the distance required for the product to travel through the factory has been divided in half.

By reducing handling and the time it takes to move products, we can reassign workers and increase productivity. Increased productivity means greater profits. Arranging the factory properly also means giving the workers the space needed to do their jobs. By improving their workplace, we help them do their jobs more quickly, and productivity again can increase.

THE FACILITY

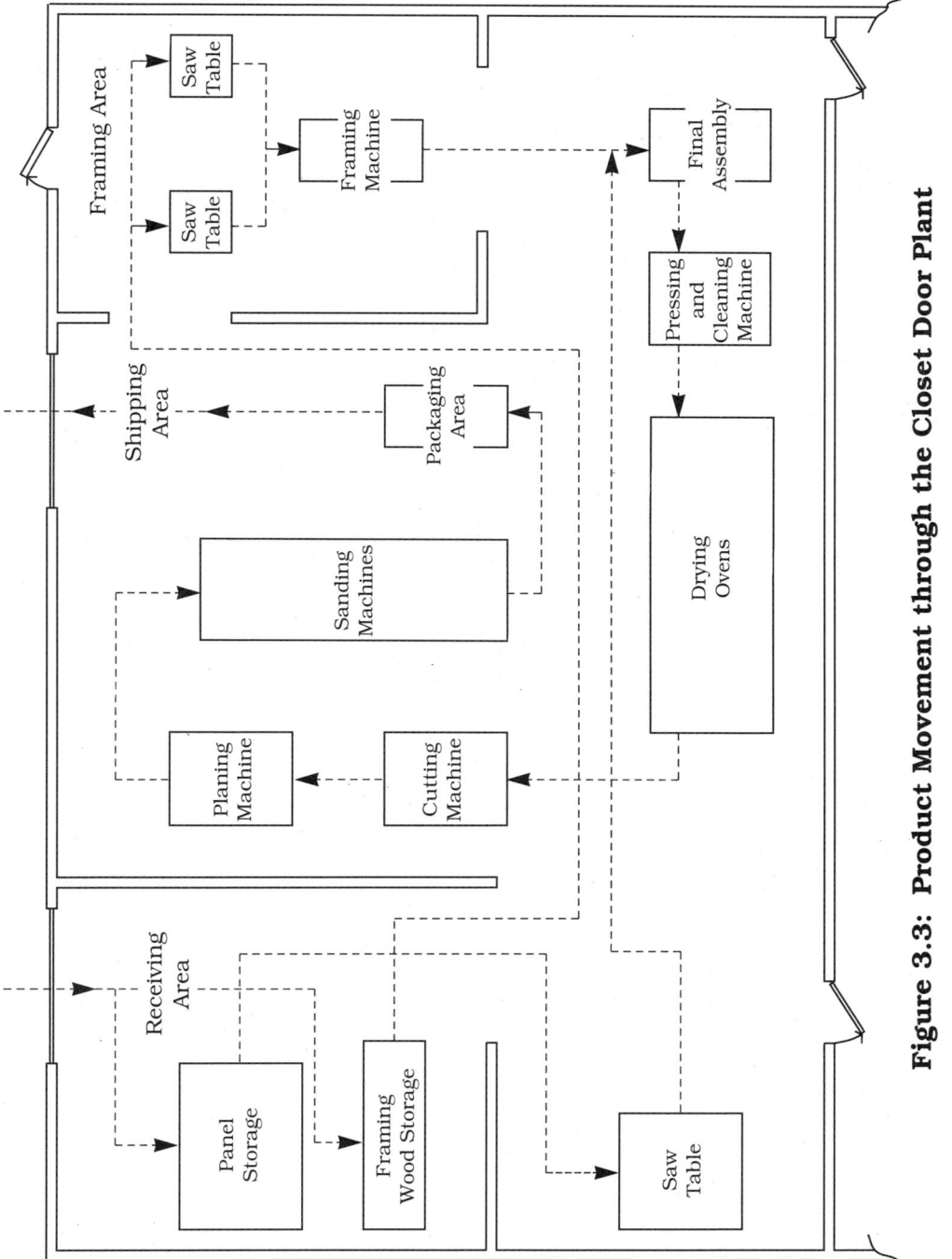

Figure 3.3: Product Movement through the Closet Door Plant

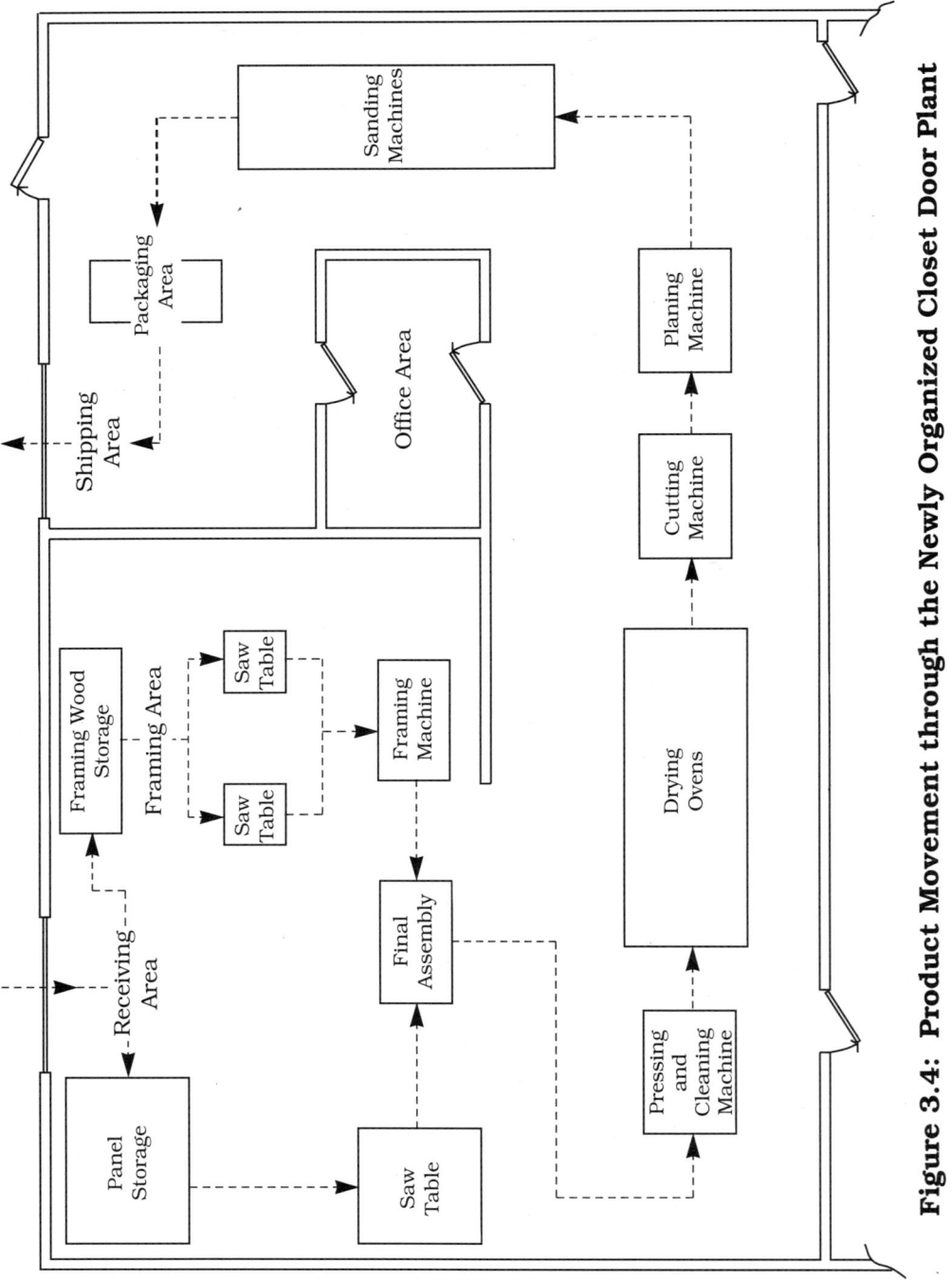

Figure 3.4: Product Movement through the Newly Organized Closet Door Plant

THE FACILITY

Chapter Summary

1. The manufacturing plant can be divided into four areas: receiving, product processing, packaging, and shipping.

2. The main objective in arranging a plant layout is to reduce handling of raw materials, components, subassemblies, and final products. Unnecessary product handling leads to increased damage and wasted staff time.

3. Job shops produce a variety of products and arrange equipment according to the types of processes they perform. Process layouts do the least to minimize product movement and handling between workstations. The advantages of process layouts are flexibility in processing different products and reduced equipment requirements.

4. Product layouts are used by production line shops that manufacture only one product or a limited series of products. These products require similar process steps in approximately the same sequence. Product layouts arrange equipment and workstations based on the flow of raw materials and components through the steps in the production process. Product layouts mirror process flowcharts and keep the distance between manufacturing steps as short as possible.

5. Factors other than product flow, such as temperature considerations or ventilation needs, also affect the arrangement of process steps and support functions.

6. Plant layouts must leave enough space for the equipment. There must be enough space around equipment so that it can be controlled, maintained, and repaired. There must be sufficient space for the product to move freely and easily from one area to the next and for the workers to do their jobs easily. This improves productivity.

Questions for Chapter 3

1. Using the flowchart that you drew for the AM radio manufacturing process at the end of chapter 2, associate each workstation in Figure 3.5 with its appropriate processing step.

2. Draw arrows in the diagram to show the movement of the radio through various stages of production.

In answering the questions at the end of chapter 2, you drew a flowchart for manufacturing a framed picture. Use this flowchart to answer the following.

3. Describe the type of machines and assembly areas you will need to perform each step.

4. Describe the type of maintenance each machine will require. Decide whether each machine requires a significant amount of space for control, maintenance, and repair.

5. Is storage space necessary during the manufacturing process? List the steps that might require a storage area after completion.

6. Draw a layout for the manufacture of the picture frame similar to the layouts provided in this chapter for the bread manufacturing process and the closet door manufacturing process.

7. Diagram the movement of the product through various stages of production. Does the layout provide short distances between manufacturing steps? Do the steps proceed in a straight line? Are processing steps that may have an undesirable relationship sufficiently separated from each other? Redraw the layout if necessary.

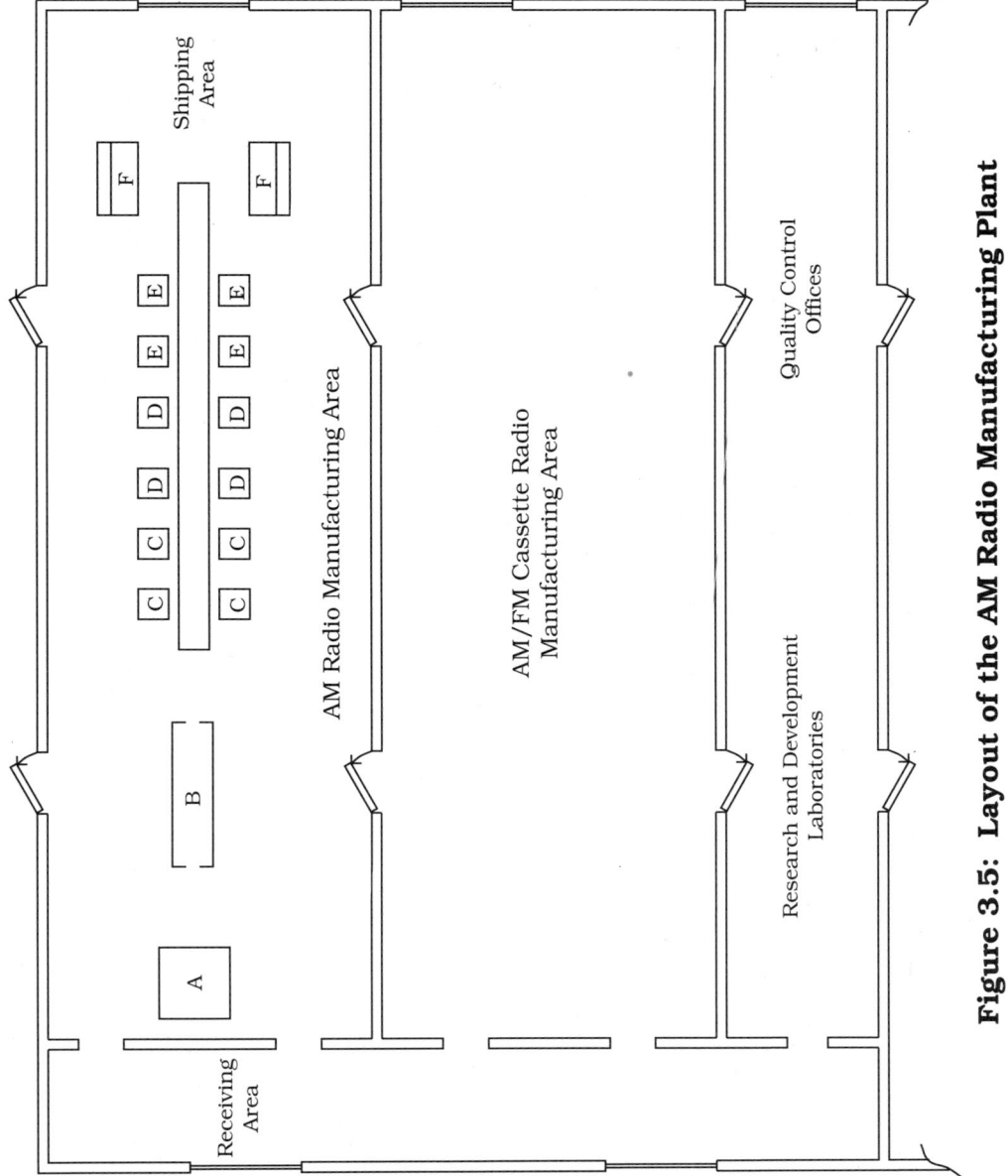

Figure 3.5: Layout of the AM Radio Manufacturing Plant

Chapter 3 Project

For the product you chose in chapter 1, you will draw a layout. The steps closely parallel questions 3–7 at the end of chapter 3.

1. Describe the type of machines and assembly areas you will need for each processing step.

2. Describe the type of maintenance required for each machine. Decide how much space must be provided for controlling, maintaining, and repairing the machine.

3. Is storage space necessary? List the processing steps that will require storage space after completion.

4. Draw a layout for the plant that will manufacture this product.

5. Diagram the movement of the product through the various stages of production. Does the diagram provide short distances between steps? Do the steps proceed in a straight line? Are processing steps that have undesirable relationships sufficiently separated? Redraw the layout if necessary.

QUALITY CONTROL

4.1 Introduction

The time has come to bring quality control into the production process. The manufacturers have identified and carefully specified a product that satisfies their customers' needs. They have identified the steps in the production process and laid out their equipment and work areas to accommodate this process. Finally, they have committed themselves to the production of a quality product—one that meets specifications each and every time. Their goal is "no rejects."

The question now is how can they accomplish this goal of quality production. What steps must they take to ensure that their factory produces a finished product that consistently meets specifications?

In this chapter, we will survey the general procedures that make up a quality control program in a manufacturing process. We will explore the role of product inspection and examine the reasons for conducting inspections at various points in the production process. We will discuss incoming inspection, process control points, and final inspection.

4.2 Inspection and the Quality Product

You will remember from chapter 1 that the closet door manufacturer is concerned about the quality of his finished product. He had learned that many customers were dissatisfied with the doors. Some of these doors didn't fit in the standard-size door openings; others were too small. Many customers were sending the doors back for replacement, and the manufacturer had to pay the shipping cost both ways. Others simply wanted a refund and were taking their future business elsewhere.

To solve the problem, the manufacturer has begun to inspect each finished door. An inspector measures the height, width, and thickness and compares them to the specified minimum and maximum tolerances. He also checks the surface of the door and the cutouts for locks and the mortises for hinges.

This final inspection procedure has been very successful; now the company almost never sells an imperfect door to a customer. The closet doors consistently conform to the specifications.

Unfortunately for the manufacturer, this final inspection has not eliminated a serious quality control problem that threatens to put the company out of business. The company still has to manufacture 10 closet doors to find six that will meet specifications. The four finished doors which the manufacturer rejects are increasing his costs substantially. Each unacceptable door costs the company $12.29 in scrap costs, and the 40 percent reject rate adds $4.00 in fixed costs to each finished product actually sold. The company's quality problems are increasing the per-unit production costs by over 66 percent (see Table 1.7).

The use of a final inspection procedure has saved the manufacturer's reputation with customers. It has also eliminated the costs incurred when replacing defective doors for clients. However, the final inspection has not reduced any of the actual production costs associated with manufacturing doors that don't meet specifications.

This example illustrates several crucial points concerning the value of quality control procedures and their placement in the production process.

Product inspections do not eliminate quality problems; they merely identify them. As we've seen, the manufacturer has not solved problems merely by implementing a final inspection. He has, however, learned exactly how bad the situation is—a 40 percent reject rate. Final inspection has also identified the general areas where these problems arise. Customers are not returning the doors because of blemishes in the wood or problems with installing locks and hinges but because the doors do not meet the size specifications.

The quality problems that product inspections identify have already occurred "upstream" in the production process. Until the manufacturer implemented the final inspection procedure, it was possible that customers were returning doors that had been damaged after being shipped from the factory. By using final inspection, the manufacturer now knows that at least 40 percent of his products are defective when they complete the production process.

Quality problems generally become more expensive as they move "downstream" in the production process. Our earlier cost analysis showed that the manufacturer's 40 percent defect rate led to a 66 percent increase in production cost. However, this cost calculation represented only the increased cost at the end of the manufacturing process. Once the product was shipped, the company incurred substantial additional costs in time lost to salesmen during the complaint process, shipping costs to return the defective product and deliver a replacement, expenses to correct billings, and, most important, lost customers.

Moreover, costs resulting from quality problems begin to grow long before the product leaves the factory. All work done on a rejected product is wasted work. This means the manufacturer is losing money on employee salaries, space costs, equipment, and so on. The sooner defective products are identified, the sooner this wasteful allocation of valuable resources can be corrected. Further processing of a defective product may also reduce the likelihood that materials and component parts can be repaired or salvaged for reuse. The cost of this repair or salvage effort is also likely to rise as the product nears the end of the production process. In short, the further defective products travel along the production process, the more expensive they become to reject.

Although the final inspection procedure has not solved all the difficulties, it has been extremely valuable to our closet door manufacturer. It has identified both the magnitude and the general area of his quality problems. Moreover, the manufacturer has avoided alienating customers and further increasing costs by passing along a defective product.

The manufacturer will reap one additional major benefit from this final inspection procedure.

Product inspections identify opportunities to correct quality problems on finished products, processed materials, or components. In chapter 1, we listed the specifications of 10 doors which the manufacturer produced. Four doors had to be rejected because they did not meet the size specifications. Three of the four were smaller than the minimum tolerances for either height, width, or thickness. One of the four, however, was rejected because it was too wide—2'7" instead of the stated maximum acceptable width of 2'6 1/8".

Since the manufacturer has now identified defective products before they were shipped to the customer, he may correct the defects wherever possible. Nothing can be done about the doors that have been cut too small, but the manufacturer can recut the door that is too wide. Removing one additional inch from the width of this door can transform a reject product into one which matches specifications perfectly. This corrective action reduces the company's defect rate from 40 percent to 30 percent and has a major positive effect on production costs.

4.3 Inspection Points and the Manufacturing Process

In light of the benefits that we have seen from the door manufacturer's inspection of finished products, it seems obvious that the company would benefit from additional inspections at other points in the manufacturing process. The question, however, is where in the process the manufacturer should install these quality control procedures.

Incoming Inspection

As we have seen, inspections can only identify problems which have occurred "upstream." Moreover, unidentified quality problems lead to increasing costs as they move "downstream" through the production process. Therefore, a manufacturer should implement inspections at the earliest point where they are likely to detect quality problems. For almost all manufacturing companies, the earliest point in the production process is the receiving of raw materials and component parts.

Manufacturers usually play two roles in the business world. On one hand, they produce goods which they hope eventually to sell. At the same time, they are also customers who purchase needed raw materials and component parts from their own suppliers. Like any other customers, manufacturers set specifications for the raw materials and component parts they buy. Manufacturers, however, are unlike many customers in that their specifications are extremely precise. Since materials and component parts become part of the finished product, the manufacturer sets these specifications based on the specifications for their own final products.

Therefore, it is easy to understand the importance of raw material and component specifications. If manufacturers start with parts or components that do not comply with specifications, they cannot expect the final products to be acceptable. The process of verifying the acceptability of components and raw materials before the manufacturing process begins is called *incoming inspection.*

As the name Incoming Inspection suggests, components and parts are inspected as soon as they arrive at the manufacturing facility. If they are not acceptable (i.e., they do not conform to specifications), they can be sent back to the supplier immediately. The supplier must quickly substitute acceptable components and/or parts to keep the manufacturing process from being interrupted.

Let's take a quick look at how the use of incoming inspection procedures can help the closet door manufacturer eliminate quality problems before production begins.

As you remember from chapter 1, the door manufacturer had set a specification of 1 3/8", with a tolerance of ±1/8", for the door's thickness. The maximum acceptable thickness, therefore, was 1 1/2". The minimum acceptable thickness was 1 1/4".

To construct a finished closet door which conforms to these specifications, the manufacturer set precise specifications for the materials used in the production process. The wood for constructing the door's inner frame was specified to have a thickness of 1 1/8", with allowable tolerances of ±1/16". Each of the two surface panels which are glued to the frame were specified to have a thickness of 1/8", ±1/32".

Based on these raw material specifications, the finished door would meet its own thickness specification if the components conformed to specifications. Table 4.1 shows how the finished door's thickness will vary within its specification as the materials vary within their own minimum and maximum thicknesses.

	Stated Specification	Minimum Specification	Maximum Specification
Framing wood	1 1/8"	1 1/16"	1 3/16"
Surface panel #1	1/8"	3/32"	5/32"
Surface panel #2	1/8"	3/32"	5/32"
Finished door	1 3/8"	1 1/4"	1 1/2"

Table 4.1: Variations in Finished Door

If each of the raw materials exactly matches its stated specification, the finished door will exactly match its own stated specification of 1 3/8". If each of the components is at the minimum limit of its specification, the finished door will have a thickness of 1 8/32" or 1 1/4"—exactly the minimum acceptable size. If each of the components is at the maximum limit of its specification, the finished door will be 1 16/32" or 1 1/2" thick—exactly the maximum acceptable size.

It is true that the finished door may still fall within its overall specification if only one piece of material is "out of spec" by a small margin. However, the manufacturer can only be assured of meeting overall product specifications if all raw materials meet the specifications. Therefore, the quickest way to prevent potential quality problems from moving downstream in the production process is to inspect incoming raw materials and component parts.

To improve the quality of finished product, the closet door manufacturer has begun to inspect incoming shipments of framing wood and surface panels. We will take a closer look at these inspections in chapter 6. For the moment, however, let's see what the manufacturer learns from this effort. All of the surface panels have met specifications. In some shipments of framing wood, however, several pieces measure 1 1/4" in thickness—a full 1/8" over the maximum acceptable size.

You may remember that one of the doors in our manufacturer's batch of 10 finished products was rejected because it had a thickness of 1 5/8"—1/8" more than the maximum acceptable thickness. Now we know how it came to be that size. This defect wasn't the result of problems in the production process. The manufacturer was actually buying a quality problem from the supplier and installing it in the finished product. If the unacceptable material had been caught at incoming inspection, the manufacturer could have reduced the reject rate by 25 percent. Just as important, early detection could have prevented a potential quality problem from becoming more expensive as it moved through the production process.

Process Control Points

Like most manufacturers, however, the closet door company can't blame all its quality problems on its suppliers. We have already seen that the manufacturer processes these raw materials and components in a number of ways to produce the finished product. The door manufacturer cuts both the panels and the framing wood to specified sizes. He assembles the frame out of the components that have been cut and then glues the panels to it, using a press and a drying oven. Holes and mortises are cut for doorknobs and hinges. The door's edges and surfaces are planed and sanded to an acceptable finish. Finally, he packages the finished product for shipping.

Quality problems can arise during any one of these operations. The panels and framing wood can be cut to the wrong size, or the cuts themselves can be crooked. The frame can be assembled incorrectly—out of square or badly fastened. Workers may position the panels improperly when gluing them on the frame, or damage the panels when putting them in the press or the drying oven. Equipment settings used to cut the holes or mortises can loosen, and sanding equipment can slip. Every time we do anything during the production process, there is the potential of doing it wrong.

As a result of these potential production problems, the manufacturer must implement quality control measures throughout the production process. These test and inspection points are called *process control points* and usually occur when the product moves from one step to another in the production process.

Each process control point added to the production process represents at least two additional steps in the manufacturing flowchart.

The first step in a process control point is the inspection itself. The manufacturer will inspect the product, material, or component that has just completed a step in the production process. The manufacturer wants to see whether it conforms to specifications set for it at that point. The door manufacturer, for example, will measure the exterior door panels after they have been cut to ensure that they fit the door frame. Similarly, the individual frame components will be measured after cutting to ensure that they are the correct length.

The inspection is a decision step. It allows the manufacturer to decide whether the product meets specifications and can continue along the production process. Even more important, the inspection tells the manufacturer whether the production process itself is working correctly. It allows the manufacturer to decide whether the equipment, employees, and processing procedures are producing a product which meets specifications.

The second step in a process control point is the action step. If a manufacturer has decided that a product or component does not meet its specifications at a certain point in the production process, steps must be taken to correct the problem. This, again, is a two-part process. First, he must correct the defect in the component which has completed processing; then he must identify and correct the actual problem in the production process which caused the defect.

The manufacturer must decide where to locate process control points in the production process. This decision will be based on the type of defects which individual production steps can create.

Sometimes a production process may create a defect that will have no effect at all on whether the finished product meets its specifications. If a piece of wood used in the closet door frame is scratched during handling, it doesn't matter. The frame will be covered by the surface panel, and no one will ever see the scratch. There is no need, therefore, to implement an inspection procedure for the framing wood after it is brought to the cutting station from the manufacturer's storehouse. The wood has already been inspected for conformance to specifications upon receipt from the supplier. Surface damage due to handling after that inspection won't affect the finished product.

In other cases, the production error will affect the finished product's quality but can be easily corrected if it is caught soon enough. An improperly positioned door panel can be repositioned correctly if it is spotted before the glue dries. Excess glue which was not removed earlier can be eliminated any time before packaging. A length of framing wood that is cut too short can be recut for use as another, smaller component in the frame.

If, however, the manufacturer continues to process the product after this initial error, he may no longer be able to correct the problem easily or at all. The improperly positioned door panel may result in the loss of both the panel and the frame if the glue is allowed to set. The framing wood which is cut too short will weaken the entire frame. To correct the problem at this point, the manufacturer will have to disassemble the frame before replacing it.

Finally, some production errors simply make the material or finished product unusable. They cannot be corrected. The product or material must be discarded. If a surface panel is cut too short or is deeply scratched during handling, it may be unusable. If the doorknob hole is cut incorrectly, the whole door may have to be discarded.

Process control points should be inserted in the manufacturing process at any point where defects can affect the finished product's conformance to specifications. The sooner defects are caught, the less expensive they are to correct. Even more important, the sooner defects are identified, the quicker the production process can be corrected so that additional defective pieces won't be produced.

In many cases, the manufacturer may only decide to inspect the first piece processed in a specific production lot. In others, he may opt to test a sample of components that have completed a step in the production process. In still other cases, the decision may be to inspect every piece processed. In chapter 6 we will look in detail at specific techniques for setting up and using process control points.

For the moment, however, let's see how the closet door manufacturer can use process control inspections to identify defects and correct the production process.

As we've seen, the manufacturing process for producing the closet door is relatively straightforward. (The basic flowchart for this production process appears in Figure 4.1.) The manufacturer begins by purchasing two types of wood to construct the frame and the exterior panels. Both materials go to the appropriate cutting stations. Panels are cut to the specified size. The framing wood is also cut into appropriate sizes for use as components in the door frame. As shown in the original flowchart, the manufacturer would simply send the cut framing wood on to the station where they would be assembled into the door frame. Similarly, the cut exterior panels would simply be forwarded for gluing onto the frame.

Our door manufacturer has now modified the production process to incorporate several quality control steps. The revised flowchart appears in Figure 4.2. Let's take a look at the additional steps that these quality control efforts have added to the production process up to this point.

First, the manufacturer has added the incoming inspection

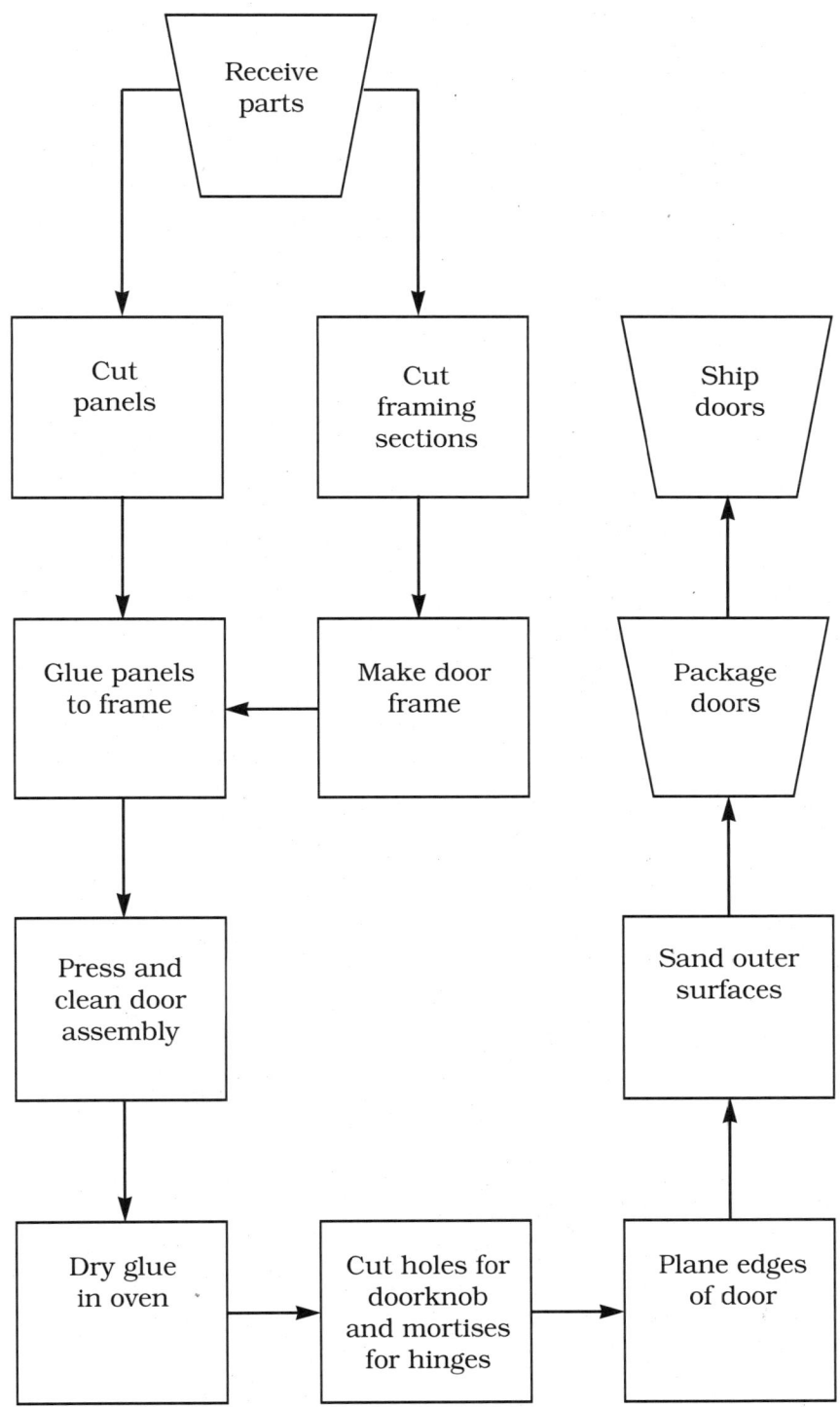

Figure 4.1: Flowchart of the Closet Door Manufacturing Process

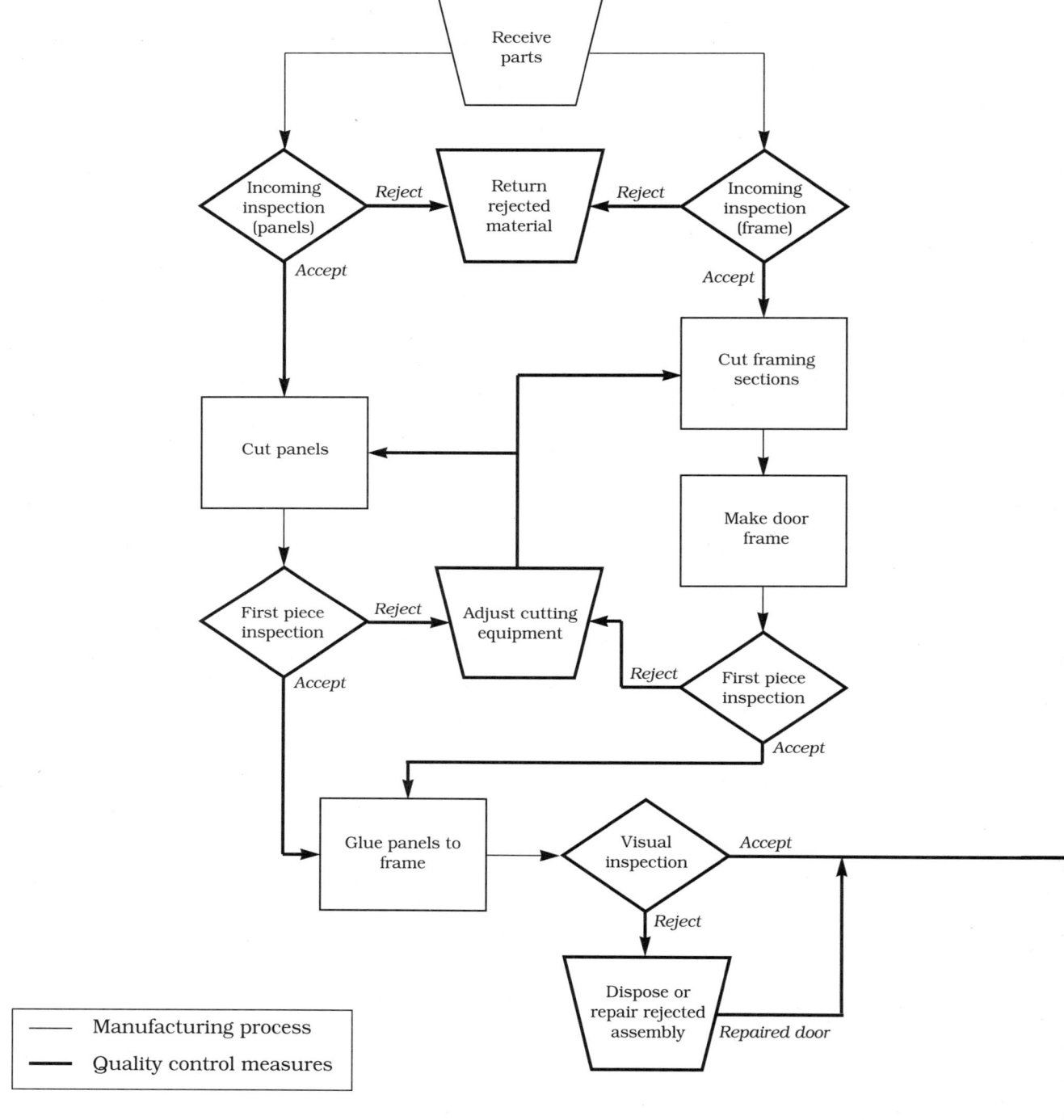

Figure 4.2: The Closet Door Manufacturing

QUALITY CONTROL

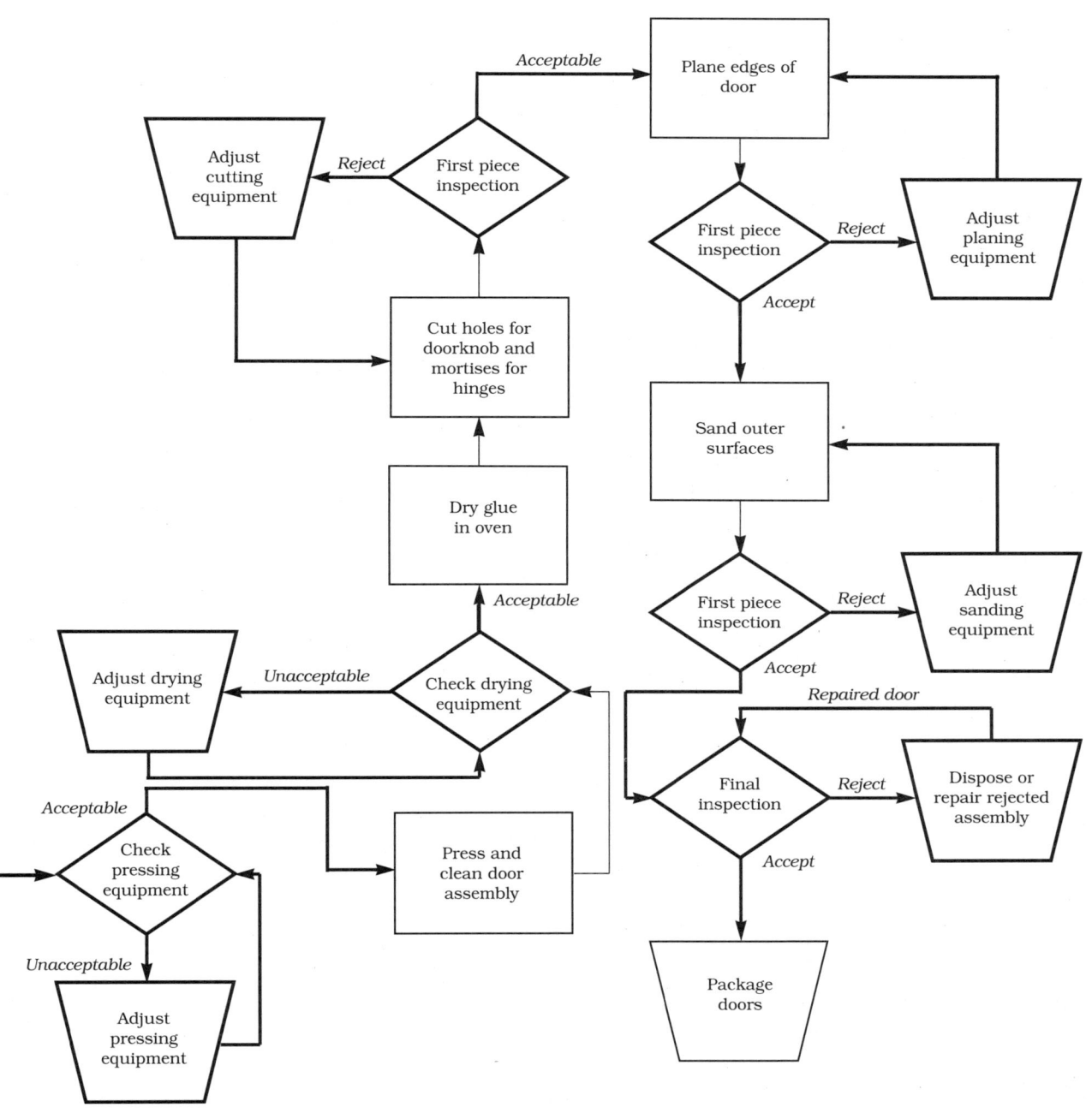

Process, Including Quality Control Measures

that we have already discussed. The inspection (decision step) is shown in the diamond shaped box. If the incoming material is acceptable, it passes along to the cutting station. If the material doesn't meet specifications, the manufacturer returns the rejected material to the supplier (action step), shown in the trapezoidal shaped box.

Second, the manufacturer has implemented inspection procedures for panels and frame components after they are cut (decision steps). If these pieces do not meet specifications, the manufacturer readjusts the cutting equipment (action step). As you can see, *this first process control point identifies the defect in the processed component and corrects the problem in the production process that created the defect.*

As you will remember, the door manufacturer had found that two out of 10 finished doors were being rejected because they were either too short or too narrow. By inspecting the cut frame components, the manufacturer has identified pieces which do not meet specifications. If these pieces had been used, the door would not meet its overall specifications. The manufacturer is now able to eliminate these pieces from the production process and replace them with freshly-cut pieces which do meet specifications. In turn, this allows him to produce a quality door—one that conforms to its overall specifications.

The manufacturer has gone on to add process control points at critical steps further downstream in the production process. Originally, the manufacturer would have simply assembled the door frame, glued the panels to it using a press and a drying oven, cut holes and mortises for the hardware, planed and sanded the assembled door, and packaged it for shipping. Figure 4.2 shows the quality control steps that have been added to the process.

- Glued panels and frames are visually inspected before going into the press. If unacceptable in any way, they go back for recutting and/or reassembly. The cutting equipment and assembly jigs would be readjusted.

- After the doorknob hole and hinge mortises are cut, the doors are again inspected. If the holes and/or mortises have been cut incorrectly, the piece is returned for rework or rejection and the hole-cutting equipment is readjusted.

- After planing the door edges, another visual inspection takes place. Once again, if found unacceptable, the piece is reworked or rejected. Most important, the planing equipment is readjusted to avoid the production of additional defective pieces.

- A similar inspection takes place after the sanding operation and, as with the other process control points, any variation from specifications will lead to a readjustment of the sanding equipment.

Final Inspection

The last quality control step in the revised manufacturing flowchart is the final inspection of the finished closet door prior to packaging and shipment to the customer. Our door manufacturer has now come full circle. At the beginning of this chapter, he took the first steps toward a quality control program by implementing final inspection. He found a 40 percent reject rate and identified a serious quality problem.

To solve this quality problem, the door manufacturer has implemented quality control procedures "upstream" in the manufacturing process. An incoming inspection program was started that identified quality problems in the materials purchased from suppliers. Process control points were added at critical points in the manufacturing process which identified and corrected problems in the dimensions of cut components.

As a result of these "upstream" efforts, the manufacturer now hopes to find no product defects at final inspection. He will have achieved "zero defect" production by catching and correcting quality problems at the earliest possible stage in the production process.

Additional Examples of Quality Control Procedures

The closet door manufacturer isn't the only company that can benefit from implementing quality control procedures during the production process. Use of incoming inspections, process control points, and final inspections will provide comparable benefits for the bakery and the AM radio manufacturer. Let's take a quick look at how the baker would incorporate these procedures into the bread baking process.

The bakery has a particularly keen interest in controlling both the quality of its raw ingredients and its production process. Figure 4.3 shows the ways the bakery has modified its production flowchart to accommodate these quality control concerns.

In addition to an incoming inspection, the bakery has also implemented a second inspection for ingredients coming out of storage at the start of the baking process. This additional inspection is necessary because the bakery's ingredients are perishable and may have spoiled while being stored after incoming inspection.

A BEGINNER'S GUIDE TO QUALITY IN MANUFACTURING

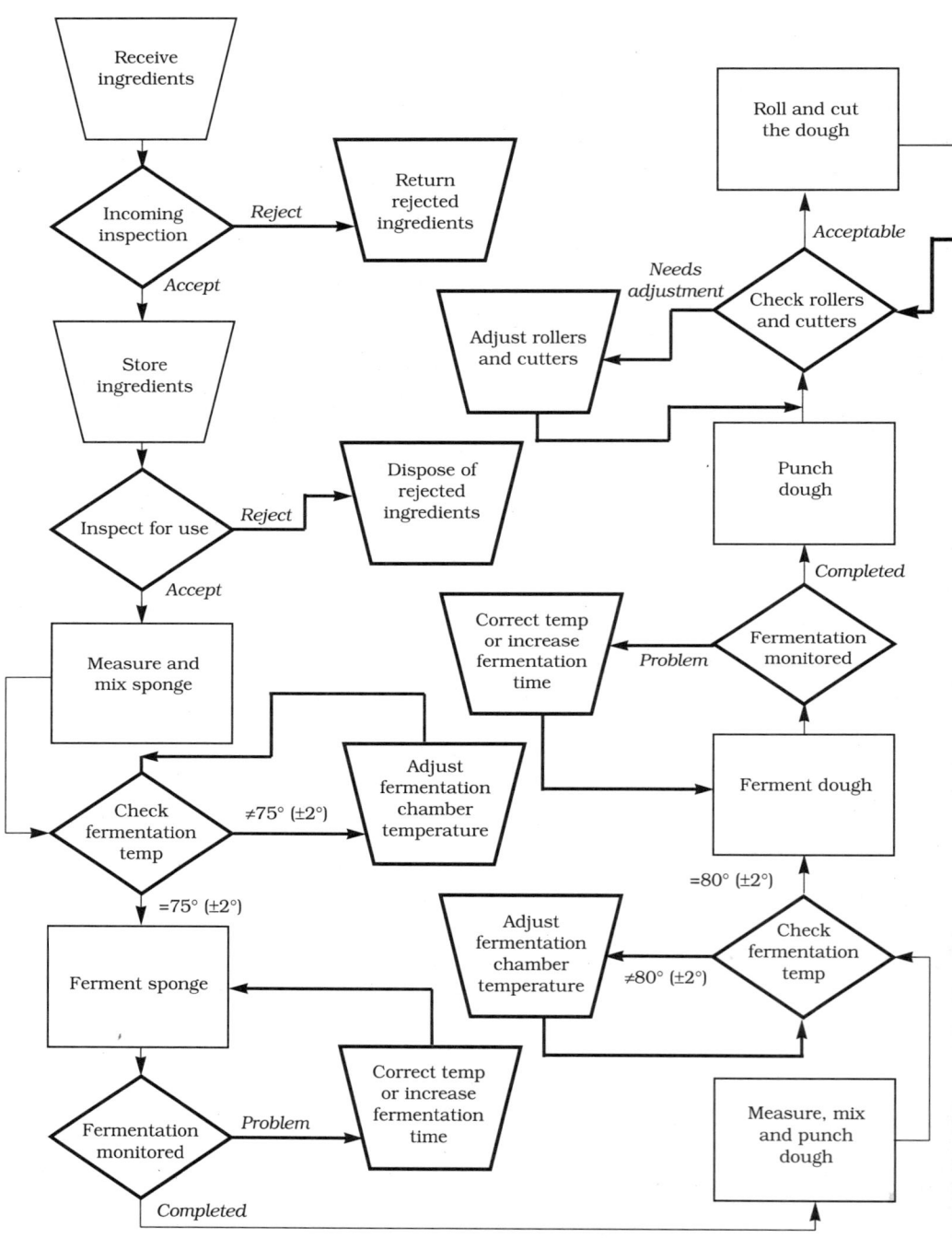

Figure 4.3: The Bread-Making Process

QUALITY CONTROL

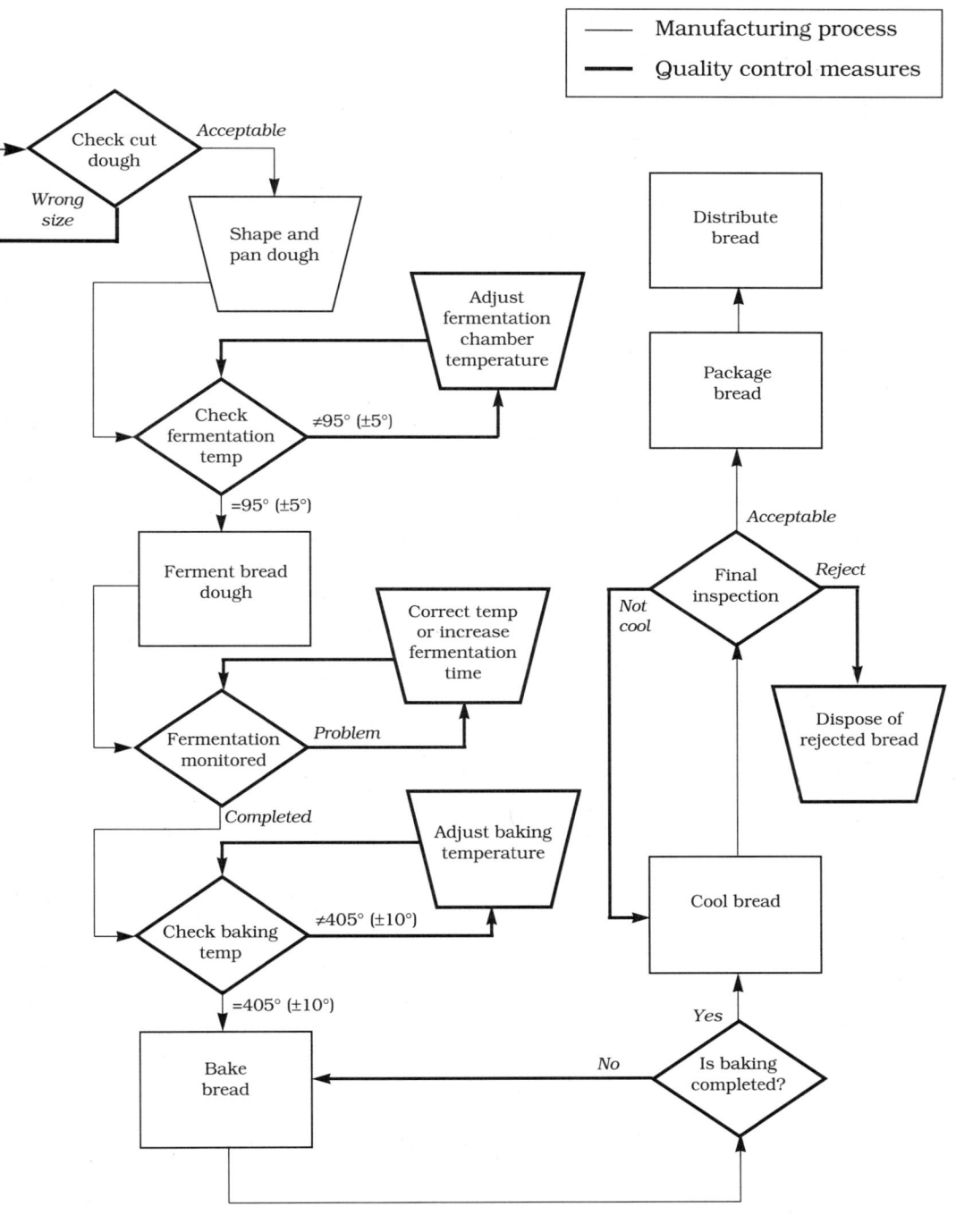

Including Quality Control Measures

The temperature of the bakery's fermentation chamber and the length of time the dough stays in the chamber are also of critical importance at several points in the process. If the chamber is not at the correct temperature for the specific fermentation process, the dough may not rise appropriately. Likewise, if the dough stays in the chamber for too long or too short a time, similar problems will result.

Consequently, the bakery uses a number of process control instruments to ensure that the bread is being baked correctly. The fermentation chamber is set for the appropriate temperature at each of the three fermentation steps. If the temperature varies by more than a specified number of degrees, a buzzer will sound and the chamber must be manually corrected. There is also a timer on the chamber that monitors fermentation time. The timer sounds an alarm when the fermentation period is completed. The mixture is checked to determine if it has risen properly. When it has, the next process starts.

The bakery uses a similar procedure to control the actual baking of the bread. The oven temperature is set to 405°F, ±10°. Both the baking temperature and time are monitored. If the oven temperature goes lower than 395° or higher than 415°, a bell rings. The oven is adjusted to maintain the correct temperature. A buzzer will sound when the baking period is supposed to be completed. The bread is inspected for color. If it is not completely cooked, it goes back into the oven. Monitoring the temperature and time, and inspecting for color, are examples of process control.

As you can see on Figure 4.3, the bakery uses several other process control points at various steps in the production process to ensure the quality of its finished product.

The bakery, like the closet door manufacturer, ends its production process with a final inspection. Loaves of bread are randomly chosen and checked for taste, weight, size, moisture, and color. If these first loaves are acceptable, final inspection of the remaining loaves begins. All are visually checked and, if acceptable, are packaged. The packaged loaves are loaded onto the delivery truck and delivered.

If any loaves are found unacceptable, they must be discarded. However, if the process controls we have discussed are successful, we should have no rejected loaves.

4.4 Basic Resources for a Quality Control Program

Adding quality control procedures to a manufacturing process does more than just change the factory's production flowchart. A successful quality control program requires the commitment of resources in the form of staff, facilities, and equipment.

Staff

The most important element in any quality control program is the staff who will carry it out. In a later chapter, we will look in detail at the specific role of the quality control department in implementing a quality control program. We will also explore the ways in which all company staff can be educated to recognize the critical importance of general product quality, trained in specific quality control techniques, and motivated to implement these techniques.

Facilities

Inspections of incoming materials, work in process, and finished products require the use of physical space within the factory. Similarly, rework stations to repair defective products and components identified through these inspections also require the assignment of space on the shop floor.

The space requirements of implementing quality control inspections in the bakery can be seen in a revised facility diagram (Figure 4.4). An inspection area has been added to perform incoming inspection on the ingredients and to inspect samples of the final product.

Equipment

Quality control programs also require the use of carefully selected equipment for the measurement and testing of product specifications. For example, the bakery's quality control equipment needs are also illustrated in Figure 4.4. Thermometers, timers, and sounders have been added to the fermentation chamber and baking ovens. Scales and rulers have been added to the rolling, cutting, and packaging areas. A timer and sounder have been added to the cooling area.

Manufacturers must specify their quality control equipment based on the product characteristics they wish to measure. The quality control equipment used by the bakery does not seem particularly exotic. Test equipment used by the AM radio manufacturer, on the other hand, is extremely sophisticated. In chapter 11, we will discuss the selection, use, and maintenance of test equipment appropriate for various quality control programs.

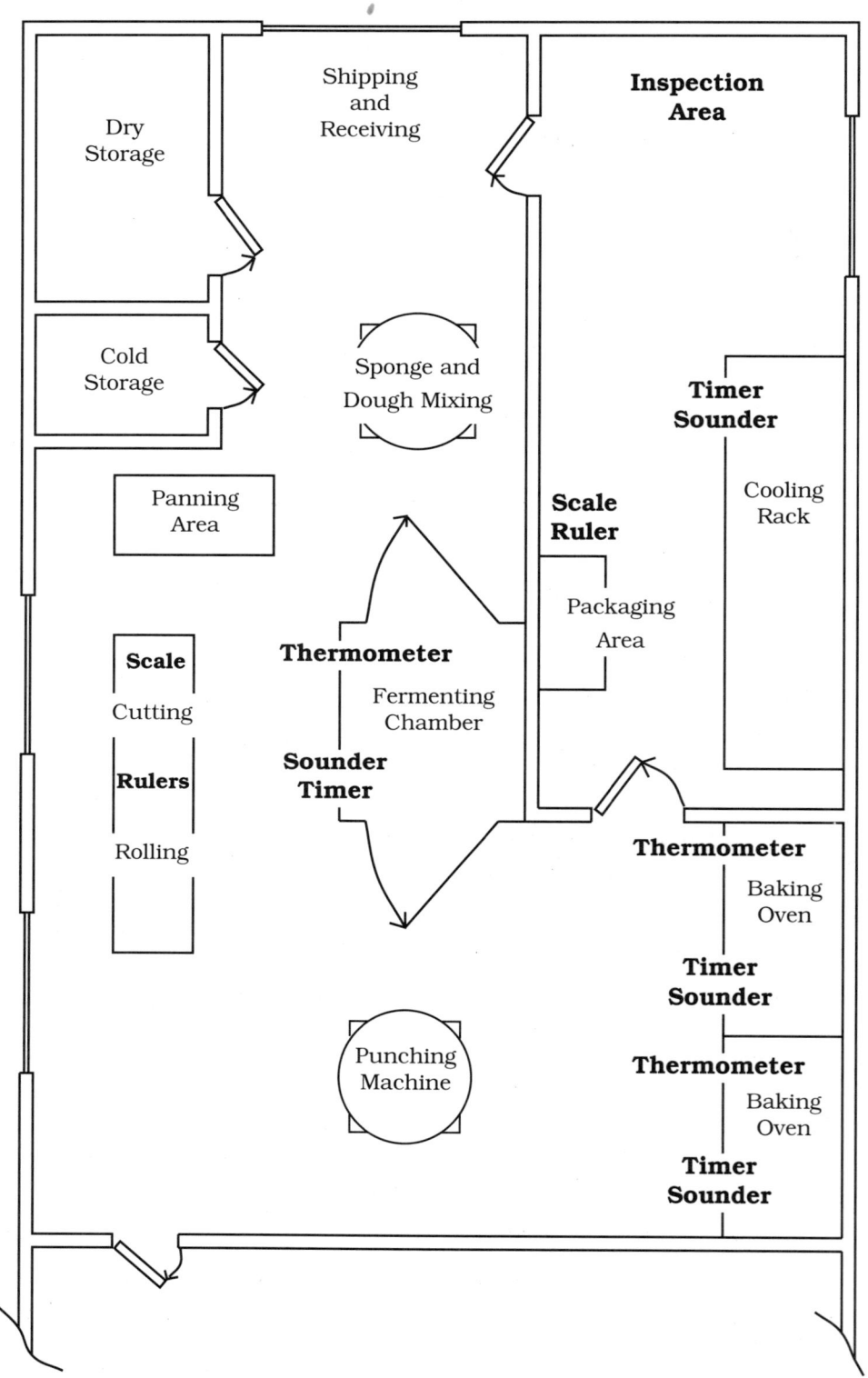

Figure 4.4: Bakery Layout with Quality Control Areas and Equipment

QUALITY CONTROL

Chapter Summary

1. A quality product is one that conforms to its specifications and requirements.

2. Product inspections do not eliminate quality problems; they merely identify them.

3. Defects identified by inspections are the result of quality problems "upstream" in the production process.

4. Quality problems become more expensive as they move "downstream" in the production process.

5. Product inspections identify opportunities to correct quality problems on finished products and processed materials or components.

6. Incoming inspections of purchased raw materials and component parts offer the opportunity to catch quality problems before the production process begins.

7. Process control points are inspection procedures placed between two steps in the production process.

8. Process control points consist of two steps. The inspection is a decision step which identifies defects in the processed component and a problem in the prior production process which caused the defect. The resulting action step repairs or replaces the defective piece and corrects the production process so that it will not turn out additional defective pieces.

9. Final inspection is the inspection of the finished product prior to packaging and shipment to the customer. If incoming inspections and process controls are adequate, the final inspection will not find any quality problems in the finished product because there will be none.

Questions for Chapter 4

For questions 1–3, refer to Figure 4.5.

1. List all the manufacturing process steps.

2. List all the quality control steps.

3. Quality control steps usually occur in pairs: the decision step followed by the action step. From the list in question 2, identify the decision steps and the corresponding action steps.

4. Complete a plant layout diagram similar to Figure 4.4 for the AM radio manufacturing process, with all quality control areas.

QUALITY CONTROL

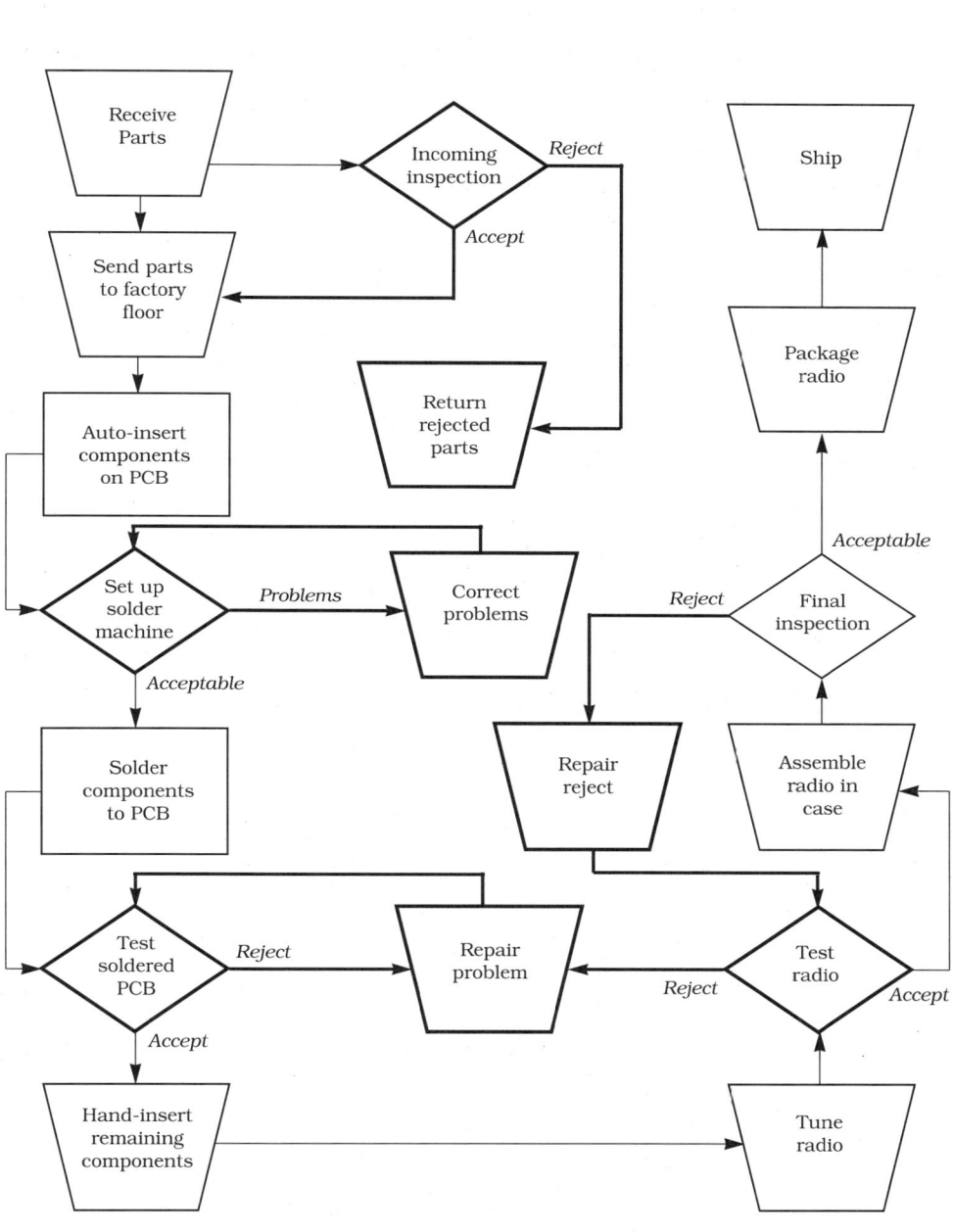

Figure 4.5: Flowchart of AM Radio Manufacturing Process, Including Quality Control Measures

A BEGINNER'S GUIDE TO QUALITY IN MANUFACTURING

Chapter 4 Project

In chapters 2 and 3, you made a flowchart and a plant layout drawing for your product. Update these charts and drawings by completing the following:

1. Redraw your flowchart by adding quality control steps. Remember to include incoming inspection, process control, and final inspection.

2. Redraw your plant layout drawing to include all the quality control inspection points. Indicate what equipment or personnel are needed to make the necessary checks.

CHAPTER 5

INCOMING INSPECTION

5.1 Introduction

In the previous chapter, we learned that unidentified quality problems become more expensive as they move along the manufacturing process. It is advantageous, therefore, to identify a quality problem as soon as possible. The first place in our manufacturing process that a quality problem can be identified is in receiving. The testing, checking, measuring, and examining of raw materials and components as they arrive at the manufacturing location is called incoming inspection.

Each raw material and component has its own specifications. Raw materials and components are compared to these specifications during incoming inspection. If they comply with their specifications, they will not cause quality problems. Those that do not comply must be removed from the manufacturing process.

In this chapter, we will learn how to measure the overall level of quality in large batches of incoming materials and outgoing finished products. Two such useful measurements are *percent defective* and *defects per hundred units*.

Using these measuring tools, we will then identify the Acceptable Quality Level (AQL) which we can tolerate in our own output of finished products. The AQL for finished products can be used to determine AQLs for all incoming raw materials and component parts.

We will learn to keep inspection costs to a minimum by using a small sample of incoming components to identify the overall quality level of a whole shipment. The AM radio manufacturer receives 580,800 fixed resistors every month. She does not have to inspect each and every one. After comparing the results of the sample with the required AQL, she will accept or reject whole deliveries.

Military Standard 105E (MIL-STD-105E) is one of several formal guidelines developed to help manufacturers select and inspect samples of incoming deliveries. Through MIL-STD-105E, we will learn how the careful use of acceptance sampling plans can minimize costs and assure our required AQLs in a wide variety of circumstances.

Finally, we will examine how a manufacturer's ongoing relationship with suppliers can be structured to eliminate the need for incoming inspections.

5.2 Measuring Quality

In chapter 1, we defined quality as conformance to specifications. Given this definition, it is easy to measure the level of quality for a single unit of finished product. It either meets specifications or it does not.

The issue becomes a little more complicated when we want to measure the overall level of quality for a large shipment of finished products or incoming raw materials. Some of the individual units will conform to their specifications and some may not.

Several different mathematical yardsticks have been developed to measure this overall quality based on how individual units meet specifications.

The Percent Defective

One such measure of overall quality is the *percent defective*. This is defined as the number of defective units in a shipment, divided by the total number of units shipped, times 100.

$$\text{Percent Defective} = \frac{\text{Number of Defectives}}{\text{Number of Units Inspected}} \times 100$$

Let's use the percent defective to measure an incoming shipment of variable resistors which the AM radio manufacturer uses for switch/volume controls. After completely inspecting all 26,400 incoming units, the manufacturer finds that 132 fail to meet specifications. The shipment has a percent defective measure of 0.5 percent. Let's look at the calculation.

$$\text{Percent Defective} = \frac{\text{Number of Defectives}}{\text{Number of Units Inspected}} \times 100$$

$$\text{Percent Defective} = \frac{132}{26,400} \times 100$$

$$\text{Percent Defective} = \frac{1}{200} \times 100 = 0.5\%$$

The percent defective measure tells us the number of units in a batch of components or finished product that do not meet specifications.

Defects Per Hundred Units

Each individual unit of raw material or finished product may have several different specifications. Therefore, a manufacturer will have to test them to see if they conform to each of these specifications.

The AM radio manufacturer's variable resistors, for example, turn the radio on and adjust the sound level. These resistors regulate the flow of electrical current through an electric circuit. The ability to do this is measured in ohms. This switch/volume control also takes up space on the circuit board. Consequently, it must be the correct size and shape to fit in the radio.

The manufacturer, therefore, inspects each switch/volume control to determine whether it conforms to five different specifications: electrical resistance in ohms, body length, body diameter, shaft length, and shaft diameter.

A second mathematical yardstick, *defects per hundred units*, measures the extent to which a shipment of components or finished products conforms to all of its different specifications. Rather than counting the number of defective units, this measure counts the number of "out-of-tolerance" measurements, or defects. Defects per hundred units is defined as the number of defects found in a shipment, divided by the number of units in the shipment, times 100. The formula is as follows:

$$\text{Defects per Hundred Units} = \frac{\text{Number of Defects}}{\text{Number of Units Inspected}} \times 100$$

Let's take another look at the overall quality of the radio manufacturer's shipment of variable resistors using the defects per hundred units measure.

As we've seen, the manufacturer found that 132 units in the incoming shipment of 26,400 variable resistors were defective. Seventy-five of these units did not have the specified electrical resistance. Fifty failed inspection because they did not have adequate electrical resistance *and* they had shaft lengths which exceeded specifications. The seven remaining defective units had larger-than-acceptable body diameters but met all their other specifications. The manufacturer found a total of 182 individual defects in the 132 defective units. The resistor shipment is summarized in Table 5.1.

Number of Defective Units	Specific Defect	Number of Defects
75	Incorrect resistance	75
50	Incorrect resistance and excessive shaft length	50 50
7	Excessive body diameter	7
Totals 132		182

Table 5.1: Defects in the Resistor Shipment

Now we can evaluate the overall quality of this incoming shipment using the defects per hundred units measurement.

$$\frac{\text{Defects per}}{\text{Hundred Units}} = \frac{\text{Number of Defects}}{\text{Number of Units Inspected}} \times 100$$

$$\frac{\text{Defects per}}{\text{Hundred Units}} = \frac{182}{26,400} \times 100 = 0.69$$

In general, defects per hundred units offers the most information about the quality of the product from an engineering point of view. While inspecting the unit, the inspector normally lists the defects that are found. This information is valuable for correcting quality problems. Calculating defects per hundred will always lead to a defect rate that is either higher than or equal to the results found by calculating the percent defective. Defects per hundred units is a more severe measure of quality, and recordkeeping for its calculation can result in more information for quality problem solving.

Measuring quality levels using percent defective has its advantages also. Since the inspector needs to keep track of defective units and not each and every defect, recordkeeping is reduced. For purposes of accounting, percent defective is, in general, a more useful number. Scrap costs and rework costs can be calculated directly from the percent defective.

Parts Per Million

As manufacturers continually strive to improve the quality levels of their product, they need measurements which can assess fewer and fewer variations from specifications. One measure which is now widely used is parts per million (ppm). This quality yardstick can refine our measurement of the number of defects found in a shipment. Rather than calculating the defects per hundred units, we now calculate the number of defects which would be found in a sampling of one million units. Similarly, rather than counting

INCOMING INSPECTION

the number of defective units in a sampling and calculating the percent defective, we can change the scale and measure defective units in parts per million.

These measurements are normally used for measuring quality in products which have extremely low defect rates.

The quality level (QL) for defects in parts per million is calculated as follows:

$$\text{QL Defects (ppm)} = \frac{\text{Number of Defects}}{\text{Number of Units Inspected}} \times 1{,}000{,}000$$

$$\text{QL Defectives (ppm)} = \frac{\text{Number of Defective Units}}{\text{Number of Units Inspected}} \times 1{,}000{,}000$$

Let's look at our shipment of incoming resistors and calculate the quality level in parts per million.

$$\text{QL Defects (ppm)} = \frac{\text{Number of Defects}}{\text{Number of Units Inspected}} \times 1{,}000{,}000$$

$$\text{QL Defects (ppm)} = \frac{182}{26{,}400} \times 1{,}000{,}000$$

$$\text{QL Defects (ppm)} = .0069 \times 1{,}000{,}000$$

$$\text{QL Defects (ppm)} = 6{,}900$$

The QL(ppm) for our shipment of variable resistors is actually pretty high. The AM radio manufacturer doesn't need a measure this precise to assess the overall quality of her shipments of this component—at least not yet. In many industries, on the other hand, manufacturers will measure quality with extremely low QL(ppm) levels. Some transistor manufacturers report quality levels as low as 100 ppm.

Manufacturers can translate quality measurements from percent defective or defects per hundred units to a parts per million measure using the following formula:

ppm = Percent Defective (or defects per hundred units) × 10,000

Let's calculate the QL(ppm) for our shipment of variable resistors based on the percent defective measurement we did a little earlier.

$$\text{QL Defective (ppm)} = \text{Percent Defective} \times 10{,}000$$

$$\text{QL Defective (ppm)} = 0.5\% \times 10{,}000 = 5{,}000$$

Reversing the calculation will allow the manufacturer to translate from QL(ppm) to percent defective or defects per hundred units.

5.3 Acceptable Quality Level

Now we know how to measure the overall level of quality in large numbers of components or finished products. We can use these measures to rate our own manufacturing performance. We can also use them to evaluate the raw materials and component parts we purchase to make our finished product.

Our own goal, as we have stated previously, is to manufacture finished products that consistently conform to specifications. They will have no defects. Our percent defective and defects per hundred units measurements will be zero.

This does not mean, however, that we will never produce any rejects. Our goal, rather, is to produce as few as possible and catch them as early as possible in the production process, long before they can be shipped to our customers.

As we learned in chapter 4, the quality of our incoming raw materials and component parts plays a critical role in determining the ultimate quality of our finished product. Defects in raw materials and components eventually become defects in final products. The more materials and component parts per product, the greater the likelihood that defects will appear in the finished product.

To assure our own production of defect-free products, therefore, we should purchase only defect-free raw materials and component parts. Unfortunately, suppliers who will promise and actually deliver absolutely perfect materials and components aren't always available.

Given the improbability of finding defect-free suppliers, what level of quality should we look for when purchasing and accepting raw materials and component parts? To answer this question, we must first ask ourselves another one. How many incoming defects can our manufacturing process tolerate? How many defective products can we afford to produce, and how many can we catch before they are shipped to customers? Once we know our own goals and capabilities, we will know what we need to get from our suppliers.

Let's look at how the AM radio manufacturer approaches the question. She has determined that the company can tolerate a percent defective for finished radios of approximately 1.5 percent. This means that out of every 200 radios made, three may be unacceptable. The manufacturer is confident that she can find these unacceptable radios and correct them during the manufacturing process before they get to the consumer.

Now that the radio manufacturer has identified quality targets for radios in process, she can identify the quality levels for all the materials and component parts which go into the radios.

As discussed earlier, the limit of incoming defects which a manufacturer can tolerate for a given raw material or component part is the AQL. The AQL can be measured in percent defective, defects per hundred units, or parts per million. The AQL is assumed to be an average value over the course of many shipments. An AQL should be assigned to every incoming component, part, and/or raw material.

Incoming parts and components must have AQLs which are much lower than the target quality level for the finished product as a whole. Individual AQLs for each component are added together to determine the probability that a defect will appear in the final product.

Table 5.2 shows the bill of materials for the AM radio and lists the individual AQLs necessary for various components to reach the manufacturer's target quality level of 1.5 percent defective for the radio as a whole.

Quantity	Material	AQL/Part	AQL/Radio
1	Antenna	0.065%	0.065%
1	Tuner capacitor	0.04%	0.04%
4	Transformers (tunable)	0.025%	0.1%
7	Transistors	150 ppm (0.015%)	1050 ppm (0.105%)
22	Resistors (fixed)	100 ppm (0.010%)	2200 ppm (0.22%)
1	Resistor (variable)	0.04%	0.04%
17	Capacitors (fixed)	100 ppm (0.01%)	1700 ppm (0.17%)
2	Capacitors (variable)	0.04%	0.08%
2	Diodes	100 ppm (0.01%)	200 ppm (0.02%)
1	Speaker	0.065%	0.065%
1	Earphone jack	0.05%	0.05%
1	Switch/volume control	0.04%	0.04%
1	Printed circuit board	0.05%	0.05%
1	Case	0.01%	0.01%
1	User's manual	0.01%	0.01%
1	Packaging	0.025%	0.025%

Total Quality Level for All Incoming Parts and Components = 1.09%

Table 5.2: AQL for Bill of Materials for AM Radio

The column labeled "AQL/Part" shows the Acceptable Quality Level for one part or component. The column marked "AQL/Radio" is the resulting total quality level for all similar parts used in the radio. For example, the AQL of one resistor is 0.01. This means that approximately one out every 10,000 resistors will be defective in some way. The radio uses 22 resistors. If each has an AQL of 0.01, then all 22 resistors, added together, have an AQL of approximately 0.22. Adding AQLs together to find the worst-case quality level for a product is a good approximation as long as the total quality level is small.

If we add all the AQLs for all the parts and components, as shown in the last column, we find that our quality level for the radio as a whole is approximately 1.09 percent. We see that the manufacturer has assigned AQLs for each component, which keeps the total product quality level within the target range of 1.5 percent defective. The AM radio manufacturer has defined both the finished product and the incoming components in terms of percent defective. The AQL could also have been measured in defects per hundred units. MIL-STD-105E allows the use of either percent defective or defects per hundred units for AQL values less than 10. For AQL values greater than 10, AQL must be expressed in defects per hundred units only.

It is important to remember that a measure of total product quality level based on individual component AQLs is only an approximation. Suppliers may be delivering products at quality levels that exceed the AQLs specified. In such a case, the quality level of our radio will be better than 1.09 percent. On the other hand, if actual shipments of supplies and materials fall outside the AQL ranges, the quality level due to the components and parts is worse than 1.09 percent. Later in the chapter we will discuss monitoring a supplier's actual Average Quality Level.

5.4 Measuring Quality Through Sample Inspections

As we have already seen, manufacturers frequently are faced with the need to measure quality of shipments or production runs with extremely large numbers of units. Our radio manufacturer, for example, has taken delivery of 22,400 variable resistors. Other manufacturers are talking about quality levels in parts per million.

The only way to determine the quality level of such shipments with complete accuracy is to inspect every unit for conformance to all of its specifications. This type of 100 percent inspection plan might well be more expensive than the raw materials themselves and could quickly put a manufacturer out of business.

INCOMING INSPECTION

To avoid this expense, yet still protect themselves from costly defects in materials and components, manufacturers rely on the use of sample inspections. By using the laws of statistics, producers may confidently estimate the overall quality level for large shipments of components after inspecting only a relatively small, randomly selected sample.

Over the years, detailed guidelines have been developed by a variety of sources to assist manufacturers in sampling incoming raw materials and component parts. These procedures allow a manufacturer to make sure that purchased components will have required AQLs by accepting or rejecting shipments according to the outcomes of specified sample inspection plans.

MIL-STD-105E

We will examine one of these guidelines for sampling—Military Standard 105E (MIL-STD-105E) entitled "Sampling Procedures and Tables for Inspection by Attributes"—to see how our manufacturers can minimize their inspection expenses and still ensure that purchased components and raw materials have the quality levels they require.

First, let's look at what MIL-STD-105E means when it talks about *sampling and inspection by attributes.*

The inspector begins by selecting a sample of units out of a total lot to test. The size of this sample will be determined by a number of factors, including the size of the total shipment, the required AQL, the manufacturer's confidence in the supplier, and the types of defects which may occur.

After choosing the sample units, the inspector tests them to see whether they conform to specifications. When we inspect by attribute, there are only two outcomes: either the sample unit is acceptable or a defect is recorded. No measurement value is recorded or used to determine the size of the variance from specifications. Either sample units are acceptable or they have defects.

The inspector then compares the total number of defects found to the sampling plan outlined in MIL-STD-105E. Based on this comparison, a decision is made whether or not to accept the entire shipment.

Selecting a Sample Size

Now let's look at how MIL-STD-105E guides us in selecting the appropriate sample size for our inspection. The sample size will depend on several factors, including the size of the total shipment and degree of confidence we wish to have in our findings.

MIL-STD-105E allows us to achieve our required degree of confidence by offering seven different inspection levels. There are three General Inspection Levels (I, II, and III) and four Special Inspection Levels (S-1, S-2, S-3, and S-4). The inspection levels determine how large the sample size should be, based on the size of the incoming lot. The larger the sample size, the more accurate your assessment of the quality of a particular lot. If your sample size was zero, you would have no idea of the quality level of a lot. If your sample size was the entire lot (100 percent inspection), you would know the quality level of the lot exactly.

Special Inspection Level S-1 requires the smallest sample size of any inspection level. As we change Special Inspection Levels from S-1 to S-2 to S-3 and finally to S-4, the sample sizes will, in general, increase. As we move through General Inspection Levels, from I to III, the sample size will also increase. General Inspection Level III requires the largest sample size of any inspection level. MIL-STD-105E recommends using General Inspection Level II unless otherwise specified.

Table 5.3 is a copy of a sample size code letter table from MIL-STD-105E. The first column lists lot size ranges. The next seven columns list sample size code letters for each of the inspection levels. As the letters go from A to R, the sample sizes increase. The actual size of our sample will depend on the specific sampling plan we wish to use. To see how this table works, let's take a simple example.

The closet door manufacturer receives approximately 1,900 boards of framing wood each week from supplier A. Our door manufacturer uses General Inspection Level II. To find the correct sample size code letter, we go down the lot size ranges in the left column until we reach lot size range 1,201–3,200. We then go across to the General Inspection Level II column, where we determine that the correct sample size code letter is K.

The sample size code letter will be used for different types of plans. The door manufacturer uses a Single Sampling Plan for Normal Inspection. This means that the manufacturer will take only one sample for inspection from the shipment in question. Normal inspection is used for deliveries where the company has no preconceived notions about the probable level of quality in the delivery. We will talk about other types of inspection plans later in the chapter.

The MIL-STD-105E table for the Single Sampling Plan for Normal Inspection is shown in Table 5.4.

The door manufacturer requires an AQL of 0.65 percent for incoming pieces of framing wood. This means the manufacturer expects fewer than seven rejects in every thousand units. Based on the information we have so far, let's use Table 5.4 to tell us what the actual sample size should be. Remember that the sample size code letter is K and the AQL is 0.65 percent.

Lot or batch size	Special inspection levels				General inspection levels		
	S-1	S-2	S-3	S-4	I	II	III
2–8	A	A	A	A	A	A	B
9–15	A	A	A	A	A	B	C
16–25	A	A	B	B	B	C	D
26–50	A	B	B	C	C	D	E
51–90	B	B	C	C	C	E	F
91–150	B	B	C	D	D	F	G
151–280	B	C	D	E	E	G	H
281–500	B	C	D	E	F	H	J
501–1,200	C	C	E	F	G	J	K
1,201–3,200	C	D	E	G	H	K	L
3,201–10,000	C	D	F	G	J	L	M
10,001–35,000	C	D	F	H	K	M	N
35,001–150,000	D	E	G	J	L	N	P
150,001–500,000	D	E	G	J	M	P	Q
500,001 and over	D	E	H	K	N	Q	R

Table 5.3: Sample Size Code Letters (Table 1 in MIL-STD-105E)

Sample size code letter	Sample size	0.010		0.015		0.025		0.040		0.065		0.10		0.15		0.25		0.40		0.65		1.0		1.5		2.5		4.0		6.5		10		15		25		40		65		100		150		250		400		650		1,000	
		Ac	Re	Ac	Re	Ac	Re	Ac	Re	Ac	Re	Ac	Re	Ac	Re	Ac	Re	Ac	Re	Ac	Re	Ac	Re	Ac	Re	Ac	Re	Ac	Re	Ac	Re	Ac	Re	Ac	Re	Ac	Re	Ac	Re	Ac	Re	Ac	Re	Ac	Re	Ac	Re	Ac	Re
A	2	↓																															0	1	↓		↑		1	2	2	3	3	4	5	6	7	8	10	11	14	15	21	22	30	31	44	45
B	3																															0	1	↓		↑		1	2	2	3	3	4	5	6	7	8	10	11	14	15	21	22	30	31	44	45	←	
C	5																									0	1	↓		↑		1	2	2	3	3	4	5	6	7	8	10	11	14	15	21	22	30	31	44	45	←			
D	8																					0	1	↓		↑		1	2	2	3	3	4	5	6	7	8	10	11	14	15	21	22	30	31	44	45	←					
E	13																		0	1	↓		↑		1	2	2	3	3	4	5	6	7	8	10	11	14	15	21	22	←											
F	20																0	1	↓		↑		1	2	2	3	3	4	5	6	7	8	10	11	14	15	21	22	←													
G	32													0	1	↓		↑		1	2	2	3	3	4	5	6	7	8	10	11	14	15	21	22	←															
H	50											0	1	↓		↑		1	2	2	3	3	4	5	6	7	8	10	11	14	15	21	22	←																	
J	80									0	1	↓		↑		1	2	2	3	3	4	5	6	7	8	10	11	14	15	21	22	←																			
K	125							0	1	↓		↑		1	2	2	3	3	4	5	6	7	8	10	11	14	15	21	22	←																					
L	200					0	1	↓		↑		1	2	2	3	3	4	5	6	7	8	10	11	14	15	21	22	←																							
M	315			0	1	↓		↑		1	2	2	3	3	4	5	6	7	8	10	11	14	15	21	22	←																									
N	500	0	1	↓		↑		1	2	2	3	3	4	5	6	7	8	10	11	14	15	21	22	←																											
P	800	↓		↑		1	2	2	3	3	4	5	6	7	8	10	11	14	15	21	22	←																													
Q	1,250	↑		1	2	2	3	3	4	5	6	7	8	10	11	14	15	21	22	←																															
R	2,000	1	2	2	3	3	4	5	6	7	8	10	11	14	15	21	22	←																																	

↓ = use first sampling plan below arrow. If sample size equals or exceeds lot or batch size, do 100% inspection.
↑ = use first sampling plan above arrow.
Ac = acceptance number.
Re = rejection number.

Table 5.4: Single Sampling Plan for Normal Inspection (MIL-STD-105E Table II-A)

The sample size code letters are found in the first column on Table 5.4. When we find sample size code letter K, we move across to the second column. The sample size required for this sample plan is 125 door frame boards.

Accepting or Rejecting the Shipment

Once we know the size of our required sample, MIL-STD-105E goes on to indicate when we should accept or reject the shipment based on the results of our sample inspection.

Continuing from our sample size of 125 in the second column on Table 5.4, we now move across the page. The remaining columns show inspection requirements for varying AQLs, starting at 0.010 and going to 1,000.

Let's go to the column for 0.65 percent AQL, our manufacturer's target level. We are told to accept (Ac) a lot if we find two or fewer defects. We are told to reject (Re) a lot if we find three or more defects. The manufacturer's decision is made automatic by simply following the rules laid out in the inspection plan.

Let's summarize the door manufacturer's incoming inspection plan for framing wood, as follows:

Incoming Inspection Plan for Framing Wood

Sampling plan:	Single Sampling Plan for Normal Inspection (MIL-STD-105E)
AQL:	0.65 percent
Lot size:	1,900 boards
Sample size:	125 boards
Acceptance number (Ac):	Accept the lot if two or fewer defects are found.
Rejection number (Re):	Reject the lot if three or more defects are found.
Inspections required:	Length: >14' Thickness: 1 1/8" (±1/16") Width: 6" (+1/4", −0")

The inspections (measurements) that are required during the incoming inspection have been added to complete the sampling plan.

This is the type of plan a quality control inspector needs to make an inspection and record the results. As we will discuss later in the chapter, these results would then be averaged with the results of other inspections, and a more accurate quality level for this supplier will be calculated.

The Radio Manufacturer's Antennas

The radio manufacturer receives approximately 26,400 antennas per month. Table 5.2 shows that the required AQL for these incoming components is 0.065 percent. As in our previous example, the radio manufacturer uses the Single Sampling Plan for Normal Inspection. Similarly, she also has selected General Inspection Level II. Using MIL-STD-105E, we will determine what the sampling size should be and what the acceptance and rejection numbers are.

First, let's turn to Table 5.3, which will tell us the sample size code letter. For a lot size of 26,400 antennas, and using General Inspection Level II, the code letter is M.

Next, we refer to the Single Sampling Plan for Normal Inspection in Table 5.4. Using the sample size code letter M, we determine that the sample size should be 315.

From here we move across the table to the 0.065 percent AQL column. The arrow pointing up tells us that the acceptance and rejection numbers are the first numbers we come to when we proceed up the column. The acceptance number is zero and the rejection number is one. This means that the lot will be accepted if no defects are found and rejected if one defect is found.

Below is a summary of the inspection plan for the incoming inspection of the radio antenna.

Incoming Inspection Plan for the Radio Antenna

Sampling plan:	Single Sampling Plan for Normal Inspection (MIL-STD-105E)
AQL:	0.065 percent
Lot size:	26,400 antennas
Sample size:	315 antennas
Acceptance number (Ac):	Accept the lot if no defects are found.
Rejection number (Re):	Reject the lot if one or more defects are found.

The actual inspection procedure for incoming antennas is kept in a separate document. When an antenna shipment arrives at the plant, the quality control inspector will randomly pick 315 samples from the incoming lot and follow the required procedure to test the antennas. If one defect is found in the sampling, the lot is rejected and would normally be sent back to the supplier. If no defects were found during incoming inspection, the inspector would accept the lot and send the antennas to the factory floor.

5.5 Normal, Tightened, and Reduced Inspection

Both the closet door company and the radio manufacturer have been using sampling plans for normal inspection. As we've already noted, normal inspection is used for deliveries where the company has no preconceived notions about probable level of quality in the delivery. This is the type of plan, for example, that a manufacturer would institute for a new supplier.

There are, however, circumstances that might lead us to change the sampling plan. A certain supplier may be providing shipments of components that are never rejected. The supplier's quality is so consistent that we may want to do fewer inspections. It is important to remember that inspections cost money and, therefore, reduce profit. If we can eliminate unnecessary product inspections, we should. Reduced inspection plans allow us to use a smaller sample size for incoming shipments. By reducing the number of sample units we must inspect, we save time, human resources, and money.

On the other hand, we also want to revise our inspection plan if a supplier begins to have quality problems. If incoming quality is poor, then our finished products will be defective. These rejected finished goods must be reworked or written off as scrap. This costs money and erodes profits. During normal inspection, we may notice that shipments from an individual supplier are being rejected with increased frequency. Switching to a tightened inspection plan will increase our quality target so that the incoming AQL is not jeopardized.

MIL-STD-105E offers precise guidelines for moving between normal, tightened, and reduced inspection plans based on the results of our inspections for an individual vendor over a period of time. Let's look at the door manufacturer's experience with one particular supplier to see how these guidelines work.

Tightened Inspection Plans

The closet door producer receives approximately 1,900 framing boards every month. The AQL level for this material is 0.65 percent, and 125 boards are inspected every shipment. With the normal inspection plan, the lot will be accepted if two or fewer defects are found. The lot will be rejected if three or more defects are found.

The manufacturer has found, however, that approximately four out of every 10 lots delivered are rejected. These inspections and rejections are costing money. They are also raising questions about the actual quality level of the shipments which have been accepted.

MIL-STD-105E has a simple rule for moving from normal inspections to tightened inspections. When two out of five consecutive lots or batches have been rejected on original inspection using normal inspection procedures, the manufacturer should switch to a tightened inspection plan for the vendor in question. By original inspections, we mean inspections of lots delivered to the manufacturer for the first time. Inspections of lots that have been previously rejected and redelivered by the supplier are not counted as original inspections.

The door manufacturer's shipments from the framing wood supplier meet this threshold criteria. Therefore, the quality control group changes the inspection plan from normal to tightened.

Let's look at how the new plan works by referring to Table 5.5. As we've previously noted, the sample size code letter for a given lot size stays the same for all sampling plans. The sample size code letter for our shipment of 1,900 boards is K. Using Table 5.5, we can see that the sample size for the tightened inspection plan is 125. This is no different than under a normal inspection plan.

To find the acceptance and rejection criteria, we move across the table to the 0.65 percent AQL column. The manufacturer will now only accept a shipment with no more than one defect. He will reject the shipment if there are two or more defects. Under normal inspection, the manufacturer would have accepted the shipment if up to two defects were found. The criteria for accepting or rejecting the shipment has been "tightened." This is the only thing which has changed in the move from normal to tightened inspection plans.

The tightened inspection plan for the framing wood is detailed as follows:

Tightened Incoming Inspection Plan for Framing Wood

Sampling plan:	Single Sampling Plan for Tightened Inspection (MIL-STD-105E)
AQL:	0.65 percent
Lot size:	1,900 boards
Sample size:	125 boards
Acceptance number (Ac):	Accept the lot if one defect or no defects are found.
Rejection number (Re):	Reject the lot if two or more defects are found.
Inspections required:	Length: >14' Thickness: 1 1/8" (±1/16") Width: 6" (+1/4", −0")

INCOMING INSPECTION

Sample size code letter	Sample size	Acceptable Quality Levels (tightened inspection)																										
		0.010	0.015	0.025	0.040	0.065	0.10	0.15	0.25	0.40	0.65	1.0	1.5	2.5	4.0	6.5	10	15	25	40	65	100	150	250	400	650	1,000
		Ac Re	Ac Re	Ac Re	Ac Re	Ac Re	Ac Re	Ac Re	Ac Re	Ac Re	Ac Re	Ac Re	Ac Re	Ac Re	Ac Re	Ac Re	Ac Re	Ac Re	Ac Re	Ac Re	Ac Re	Ac Re	Ac Re	Ac Re	Ac Re	Ac Re	Ac Re
A	2																				1 2	2 3	3 4	5 6	8 9	12 13	18 19	27 28
B	3																			1 2	2 3	3 4	5 6	8 9	12 13	18 19	27 28	41 42
C	5																		1 2	2 3	3 4	5 6	8 9	12 13	18 19	27 28	41 42	←
D	8																	1 2	2 3	3 4	5 6	8 9	12 13	18 19	27 28	41 42	←	
E	13																1 2	2 3	3 4	5 6	8 9	12 13	18 19	27 28	41 42	←		
F	20															1 2	2 3	3 4	5 6	8 9	12 13	18 19	←					
G	32														1 2	2 3	3 4	5 6	8 9	12 13	18 19	←						
H	50													1 2	2 3	3 4	5 6	8 9	12 13	18 19	←							
J	80												1 2	2 3	3 4	5 6	8 9	12 13	18 19	←								
K	125										0 1	→	1 2	2 3	3 4	5 6	8 9	12 13	18 19	←								
L	200									0 1	→	1 2	2 3	3 4	5 6	8 9	12 13	18 19	←									
M	315								0 1	→	1 2	2 3	3 4	5 6	8 9	12 13	18 19	←										
N	500							0 1	→	1 2	2 3	3 4	5 6	8 9	12 13	18 19	←											
P	800						0 1	→	1 2	2 3	3 4	5 6	8 9	12 13	18 19	←												
Q	1,250					0 1	→	1 2	2 3	3 4	5 6	8 9	12 13	18 19	←													
R	2,000	0 1	←	→	1 2	2 3	3 4	5 6	8 9	12 13	18 19	←																
S	3,150		0 1	1 2																								

↓ = use first sampling plan below arrow. If sample size equals or exceeds lot or batch size, do 100% inspection.
↑ = use first sampling plan above arrow.
Ac = acceptance number.
Re = rejection number.

Table 5.5: Single Sampling Plans for Tightened Inspection (MIL-STD-105E Table II-B)

Manufacturers should always notify the supplier in question when going to a tightened inspection plan. Working with a vendor to upgrade quality may be significantly less expensive than seeking additional sources for a component or raw material. This is what the door manufacturer did, and found that the quality of the incoming door framing boards improved. Consequently, the manufacturer wanted to go back to a Normal Inspection Plan.

Once again, MIL-STD-105E offers specific guidelines for moving from a tightened inspection plan back to a normal plan. If five consecutive lots had been considered acceptable on original inspection, the procedure allows a move from tightened to normal plans. This was the case, and the inspection plan was changed from tightened to normal.

Reduced Inspection Plans

The supplier of framing material kept right on improving quality. The manufacturer also found that as reject rates decreased, profits increased. The door manufacturer noticed this continuing improvement and wanted to move the inspection plan from normal to reduced.

By consulting MIL-STD-105E, the door manufacturer found that the inspection plan could be safely reduced if experience with a vendor met all of the following conditions:

1. At least 10 consecutive lots have been accepted during original inspection using a normal plan.

2. The total number of sample units inspected from the last 10 lots or batches must meet or exceed the numbers required in Table 5.6. Different total numbers of sample units are required based on the AQL we are seeking. An AQL of 0.010, for example, requires that at least 20,000 sample units were inspected out of the last 10 consecutive shipments. For an AQL of 1.5, on the other hand, a total of only 130 sample units is needed.

   If the number of sample units from the last 10 consecutive shipments does not meet these threshold requirements, additional consecutive lots must be accepted before the manufacturer can move to a reduced inspection plan.

3. The total number of defectives or defects found in the samples from the 10 preceding lots must be equal to or less than the number given in Table 5.6 for the AQL the manufacturer is seeking.

INCOMING INSPECTION

4. The supplier's production is steady and ongoing.

5. Reduced inspection is considered desirable by the responsible authority. (This stipulation is specifically for government contracts.)

Let's look at the door manufacturer's experience with the framing board supplier to see whether he can safely move to a reduced inspection plan.

The manufacturer had accepted the last 10 deliveries from the supplier. A total of 1,250 units were inspected under a normal inspection plan. Only one defect was found in all 10 inspections. The shipments had been delivered every month.

The door manufacturer checked Table 5.6 for switching to reduced inspections. For 1,250 samples tested to an AQL of 0.65 percent, the total number of defectives found cannot be greater than four. Since only one defective was found in 10 lots, the plan allowed the door manufacturer to move to a reduced inspection schedule.

Now let's see how the reduced inspection plan works.

As with all other plans, the first step is to find the sample size code letter. For this, we'll consult Table 5.3. The sample size code letter for a 1,900-unit lot, using general inspection level 2, is K.

The next step is to find the sample size and the acceptance and rejection numbers in the Single Sampling Plans for Reduced Inspection Table, Table 5.7.

Under the reduced inspection plan, the sample size is 50. When working with a normal inspection plan, the manufacturer was required to inspect 125 boards out of each shipment. By moving to a reduced inspection plan, he has saved the time and expense of inspecting 75 boards per shipment.

On the other hand, the reduced inspection plan hasn't changed the number of defects which a manufacturer would use in deciding when to accept or reject a shipment. It has, however, added an extra wrinkle.

Table 5.7 gives an acceptance number of one and a rejection number of three for our sample of 50 units at an AQL of 0.65 percent. A gap exists between the acceptance and rejection numbers. In this case, we use the acceptance and rejection guidelines in the following way.

If the manufacturer finds three or more defects in the reduced sample, he will reject the delivery, just as with the normal inspection. If he finds one or no defects in the sample, he will accept the lot. However, if he finds two defects, the manufacturer will accept the shipment but put the supplier back on a normal inspection plan.

A BEGINNER'S GUIDE TO QUALITY IN MANUFACTURING

Number of sample units from last 10 lots or batches	0.010	0.015	0.025	0.040	0.065	0.10	0.15	0.25	0.40	0.65	1.0	1.5	2.5	4.0	6.5	10	15	25	40	65	100	150	250	400	650	1,000
20–29	†	†	†	†	†	†	†	†	†	†	†	†	†	†	†	0	0	2	4	8	14	22	40	68	115	181
30–49	†	†	†	†	†	†	†	†	†	†	†	†	†	†	0	0	1	3	7	13	22	36	63	105	178	277
50–79	†	†	†	†	†	†	†	†	†	†	†	†	†	0	0	2	3	7	14	25	40	63	110	181	301	
80–129	†	†	†	†	†	†	†	†	†	†	†	†	0	0	2	4	7	14	24	42	68	105	181	297		
130–199	†	†	†	†	†	†	†	†	†	†	†	0	0	2	4	7	13	25	42	72	115	177	301	490		
200–319	†	†	†	†	†	†	†	†	†	†	0	0	2	4	8	14	22	40	68	115	181	277	471			
320–499	†	†	†	†	†	†	†	†	†	0	0	1	4	8	14	24	39	68	113	189						
500–799	†	†	†	†	†	†	†	†	0	0	2	3	7	14	25	40	63	110	181							
800–1,249	†	†	†	†	†	†	†	0	0	2	4	7	14	24	42	68	105	181								
1,250–1,999	†	†	†	†	†	†	0	0	2	4	7	13	24	40	69	110	169									
2,000–3,149	†	†	†	†	†	0	0	2	4	8	14	22	40	68	115	181										
3,150–4,999	†	†	†	†	0	0	1	4	8	14	24	38	67	111	186											
5,000–7,999	†	†	†	0	0	2	3	7	14	25	40	63	110	181												
8,000–12,499	†	†	0	0	2	4	7	14	24	42	68	105	181													
12,500–19,999	†	0	0	2	4	7	13	24	40	69	110	169														
20,000–31,499	0	0	2	4	8	14	22	40	68	115	181															
31,500–and over	0	1	4	8	14	24	38	67	111	186																

Acceptable Quality Level

† Denotes that the number of sample units from the last 10 lots or batches is not sufficient for reduced inspection for this AQL. In this instance more than 10 lots or batches may be used for the calculation, provided that the lots or batches used are the most recent ones in sequence, that they have all been on normal inspection, and that none has been rejected while on original inspection.

Table 5.6: Limit Numbers for Reduced Inspection (MIL-STD-105E Table VIII)

INCOMING INSPECTION

Sample size code letter	Sample size	Acceptable Quality Levels (reduced inspection)†																									
		0.010	0.015	0.025	0.040	0.065	0.10	0.15	0.25	0.40	0.65	1.0	1.5	2.5	4.0	6.5	10	15	25	40	65	100	150	250	400	650	1,000
		Ac Re	Ac Re	Ac Re	Ac Re	Ac Re	Ac Re	Ac Re	Ac Re	Ac Re	Ac Re	Ac Re	Ac Re	Ac Re	Ac Re	Ac Re	Ac Re	Ac Re	Ac Re	Ac Re	Ac Re	Ac Re	Ac Re	Ac Re	Ac Re	Ac Re	Ac Re
A	2																										
B	2																		0 1	1 2	2 3	3 4	5 6	7 8	10 11	14 15	21 22	30 31
C	2																	0 1	↑	↓	3 4	5 6	5 6	7 8	10 11	14 15	21 22	30 31
D	3																0 1	↑	↓	1 2	3 4	5 6	6 7	8 10	10 13	14 17	21 24	
E	5															0 1	↑	↓	2 3	3 4	5 6	6 7	8 10	10 13	14 17	21 24		
F	8														0 1	↑	↓	1 3	2 4	3 5	5 6	7 8	10 11	13				
G	13													0 1	↑	↓	1 3	2 5	3 6	5 8	7 10	10 13						
H	20												0 1	↑	↓	1 4	2 5	3 6	5 8	7 10	10 13							
J	32											0 1	↑	↓	1 3	2 5	3 6	5 8	7 10	10 13								
K	50										0 1	↑	↓	1 3	2 5	3 6	5 8	7 10	10 13	←								
L	80									0 1	↑	↓	1 4	2 5	3 6	5 8	7 10	10 13										
M	125								0 1	↑	↓	1 4	2 5	3 6	5 8	7 10	10 13											
N	200							0 1	↑	↓	1 3	2 5	3 6	5 8	7 10	10 13												
P	315						0 1	↑	↓	1 4	2 5	3 6	5 8	7 10	10 13													
Q	500					0 1	↑	↓	1 3	2 5	3 6	5 8	7 10	10 13														
R	800				0 1	↑	↓	1 3	2 5	3 6	5 8	7 10	10 13															

↓ = use first sampling plan below arrow. If sample size equals or exceeds lot or batch size, do 100% inspection.
↑ = use first sampling plan above arrow.
Ac = acceptance number.
Re = rejection number.
† If the acceptance number has been exceeded but the rejection number has not been reached, accept the lot but reinstate normal inspection.

Table 5.7: Single Sampling Plan for Reduced Inspection (MIL-STD-105E Table II-C)

The reduced inspection plan is as follows:

Reduced Incoming Inspection Plan for Framing Wood

Sampling plan:	Single Sampling Plan for Reduced Inspection (MIL-STD-105E)
AQL:	0.65 percent
Lot size:	1,900 boards
Sample size:	50 boards
Acceptance number (Ac):	Accept the lot if two or fewer defects are found. Return to Normal Inspection Plan if two defects are found.
Rejection number (Re):	Reject the lot if three or more defects are found.
Inspections required:	Length: >14' Thickness: 1 1/8" (±1/16") Width: 6" (+1/4", −0")

When working with a reduced inspection plan, the door manufacturer must be particularly vigilant to ensure that the quality of the framing board supplier does not degrade. In addition to the guidelines laid out in Table 5.6, MIL-STD-105E recommends a return to normal inspection plans if, during incoming inspection, a lot is rejected, or production becomes irregular or delayed.

MIL-STD-105E allows a switch from reduced to normal for any condition that may warrant such a switch.

5.6 Single, Double, and Multiple Sampling Plans

The inspection plans we've examined up to this point have all been single sampling plans. In these plans, a single sample is selected from the incoming shipment, and the lot is either accepted or rejected depending on the number of defects found in that sampling. Manufacturers can also choose to use plans in which more than one sample is selected and inspected for the same shipment. The advantage of these plans is that the manufacturer may be able to reduce the total number of unit inspections needed to assure the target AQL. Let's look at how these alternative plans can conserve valuable resources by examining the MIL-STD-105E procedures for double and multiple sampling plans.

In a double sampling plan, two sample sizes are specified. The manufacturer randomly selects and inspects the number of

INCOMING INSPECTION

units indicated for the first sample. If the defects found are less than or equal to the acceptance number, the lot can be accepted immediately; no second sample is needed. On the other hand, if the number of defects found is greater than or equal to the first rejection number, the lot can be rejected immediately.

However, if the number of defects found is between the acceptance and rejection numbers, a second sampling must be done. The specified second sample is inspected, and the number of defects found in the second sampling is added to the number of defects found in the first sampling. This cumulative number is then compared to the acceptance and rejection numbers for the second sampling, and the lot is accepted or rejected.

Earlier, we detailed an inspection plan for incoming framing wood at the closet door factory. It was a Single Sampling Plan for Normal Inspection. The AQL was 0.65 percent. Let's rewrite this plan as a Double Sampling Plan for Normal Inspection.

As in the single sampling plan, we first determine the sample size code letter (see Table 5.3). Because the lot size was 1,900, the code letter remains K for General Inspection Level II. Next, we must refer to Table 5.8 for the Double Sampling Plan For Normal Inspection. We find that the first sample size is 80. For an AQL of 0.65 percent, if there are no defects, the lot can be accepted and no further sampling or inspection is necessary. If we find three or more defects, then the lot is to be rejected and no more sampling or inspection is necessary. If the number of defects is one or two, a second sampling is necessary.

The size of the second sampling is also 80. The acceptance number is three and the rejection number is four. If the total number of defects found during both samplings add up to three or fewer, the lot is acceptable. If the defects counted in both the first and second sampling add up to four or more, the lot is to be rejected.

The double sampling plan for the framing wood reads as follows:

Incoming Inspection Plan for Framing Wood

Sampling plan:	Double Sampling Plan for Normal Inspection (MIL-STD-105E)
AQL:	0.65 percent
Lot size:	1,900 boards
First sample size:	80 boards
First acceptance number (Ac):	Accept the lot if no defects are found.
First rejection number (Re):	Reject the lot if three or more defects are found.

Table 5.8: Double Sampling Plans for Normal Inspection (MIL-STD-105E Table III-A)

Incoming Inspection Plan for Framing Wood

Make a second sampling if one or two defects are found.

Second sample size:	80 boards
Second acceptance number (Ac):	Accept the lot if a total of three or fewer defects are found in both samplings.
Second rejection number (Re):	Reject the lot if a total of four or more defects are found in both samplings.
Inspections required:	Length: >14' Thickness: 1 1/8" (±1/16") Width: 6" (+1/4", −0")

The double sampling plan allows the manufacturer to reduce the number of units that must be sampled as long as the shipment can be accepted or rejected based simply on the first sample. In this case, the company only had to inspect a first sample of 80 units compared to a required sample of 125 units for the single sampling plan. On the other hand, if a second sample is required under the double sampling plan, the manufacturer will have inspected a total of 160 units, 35 more than under the single sampling plan. Despite the latter possibility, it is generally advantageous to use a double sampling plan as long as the specified first sample is smaller than the sample for the single sampling plan.

MIL-STD-105E outlines double sampling plans for normal, tightened, and reduced inspections. The rules for switching between these inspection plans are the same for double sampling plans as for single sampling plans.

Finally, manufacturers can choose to use a multiple sampling plan. In this type of plan, up to seven samples may be taken. As in the double sampling plan, the number of defects found in the sampling is compared to the acceptance and rejection numbers. If the number of defects is greater than or equal to the rejection number, the lot is rejected. If the number of defects is less than or equal to the acceptance number, the lot is accepted, unless otherwise noted. When the number of defects is between the acceptance and rejection numbers, a subsequent sampling must be taken. The number of defects found in subsequent samplings must be added to the number of defects found in previous samplings. This cumulative number is then compared to the acceptance and rejection numbers. The decision for accepting or rejecting the lot, or continuing the sampling process, follows the same rules as discussed during the first sampling.

Table 5.9: Multiple Sampling Plan for Normal Inspection (Second half of table) (MIL-STD-105E Table IV-A)

INCOMING INSPECTION

To better understand the multiple sampling plan, we will again rewrite the incoming inspection plan for the door manufacturer's framing wood. The second half of the Multiple Sampling Plan for Normal Inspection from MIL-STD-105E appears in Table 5.9. We have provided the second half of this plan because it conforms to the sample size required for the framing wood.

The multiple sampling plan as defined by Table 5.9 for the framing wood is as follows:

Incoming Inspection Plan for Framing Wood

Sampling plan:	Multiple Sampling Plan for Normal Inspection (MIL-STD-105E)
AQL:	0.65 percent
Lot size:	1,900 boards
First sample size:	32 boards
First acceptance number (Ac):	Must inspect a second sample if fewer than two defects are found.
First rejection number (Re):	Reject the lot if two or more defects are found.

Unless the batch is rejected because two or more defects are found, make a Second Sampling.

Second sample size:	32 boards
Second acceptance number (Ac):	Accept the lot if no defects are found in both samplings.
Second rejection number (Re):	Reject the lot if three or more defects are found in both samplings.

Make a third sampling if a total of one or two defects were found in both samples.

Third sample size:	32 boards
Third acceptance number (Ac):	Accept the lot if no defects are found in all samplings.
Third rejection number (Re):	Reject the lot if three or more defects are found in all samplings.

Make a fourth sampling if a total of one or two defects were found in all samples inspected.

Fourth sample size:	32 boards
Fourth acceptance number (Ac):	Accept the lot if one or no defects are found in all samplings.
Fourth rejection number (Re):	Reject the lot if four or more defects are found in all samplings.

Make a fifth sampling if a total of two or three defects are found in all samples inspected.

Fifth sample size:	32 boards
Fifth acceptance number (Ac):	Accept the lot if two or fewer defects are found in all samplings.
Fifth rejection number (Re):	Reject the lot if four or more defects are found in all samplings.

Make a sixth sampling if a total of three defects are found in all samples inspected.

Sixth sample size:	32 boards
Sixth acceptance number (Ac):	Accept the lot if three or fewer defects are found in all samplings.
Sixth rejection number (Re):	Reject the lot if five or more defects are found in all samplings.

Make a seventh sampling if a total of four defects are found in all samples inspected.

Seventh sample size:	32 boards
Seventh acceptance number (Ac):	Accept the lot if four or fewer defects are found in all samplings.
Seventh rejection number (Re):	Reject the lot if five or more defects are found in all samplings.

Based on the plan outlined above, it is clear that multiple sampling plans can significantly reduce the total number of units which a manufacturer must inspect before accepting or rejecting a lot. Good lots, i.e., those with very few defects, are accepted rapidly with relatively little inspection required. Similarly, bad lots, i.e., those with many defects, are also rejected quickly. The framing wood shipment, for example, could be rejected with a sample of only 32 boards, compared to the 125 needed for the single sampling plan. The shipment could be accepted with a sample of 64 boards. Even the need for a third sample, as outlined in the plan, will require a smaller total number of inspections than the single sampling plan.

It is true that ultimately this plan could require the manufacturer to inspect 224 units. This would be 79 percent more than the single sampling plan required before reaching a final decision on accepting or rejecting the lot. However, this increased level of sampling is only likely to occur on shipments which are extremely close to the AQL target. In these cases, it can be argued, increased sampling and inspection are appropriate.

It should also be noted that the multiple sampling plan is more complicated to administer than the single or double sampling plans. During the course of seven different samplings and inspections, record-keeping becomes very important. However, any successful quality program depends on an ability to maintain accurate records on inspection data. Forms for use by the inspectors help ensure that the job gets done correctly and provide a permanent record for future analysis. A computer terminal can be used to prompt the inspector on the proper sampling procedure. The terminal can also record the inspector's findings.

Single, double, and multiple sampling plans each have advantages and disadvantages. The single sampling plan is the easiest to administer. Procedures are simple, and record-keeping is minimal. Double and multiple sampling plans offer decreased sampling for lots that have either few defects or many defects. In general, it is cost-effective to use double or multiple sampling when their first sample sizes are smaller than those required for single sampling plans.

MIL-STD-105E is not the only sampling plan available. There are skip-lot plans, sampling by variable plans, and many more. If MIL-STD-105E does not satisfy your needs, J. M. Juran's *Quality Control Handbook* offers a number of other plans. Chapter 7 of this text presents the mathematical basis for these plans.

5.7 Classes of Defects

To this point, we have defined a defect simply as any failure to meet a product's specifications, and we have treated all defects equally. In fact, defects do vary dramatically in their basic nature and their relative importance. MIL-STD-105E defines three classifications of defects and defectives as follows:

Critical Defect: A critical defect is a defect that judgment and experience indicate is likely to result in hazardous or unsafe conditions for the individual using, maintaining, or depending upon the product. A critical defect is also likely to interfere with the proper performance of emergency service equipment or the tactical function of a major military item.

Major Defect: A major defect is a defect other than critical that is likely to result in failure, or to reduce materially the usability of the product for its intended purpose.

Minor Defect: A minor defect is a defect that is not likely to reduce materially the usability of the unit of product for its intended purpose, or one which is a departure from established standards having little bearing on the effective use or operation of the unit.

Critical defects are very serious because they make the product dangerous to use. Suppose a shipment of televisions was being inspected, and when the inspector plugged a television into a power outlet, it burst into flames. This is a critical defect because it could cause physical harm to the user. Or suppose an inspector was examining sprinkler heads for a fire protection system and found that one of the heads was clogged. Since a sprinkler head in a fire protection system is emergency equipment, the clogged head would be considered a critical defect.

Critical defects, because of their serious nature, should be treated differently than other defects. If one critical defect is found during sampling, the entire lot must be rejected. In some cases, as we will see later in the chapter, every unit in a lot may need to be inspected for a critical defect.

Major defects are those that make the product, component, or part unusable. A television may not have sound; a lawn mower may not have its spark plug and cannot be started; a resistor may be the wrong value. All of these things prevent the unit from doing what it was intended to do. Normally, a major defect is counted whenever any component or part or raw material is not within its specification tolerance. Major defects are counted and compared to the inspection plan to determine if the lot is to be accepted or rejected.

A minor defect does not prevent the unit from fulfilling its purpose, nor does it make the product hazardous. However, there is still a defect. A label may be crooked, an instruction page may

INCOMING INSPECTION

be missing from a user's manual, or there may be a small imperfection in a stereo receiver cabinet. In many cases the AQL for minor defects is different from the AQL for major defects. As such, the minor defects are counted separately and compared to a different AQL when deciding on accepting or rejecting a lot.

Let's consider the bread manufacturer. He sells bread to customers who have their own inspection procedure. Consider some of the defects the bread customer inspects for.

1. Weight and size of the loaf
2. Taste
3. Moisture content
4. Food poisoning bacteria or foreign matter in the loaf
5. Color

The bread customer considers deviations from standards for the first three to be major defects and would reject the lot if two loaves in the sample were found defective. The color of the bread is a minor defect, and the customer would only reject the lot if four loaves in the sample were below specification. But food poisoning bacteria and foreign matter are potential health hazards and are considered critical defects. If any loaves were found with food poisoning bacteria or foreign matter, all the loaves would be returned to the bread manufacturer.

5.8 100 Percent Inspection

In light of the varying nature and importance of product defects, there are times when no sampling plan may be adequate to ensure the required AQL. When incoming items can affect personal safety, then 100 percent inspection may be required. Similarly, when items received in incoming inspection are very valuable, a sampling plan may not be sufficient. For example, a diamond merchant receiving a shipment of diamonds will check each stone to ensure it meets requirements before accepting the shipment.

Sometimes a shipment of critical parts may be received and found unacceptable. However, if the supplier cannot replace the lot with acceptable units and no other suppliers are available, the manufacturing line will shut down because of this critical shortage. In this situation, it may be appropriate to inspect the entire rejected lot and remove all defective items to maintain production.

5.9 Rejects

Effective quality control procedures find defective units not only during incoming inspection but throughout the entire manufacturing process. MIL-STD-105E clearly defines the procedure for handling rejected samples. Any unit found defective can be rejected whether or not it is part of the sampling. Rejects may be repaired or replaced and resubmitted for inspection by the supplier. The customer will decide on the procedure for resubmitting these samples.

MIL-STD-105E also defines a procedure for handling rejected lots. When a lot is rejected, all units in the lot must be re-examined or retested by the supplier. All defective units are either removed or corrected. The customer will decide on the process for resubmitting these samples. The customer will choose normal or tightened inspection and may choose either to inspect only for the defect which caused the initial rejection or to inspect for all criteria.

It is important for the supplier and customer to agree in advance on the procedures for handling rejects and rejected lots.

5.10 Inspection Records and Average Quality Level

It is extremely important that manufacturers maintain records showing the results of all incoming inspections. As we have seen, these records of performance over a period of time allow a company to change inspection plans in response to fluctuations in a supplier's quality. The data gathered from incoming inspection can also be used to calculate a supplier's Average Quality Level. This will let us know if our sampling plan is working as we had hoped.

Let's use the incoming inspection record for the antenna in the AM radio to help us judge the inspection plan we had implemented. The inspection plan was as follows:

Incoming Inspection Plan for the Radio Antenna

Sampling plan:	Single Sampling Plan for Normal Inspection (MIL-STD-105E)
AQL:	0.065 percent
Lot size:	26,400 antennas
Sample size:	315 antennas
Acceptance number (Ac):	Accept the lot if no defects are found.
Rejection number (Re):	Reject the lot if one defect is found.

INCOMING INSPECTION

The history of the last 10 shipments of antennas received by the quality control group at the AM radio plant is as follows:

Lot Size	Sample Size	Defects	Disposition of Lot
26,400	315	0	Sent to the factory floor
26,400	315	1	Returned to supplier for 100 percent inspection
26,400	315	0	Resubmitted lot sent to the factory floor
26,400	315	0	Sent to factory floor
26,400	315	2	Returned to supplier for 100 percent inspection
26,400	315	0	Resubmitted lot sent to the factory floor
26,400	315	0	Sent to the factory floor
26,400	315	0	Sent to the factory floor
26,400	315	1	Returned to supplier for 100 percent inspection
26,400	315	0	Resubmitted lot sent to the factory floor

Three of the 10 deliveries were resubmissions of earlier shipments which had been rejected originally. Lots that are resubmitted should be 100 percent inspected by the supplier before they are resubmitted. Therefore, resubmitted lots do not represent the supplier's normal quality level, and we won't use them in our calculation of AQL.

There were seven original lots. A total of 2,205 samples were inspected from these seven shipments, and four defects were found. Therefore the defects per hundred units is calculated as follows:

$$\text{Defects per Hundred Units} = \frac{\text{Number of Defects}}{\text{Number of Units Inspected}} \times 100$$

$$\text{Defects per Hundred Units} = \frac{4}{2205} \times 100 = 0.181\%$$

Comparing this defect rate to the AQL of 0.065 percent indicates clearly that the supplier is not providing antennas at the level that the radio manufacturer considers acceptable. The fact that three of the seven lots submitted were rejected should have been the first indication that something was wrong. The radio manufacturer needs to work with the antenna manufacturer to improve the quality level. If this cannot be done, the radio manufacturer may have to find a new supplier.

5.11 Supplier Certification

There are also situations when our inspection records will indicate that a vendor consistently supplies us with a product that surpasses our AQL target. In these cases, even reduced inspection and multiple sampling plans may simply add up to too much inspection. In these cases we may not want to do any incoming inspection at all.

At the same time, our anticipated savings from reduced inspections must be balanced against the possible costs of producing defective units as a result of variations in incoming quality. The way to reconcile these two concerns is through *supplier certification*.

Supplier certification is a well-defined process by which a manufacturer ensures that a supplier is capable of meeting AQL requirements without the need for incoming inspection.

Let's look at the steps the AM radio manufacturer uses to certify a supplier.

AM Radio Supplier Certification Procedure

1. Ensure that the specification includes all the necessary information: a brief description of the item and all important parameters with associated tolerances. The AQL is stated.

2. Ensure that the supplier is aware of product specification and procedures in case a lot is rejected.

3. Inspect the first lot received according to MIL-STD-105E, General Inspection Level II for normal inspection. The incoming lots will remain at this level until enough lots have been received and accepted to place them on reduced inspection.

4. If the item goes from normal inspection to reduced inspection and can remain on reduced inspection for 10 consecutive lots, it is time to consider "certifying" the manufacturer so that incoming inspection can be discontinued. During the certification process, the item will be sampled according to MIL-STD-105E.

5. The supplier will be contacted and told that it has been chosen for consideration as a certified manufacturer. The supplier will be requested to describe its quality

program. This description should include procedures for incoming inspection, process controls, and final inspection, and how they achieve specified quality levels. The supplier will also describe how quality records will be kept on lots sent to the radio factory.

6. Once the supplier's quality program has been studied and approved, a visit to the supplier will be arranged. The manufacturer's quality control manager will ensure that the supplier makes inspections and keeps proper records as stated in the description of the supplier's quality program.

7. Once the factory visit has been completed and the quality control manager is satisfied with the supplier, incoming inspections will cease.

8. Periodically, the supplier will be required to send quality level data on lots shipped to the factory location.

This is only one of many possible approaches for certifying vendors. Changes in steps leading up to certification may be required based on the supplier's relationship with the manufacturer or its reputation in the industry. In other cases, modifications in the process may be necessary due to the nature of the product itself. Critical components may require a longer inspection history prior to certification. On the other hand, parts which are less crucial, being supplied by a well-known vendor, may require little or no initial inspection.

In order for a certification process to be successful, a system of checks and balances must be in place at the factory. During the manufacturing process, the product should be checked before it is sent to the customer. If a large reject rate is traced to a part or component that has "certified" status, then that status should be withdrawn and incoming inspection should be reinstituted immediately.

Vendor certification programs have become a major component in most quality control efforts. Enhancements in quality theory have enabled these programs to move far beyond the mere elimination of incoming inspection. In chapter 12, we will look at how manufacturers involve vendors in final product designs, evaluate "non-component" quality, and offer "no-bid," "life-of-the-part" contracts through quality-based target pricing.

A BEGINNER'S GUIDE TO QUALITY IN MANUFACTURING

Chapter Summary

1. The goal of incoming inspection is to ensure that only raw materials, components, and parts which conform to their specifications go into the product.

2. Unidentified quality problems become more expensive as they move through the manufacturing process. Incoming inspection is our first opportunity to detect and remove quality problems.

3. The quality of a lot or shipment can be quantified using the following measures:

$$\text{Percent Defective} = \frac{\text{Number of Defectives}}{\text{Number of Units Inspected}} \times 100$$

$$\text{Defects per Hundred Units} = \frac{\text{Number of Defects}}{\text{Number of Units Inspected}} \times 100$$

$$\text{QL Defectives (ppm)} = \frac{\text{Number of Defectives}}{\text{Number of Units Inspected}} \times 1{,}000{,}000$$

$$\text{QL Defects (ppm)} = \frac{\text{Number of Defects}}{\text{Number of Units Inspected}} \times 1{,}000{,}000$$

4. The Acceptable Quality Level (AQL) is the quality measurement for maximum number of defects or defectives which a manufacturer can tolerate in a lot, shipment, or batch. The AQL is an average value over many samplings.

5. An acceptance sampling plan is a procedure used to either accept or reject a lot based on an inspection of a percentage or portion of that lot, called a sample size. When sampling by attribute, defects (or defective units) are counted. The total number of defects (or defective units) is compared to acceptance and rejection numbers outlined in the plan. Based on these guidelines, the entire lot is either accepted or rejected, or more sampling is done.

6. MIL-STD-105E offers three degrees of inspection:

    Normal inspection is done when we anticipate the lot to be at, or slightly better than, its AQL.

    Reduced inspection is implemented when a supplier's shipments are consistently better than our AQL target. In reduced inspection, sampling sizes smaller than normal are used.

Tightened inspection is used when a vendor's deliveries frequently fall below their AQL target. In tightened inspection, stricter acceptance criteria than normal is used.

Procedures for moving from one type of inspection to another are defined in MIL-STD-105E.

7. MIL-STD-105E also offers three types of sampling plans: single, double, and multiple. The single sampling plan uses only one sampling to determine acceptance or rejection. Double and multiple sampling plans use a number of samplings.

8. MIL-STD-105E defines three classifications of defects and defectives as follows:

    Critical defect: A critical defect is a defect that judgment and experience indicate is likely to result in hazardous or unsafe conditions for the individual using, maintaining, or depending upon the product. A critical defect is also one that is likely to interfere with the proper performance of emergency service equipment or the tactical function of a major military item.

    Major defect: A major defect is a defect other than critical that is likely to result in failure, or to reduce materially the usability, of the product for its intended purpose.

    Minor defect: A minor defect is a defect that is not likely to reduce materially the usability of the unit of product for its intended purpose, or is a departure from established standards having little bearing on the effective use or operation of the unit.

9. 100 percent sampling is done

    - by suppliers on lots which have been rejected on initial inspection; or,
    - the items to be sampled are very crucial; or,
    - items in the lot are very valuable.

    During 100 percent sampling, all the items in the lot are inspected.

10. Supplier or vendor certification is a process that eliminates the need for incoming inspection for a particular item. During this process the manufacturer works with the supplier or vendor to ensure that lots delivered to the factory meet or exceed the manufacturer's AQL.

A BEGINNER'S GUIDE TO QUALITY IN MANUFACTURING

Questions for Chapter 5

1. The closet door manufacturer receives a shipment of 2,400 wood panels to be used as the front and rear exterior panels of the door. The panels must be checked for length (>6'8"), width (>2'6"), and thickness (3/16", +1/32", –0"). The panels are also checked for blemishes and for warping. The manufacturer finds that:

    6 are too short

    3 are too narrow

    5 are too thin

    10 have blemishes

    1 is warped

    12 are too short and are warped

    4 are too short and have blemishes

    16 have blemishes and are warped

    6 are too short and too thin

    3 are too short, too thin, and blemished

    a. How many panels are defective? What is the percent defective? Compute the QL Defective (ppm).

    b. What is the total number of defects? Calculate the number of defects per hundred units. Compute the QL Defects (ppm).

2. A radio manufacturer samples five batches of diodes. Each batch has 32,500 diodes. The number of defective diodes in each batch is 45, 78, 127, 60, and 250.

    a. For each batch, compute the percent defective.

    b. Change each percent defective to the QL Defective (ppm).

INCOMING INSPECTION

    c. Determine the average percent defective and average QL Defective (ppm).

3. A manufacturer needs to sample a batch of 5,000 components. It has decided to use General Inspection Level II, a single sampling plan for normal inspection, and an AQL of 0.40.

    a. Find the sample size code letter in Table 5.3 and the corresponding sample size in Table 5.4.

    b. Record the acceptance number and rejection number for this plan.

    c. Prepare an incoming inspection plan listing the sampling plan, AQL, lot size, sample size, acceptance number, and rejection number.

4. Answer the same questions as in question 3 for a batch size of 1,000 and an AQL of 1.5.

5. Under what conditions must a manufacturer change from a normal to a tightened sampling plan? When should a manufacturer change from a tightened plan to a normal plan?

6. Repeat the same questions as in question 3 using a single sampling plan for tightened inspection.

7. Repeat question 4 using a single sampling plan for tightened inspection.

INCOMING INSPECTION

8. A manufacturer has accepted 10 consecutive lots of a component and wishes to institute reduced inspection. For each number of sample units from the last 10 batches, AQL, and number of defects listed, determine if it may institute reduced inspection. Use Table 5.6 on page 100.

	Sample Units	AQL	Number of Defects
a.	900	4.0	53
b.	6,740	0.25	20
c.	7,740	0.65	30
d.	150	0.10	5
e.	3,780	0.40	8

9. Continuing to use General Inspection Level II, and a single sample plan, determine the limit number for reduced inspection if an AQL of 0.25 is chosen and each of the 10 accepted batches has 40,000 components.

10. Repeat question 9 for the given AQL and batch sizes below.

    a. 4.0; 2,000

    b. 0.065; 20,000

    c. 0.65; 1,500

A BEGINNER'S GUIDE TO QUALITY IN MANUFACTURING

✓ 11. A manufacturer is using a reduced inspection plan on a component with an AQL of 1.5 which arrives in batches of 4,000 units. Use Tables 5.3 and 5.7 to determine the sample size code letter and sample size. For each number of defects, determine if the lot is accepted or rejected and whether the manufacturer must reinstate normal inspection.

    a. 0

    b. 1

    c. 2

    d. 3

    e. 4

A   f. 5

A   g. 6

A   h. 7

R   i. 8

R   j. 9

R   k. 10

 *Tighten See*

12. Write a reduced incoming inspection plan for the model in question 11.

13. A manufacturer wishes to use a double sampling plan for normal inspection. The AQL is 0.40 and the batch size is 5,000. Using Tables 5.3 and 5.8, determine the sample size for the first and second sample. How many found defects will necessitate a second sample? Write an incoming inspection plan.

14. A manufacturer wishes to use a multiple inspection plan for the batch in question 13. Using Table 5.9, determine the sample size for each of the possible seven samples. What happens if zero defects are found in the first sample? Write an incoming inspection plan.

Chapter 5 Project

In chapter 1, you created a bill of goods for the product you would like to manufacture. For each item, list the type of defects that incoming inspection might discover. Also, for each item, decide if percent defective or defects per hundred units would be the better measure. Decide if each defect is a critical defect, a major defect, or a minor defect.

STATISTICAL QUALITY CONTROL

6.1 Introduction

In chapter 5, we completed the incoming inspection process. We now have raw materials, parts, and components with an acceptable quality level. We know this because we have conducted sample inspections and calculated quality levels for the shipments as a whole.

Now we must transform these raw materials and components into a finished product. In this chapter, we will learn quality control techniques to ensure that our own manufacturing processes consistently produce components, subassemblies, and finished products which meet specifications.

As with incoming inspection, samples will be selected from the output of each manufacturing process in question. Inspections and measurements will be made. Data will be recorded and analyzed. All this information will tell us whether the manufacturing process is performing acceptably and whether our product is meeting or exceeding its specifications.

If at any time our product is not meeting its specifications, the process must be corrected immediately. We will use the information we are gathering about the product to identify specific problems with the process and make adjustments as required.

The gathering and analysis of data during the manufacturing process so that corrective measures can be taken is called Statistical Process Control (SPC).

6.2 Process Control Sites

The first decision to make when applying SPC techniques is to determine where to take data and make observations. A process control site is an inspection station designed to determine whether the manufacturing process is functioning correctly. The process control site also allows the manufacturer to identify and remove defective parts and components. A process control site should be considered at and between each step in the manufacturing process. The decision whether to place a process control site in the manufacturing process must be based on economic criteria.

Process control sites should be placed early in the manufacturing process to catch defectives as quickly as possible. Process control sites should be placed where defects are known to occur and on equipment that can go out of tolerance. Process control sites should be situated where inspections can be made quickly. Automatic test equipment can help reduce inspection test costs.

A flowchart for the AM radio manufacturing process appears in Figure 6.1. Let's discuss why the various process control steps were included.

First the manufacturer receives the parts for the radio. She inspects some of the incoming components from suppliers that are not certified; parts from certified suppliers require no inspection.

The next step is auto-insertion. Here, parts are mechanically placed on the Printed Circuit Board (PCB). The PCB supports the components and also provides an electrical path between components. No process control is needed between receiving and auto-insertion. The parts are considered acceptable during incoming inspection and do not get damaged or deteriorate traveling from receiving to the factory floor.

Following auto-insertion, the components are automatically soldered to the PCB. The soldering machine is a complicated piece of equipment. Melted solder (a mixture of lead and tin) flows across the underside of the PCB and accumulates on the wires from the components where they come through the PCB. The solder becomes solid, and the components are firmly secured to the PCB.

Both the temperature of the solder and the speed at which it flows across the underside of the PCB are critical to the success of the soldering process. The manufacturer has had many problems with the soldering machine. Consequently, she considers this to be an important process control site. Meters attached to the equipment monitor solder temperature and flow and will alert the operator to any problems.

After soldering, the next manufacturing process is hand-insertion. However, the manufacturer has chosen to locate a process control site between these two process steps. This is a good time to test both the individual components on the PCB and the success of the soldering process. Automatic equipment checks the components quickly and determines if any have been damaged by the soldering process.

STATISTICAL QUALITY CONTROL

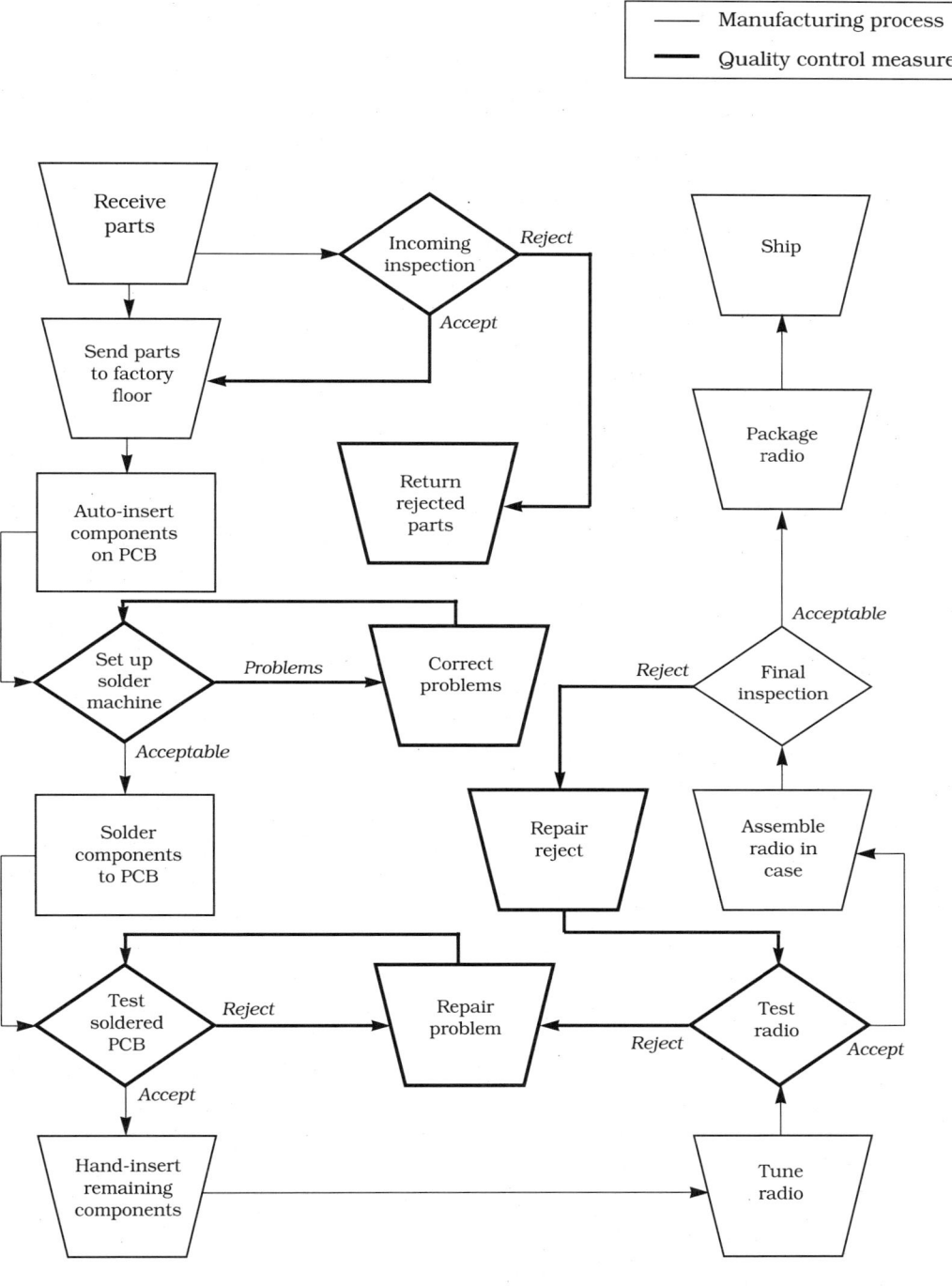

Figure 6.1: Flowchart for AM Radio Manufacturing, Including Quality Control Measures

PCBs which meet specifications at this stage go on to the hand-insertion process where a few remaining components are added. The radio goes directly from hand-insertion to tuning without a process control inspection. Only a few parts are put on the PCB at hand-insertion, and these will be checked as the radio is tuned.

The tuning process is costly, and the manufacturer wants to make sure it is done properly. The radio can be tested easily at this stage because much of the tuning equipment is used to test the radio. Therefore, the manufacturer tests the radio between the tuning and assembly stages.

Radios which are successfully tuned and tested are assembled into their cases to produce the finished product. At this point, the manufacturer visually inspects the radio for surface defects. After this last inspection, the radio will be packaged with the user's manual and sent to the customer.

The process control sites used by the AM radio manufacturer ensure that the customer will be satisfied by a product that meets specifications. At the same time, the company maximizes its profit by avoiding the production of defective components, subassemblies, and finished products.

6.3 Variations in the Manufacturing Process

As we learned in chapter 1, the actual output of any given manufacturing process will vary somewhat from one unit of production to another. Not all of our closet door panels, for example, will be exactly 2'6" wide. Some of our output will be slightly wider and some will be narrower. Our production specifications have been established with tolerances around the target specification in recognition of these variations.

The differences result from a variety of normal variations in processing performance. Equipment will only be able to process materials within certain specified tolerances. The actual panel saw used to cut the door, for example, may only be capable of cutting panels to a 1/64" tolerance. Similarly, even the performance of the most careful and conscientious operator will vary over time. Finally, the raw material may vary somewhat within its own specifications, leading to minor variations in the finished product or component part.

The theory and techniques of SPC are based on the recognition of these normal variations in process output. SPC allows us to identify the capability of an individual production process to meet specified tolerances at any given point in time, based on equipment, personnel, materials, and manufacturing procedures. SPC quantifies this capability mathematically through a series of statistical measurements. When a process is consistently producing within this capability, the process is technically *in control*. It is critically important to remember, however, that any process which is in statistical control but not meeting product specifications is totally unacceptable.

SPC then provides tools to monitor process performance to detect when a process begins to go *out of control*. SPC monitors variations in actual product measurements and compares them to the normal range of variations which we would expect. By doing so, SPC allows us to identify problems which are developing within the process (changes in equipment settings, worn tooling, decreasing operator attentiveness, etc.) and correct them prior to the production of any pieces which fail to meet our actual manufacturing specifications.

6.4 Measuring Process Capabilities

In order to see how SPC will allow us to calculate process capabilities, let's look at the closet door company's production of door panels. The stated specification for these components is 2'6" in width. Table 6.1 shows the measurements for a sample of 100 panels the company has produced.

2'6.04"	2'5.94"	2'6.01"	2'5.91"
2'5.97"	2'6.02"	2'6.06"	2'5.96"
2'5.94"	2'6.05"	2'6.03"	2'5.86"
2'5.98"	2'6.01"	2'5.96"	2'6.05"
2'5.95"	2'6.06"	2'5.97"	2'6.03"
2'5.99"	2'6.04"	2'6.00"	2'6.02"
2'5.97"	2'5.98"	2'6.07"	2'6.01"
2'5.94"	2'6.05"	2'5.88"	2'6.03"
2'5.99"	2'6.02"	2'5.95"	2'6.06"
2'6.08"	2'5.96"	2'6.02"	2'5.94"
2'6.03"	2'5.95"	2'6.01"	2'5.98"
2'6.00"	2'6.03"	2'5.99"	2'6.01"
2'5.97"	2'6.00"	2'6.02"	2'6.06"
2'5.97"	2'5.95"	2'6.04"	2'6.02"
2'6.01"	2'5.99"	2'5.99"	2'5.94"
2'6.00"	2'5.98"	2'6.03"	2'6.06"
2'6.02"	2'6.02"	2'5.98"	2'6.00"
2'5.95"	2'6.01"	2'6.03"	2'6.05"
2'6.08"	2'5.92"	2'5.96"	2'5.97"
2'6.01"	2'6.09"	2'5.99"	2'5.98"
2'6.09"	2'6.04"	2'5.96"	2'6.04"
2'6.13"	2'5.94"	2'6.01"	2'5.97"
2'5.98"	2'6.05"	2'6.03"	2'5.96"
2'6.00"	2'6.01"	2'6.06"	2'5.98"
2'5.95"	2'5.92"	2'6.02"	2'6.03"

Table 6.1: Panel Width Measurements

The capability of the process is measured by the extent of variation in these actual results.

One useful measure is the *range of variation* in the data. The range is the difference between the largest and the smallest observed values in a given sample.

The largest value in our sample data is 2'6.13". The smallest value is 2'5.86". The range is therefore calculated

Range = Largest Value − Smallest Value
Range = 2'6.13" − 2'5.86"
Range = 0.27"

Based on this sample, therefore, our actual production of door panels can vary in width by as much as .27". Since we have built in a tolerance of ± 1/8", or .25" (2 × .125"), this range of variation alone means that the process has not been capable of meeting our specifications.

The range of variation, however, is not the only measure of process capabilities in which we are interested. We also want to know how many panels were cut close to the stated specification or target value. How many were the right length? How many were short? How many were long?

We can answer these questions by arranging our sample data in a *frequency distribution*. This distribution will show us how many panels were measured at various widths.

We will construct our frequency distribution by selecting a series of size groupings, or cells, which will provide us with sufficient information to analyze our process. Let's divide our overall range of variation by 10 to get an approximate range of variation for each individual cell. Dividing the range by 10 generates a value of 0.027". This value is very close to 1/32". Since 1/32" (or 0.03125") is a value that is a factor of 1/8", which is our tolerance, we will use 1/32" as our *cell interval*. The cell boundaries are then defined by adding and subtracting 1/32" from the target value. Table 6.2 defines the cells.

Once we've identified the upper and lower boundaries for each cell, we can identify the number of door panels which fall into each of these size groupings. Cell 7, for example, contains all the data between 2'6.03125" and 2'6.0625". If we refer to Table 6.1, we find that 16 panels have been cut between the boundaries describing Cell 7. If we repeat this procedure for all the cells, the frequency distribution for the cut panels would be as shown in Table 6.3.

Our target value (2'6") is located between cells 5 and 6. As we can see from Table 6.3, most of the panels have been cut close to the target value. Some are nearer to the specification tolerances. Some are even outside the specification limits. The upper tolerance (2'6 1/8") is located between Cell 9 and Cell 10. The lower tolerance (2'5 7/8") is located between Cell 1 and Cell 2.

STATISTICAL QUALITY CONTROL

Cell Number	Lower Boundary	Upper Boundary
1	2'5 27/32" (2'5.84375")	2'5 7/8" (2'5.875")
2	2'5 7/8" (2'5.875")	2'5 29/32" (2'5.90625")
3	2'5 29/32" (2'5.90625")	2'5 15/16" (2'5.9375")
4	2'5 15/16" (2'5.9375")	2'5 31/32" (2'5.96875")
5	2'5 31/32" (2'5.96875")	2'6" (2'6.000")
6	2'6" (2'6.000")	2'6 1/32" (2'6.03125")
7	2'6 1/32" (2'6.03125")	2'6 1/16" (2'6.0625")
8	2'6 1/16" (2'6.0625")	2'6 3/32" (2'6.09375")
9	2'6 3/32" (2'6.09375")	2'6 1/8" (2'6.125")
10	2'6 1/8" (2'6.125")	2'6 5/32" (2'6.15625")

Table 6.2: Cell Intervals for Door Panel Width Data

Cell Number	Frequency of Occurrence
1	1
2	1
3	4
4	18
5	26
6	28
7	16
8	5
9	0
10	1

Note: When a data value (such as 2'6"), falls between two cells, include it with the totals of the lower-valued cell.

Table 6.3: Frequency Distribution for the Door Panels

To show more clearly the relationship between our sample results and our target specifications, the frequency distribution can be represented in a graph called a *histogram*. The histogram is made of rectangles whose height is proportional to the number of units in a cell and whose base is proportional to the cell interval. A histogram of the frequency distribution for the door panel widths appears in Figure 6.2.

A BEGINNER'S GUIDE TO QUALITY IN MANUFACTURING

The histogram is a visual picture of the results of our manufacturing process. The specification target and the upper and lower specification limits (tolerances) have been added. From this picture, we can draw some conclusions about the panel-cutting process. The majority of panels cut are within specifications, but some are not. The process is not capable of consistently meeting our specifications. The question we must answer next is whether it is capable of meeting our AQL for this particular process.

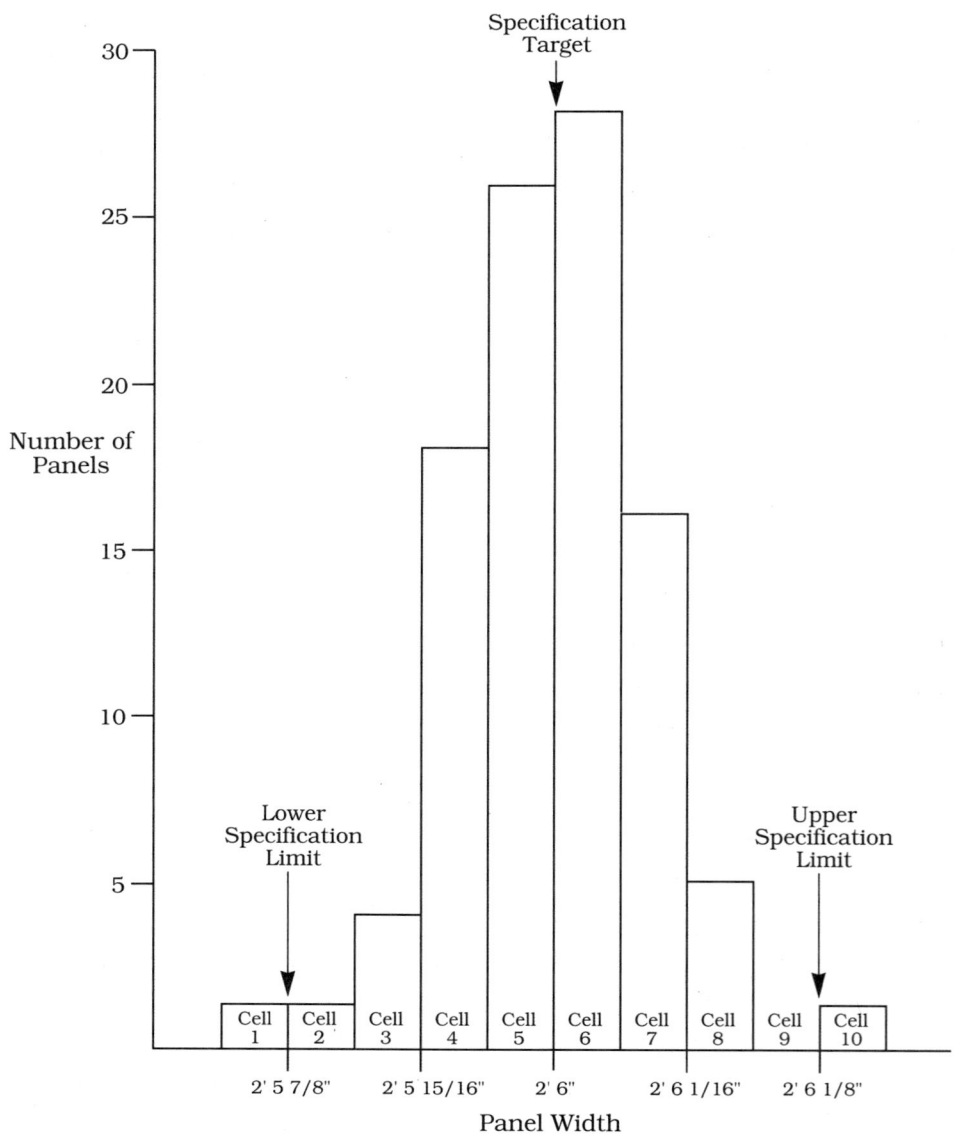

Figure 6.2: Door Panel Width Histogram

STATISTICAL QUALITY CONTROL

6.5 Process AQLs

In chapter 5, we learned that the manufacturer has established AQLs for each of the incoming component parts and materials which go into the finished product. We also saw how the manufacturer used data from the acceptance sampling plan to determine whether the shipments as a whole would meet these AQL requirements.

Similarly, the manufacturer must also establish AQLs for each of the production processes which turn out component parts and subassemblies, to ensure that the manufacturing process is capable of meeting the quality target for his finished products.

As with incoming inspection, the manufacturer will use data from sample inspections to ensure that the production processes are capable of meeting these AQL targets.

Let's continue our analysis of the closet door company to see how we can use sample data to calculate the AQL for a manufacturing process.

6.6 Normal Distribution Curves and Measures of Central Tendency

As we can see from our frequency distribution and histogram of sample data, most of the door panels have been cut to measurements which are very close to the stated specification. More than half of the 100 boards, in fact, were within 1/32" of the stated specification. Another 34 boards, or 34 percent of the total sample, were within 1/16" of the target. Less than 10 percent of the sample were found to vary by more than this margin.

This general pattern of sample results, with most measurements clustering around a central point and a symmetrical decline in the number of measurements as you move further away from that central point, is extremely common. The pattern is so common, in fact, that statisticians have been able to create a mathematical model for it, which is called a *normal distribution curve*.

We could draw a line which would roughly approximate the bell-shaped normal distribution curve by connecting the center points at the top of each cell of our histogram. Figure 6.3 would be the result of such a drawing.

This mathematical model, a normal distribution curve, is useful because it allows us to estimate how additional measurements will be distributed based on an initial sample distribution. From a quality control standpoint, this will allow us to determine the AQL for a process based on a sample of process outputs.

Let's use the statistical tools associated with the normal distribution curve to continue our analysis of the door panel process.

A BEGINNER'S GUIDE TO QUALITY IN MANUFACTURING

Population Mean

The first question we must ask regarding the normal distribution curve seems obvious in light of our target specification. Where is the mathematical center of the distribution? The answer is the *population mean*.

The population mean, or population average, conforms to the popular notion of what an average is. It is simply the sum of the data, for the entire population, divided by the number of data points in the population.

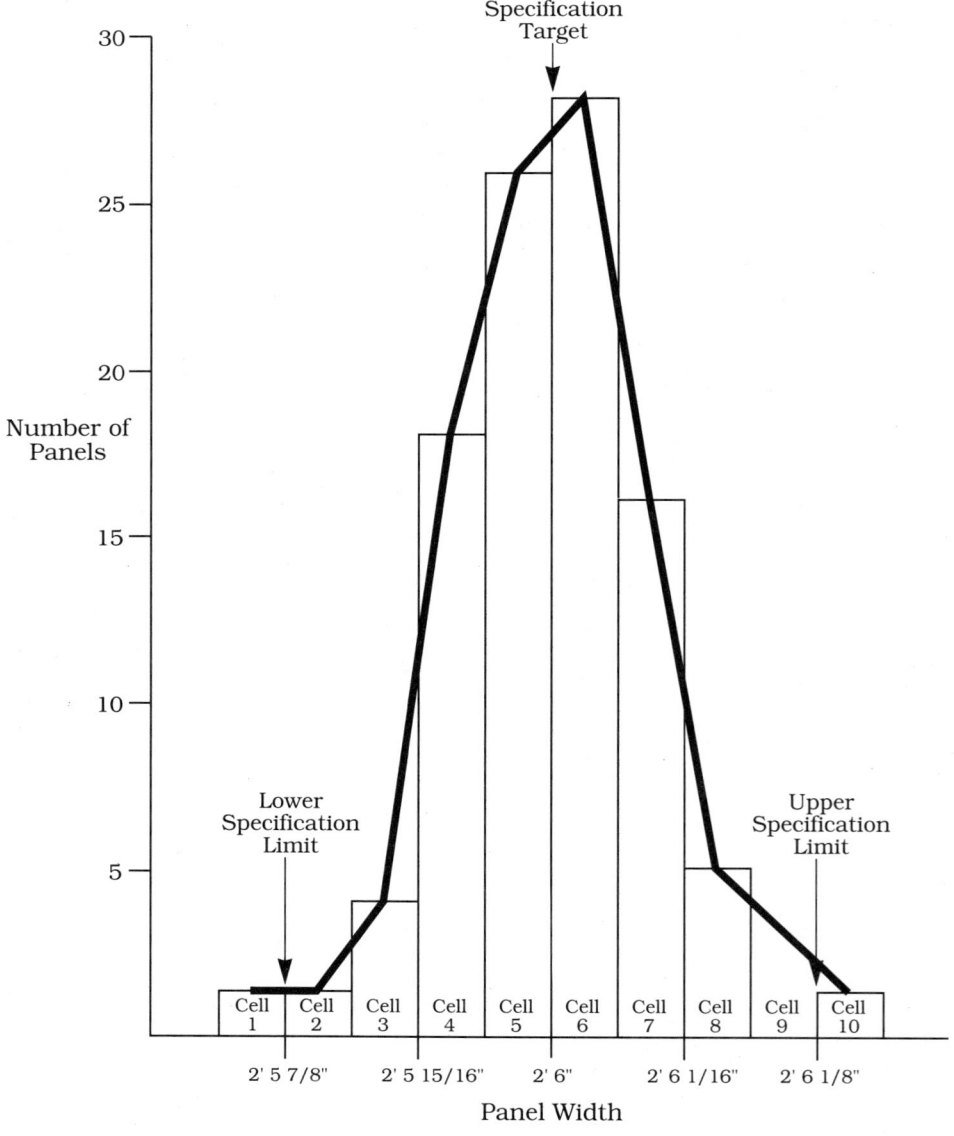

Figure 6.3: Door Panel Width Histogram

134

The formula is

$$\text{Population Mean} = \frac{\text{Sum of measurements}}{\text{Number of measurements}}$$

$$\mu = \frac{\sum X_i}{n}$$

The population mean or average is represented by the Greek letter μ (pronounced mu). Σ is the uppercase Greek letter sigma and is the symbol for sum. As such, $\sum X_i$ is the sum of all the data, where X_i represent each data point. If there are 100 data points, as in Table 6.1, then $\sum X_i$ is the sum of all 100 data points. Another way to write this is

$$\sum X_i = X_1 + X_2 + X_3 + X_4 + X_5 + \ldots\ldots X_{100}$$

The total number of data points in the sampling is represented by n.

The data in Table 6.1 is for a sampling of a population. A sample mean is represented by $\bar{X}$ and is calculated using the same procedure for calculating population mean. The sample mean for the data in Table 6.1 is calculated

$$\bar{X} = \frac{\sum X_i}{n}$$

$$\bar{X} = \frac{250'0.05"}{100}$$

where 250'0.05" is the sum of the data in Table 6.1.

$$\bar{X} = 2'6.0005"$$

From this first calculation, we can say that the sampling is centered very near to our target value of 2'6". This is a positive trend and a first indication that the doors are being cut to the correct width.

Standard Deviation

Now we've found the center of our normal distribution curve. Next, we want to know how closely our distribution of measurements is clustered around the central point. The *standard deviation* is a mathematical measure which tells us how widely our results are distributed. The larger the standard deviation, the wider the dispersion of sample results and, from a quality standpoint, the weaker our process capabilities. Calculating the standard deviation is also the first step toward estimating the percentage of defective panels which our current process will produce.

Standard deviation is the positive square root of the population *variance*. The variance is based upon the mean, or average, of the deviations from the population mean (µ) squared. The standard deviation for the population is represented by the lowercase Greek letter σ (pronounced sigma) and can be calculated by the following formula:

$$\sigma = \left\{ \frac{1}{n-1} \Sigma (X_i - \mu)^2 \right\}^{1/2}$$

where X_i = the observed values
 µ = the population mean
 n = number of observations made on the population

Because lots, or populations, can be very large, we take a sampling and calculate the standard deviation of the sampling. The results of the sampling represent the population, batch, or lot. The standard deviation of a sample is written *s* and can be calculated by the following formula:

$$s = \left\{ \frac{1}{n-1} \Sigma (X_i - \bar{X})^2 \right\}^{1/2}$$

where X_i = the observed values
 $\bar{X}$ = the sample mean
 n = number of observations made on the sample

If we consider the data in Table 6.1, we realize that there is a considerable amount of calculating to be done to arrive at our answer for standard deviation. Each data point (X_i) must be subtracted from the sample mean and squared. Then all these deviations squared must be added together. This sum is divided by 99 (100 − 1). The square root of this dividend is then taken. Upon completing these calculations, we determine that the standard deviation for the panel width measurements is 0.0467".

The distribution of door width measurements has been redrawn in Figure 6.4. A normal distribution curve has been added. Notice that the normal distribution curve closely approximates the frequency distribution. The sample mean ($\bar{X}$) and the values for the standard deviation (*s*), two standard deviations (2*s*) and three standard deviations (3*s*) have been included. Our target value (2'6") and our upper and lower specification limits (±1/8") have also been added.

STATISTICAL QUALITY CONTROL

Standard Deviations and Process AQLs

Our mathematical model, the normal distribution curve, tells us that 68.26 percent of a sample will fall within one standard deviation (1s) from the population mean. Since our calculated standard deviation is 0.0467", this means that 68.26 percent of our population should vary from the target value of 2'6" by that amount or less.

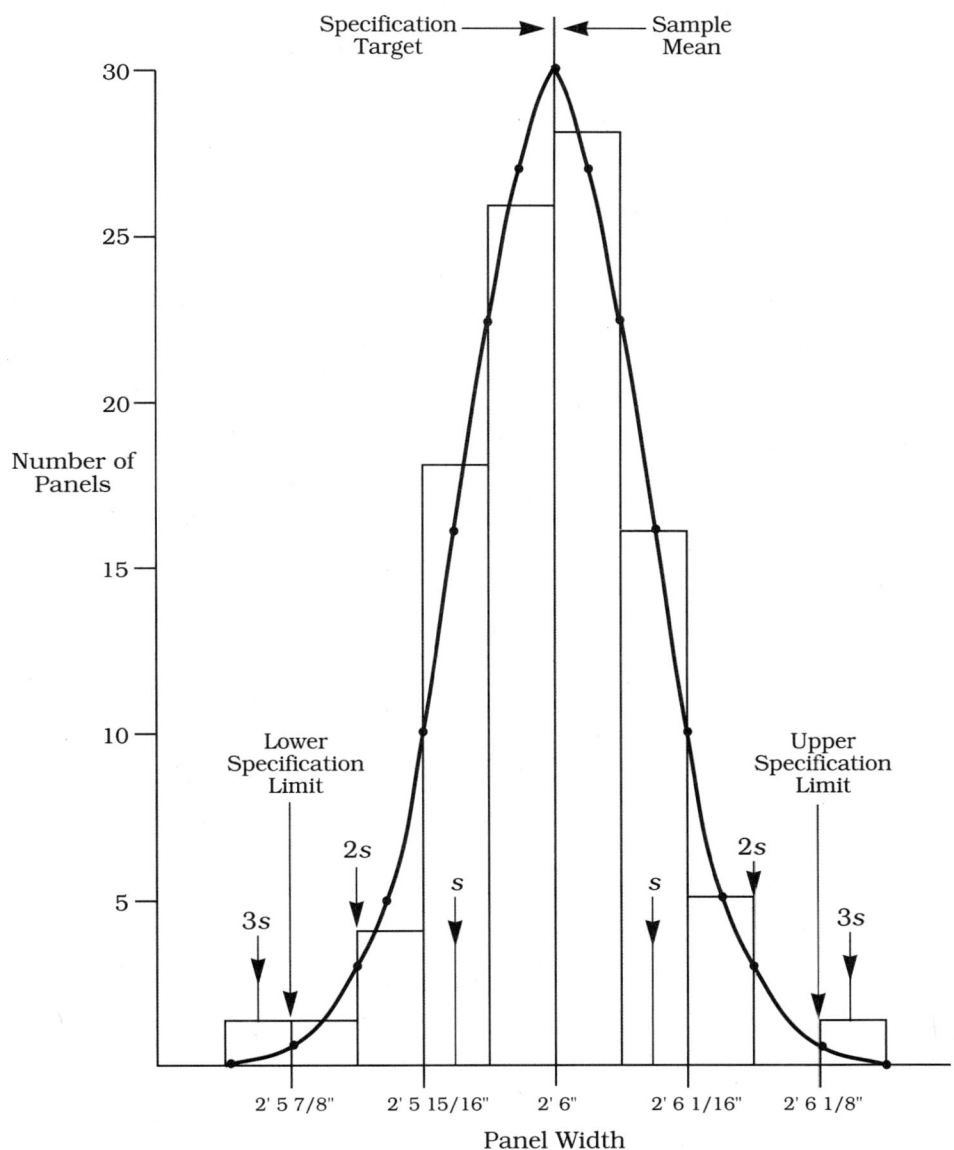

Figure 6.4: Panel Width Histogram and Normal Distribution Curve

137

The mathematical model goes on to tell us that 95.46 percent of the population should fall within two standard deviations (2s). In our case, based on the calculated standard deviation for our sample, this means that 95.46 percent of our population should vary from the target specification by 0.0934" or less. Since our specified tolerance value is ±1/8" or 0.125", we now know that at least 95.6 percent of our panels will meet specifications.

Let's see what happens as we move three standard deviations (3s or 0.140") from our central point. Since our tolerance is ±1/8" or 0.125", somewhere between 2s and 3s our process goes out of tolerance. Our mathematical model, the normal distribution curve, tells us that 99.73 percent of a population should lie within three standard deviations (3s) from the central point.

Calculating the standard deviation has given the door manufacturer a great deal of information about the quality of the panel width cutting process. The manufacturer now knows that between 95.46 percent and 99.73 percent of the panels are being cut to the correct width. This means that somewhere between 3 and 45 of every 1,000 panels will be cut to a width that is out of tolerance.

To determine the exact number of defective panels which the process produces, the manufacturer will conduct another series of calculations. He must identify exactly where the door panel specification's upper and lower tolerance limits lie on the normal distribution curve. Once this is done, the manufacturer can use the curve's mathematical formulas to calculate exactly what percentage of his population will lie between these two points. Having estimated the percentage of panels in the population which meet specification, he will then know the percent which are defective.

First, let's find out where our specification tolerances lie on the normal distribution curve which we've derived from our sample data. We do this by translating each specification point into a number of standard deviations from the mean point of our curve. We call this measurement the normalized value for these points. The formula for this calculation is as follows:

$$X_n = \frac{X_i - \bar{X}}{s}$$

where X_i = data value of interest (e.g., upper or lower specification limit)

$\bar{X}$ = sample mean

s = standard deviation

STATISTICAL QUALITY CONTROL

Let's recap the information we'll need to calculate normalized values for our own distribution curve

- The door manufacturer, as we know, sampled the panel widths of 100 panels.
- The average panel width was 2'6.0005".
- The standard deviation for the sampling was 0.0467".
- The lower specification limit is –1/8" (–0.125"), which equals a width of 2'5.875".
- The upper specification limit is +1/8" (0.125"), which equals a width of 2'6.125".

Now let's calculate the normalized value of the lower specification limit

$$X_n = \frac{X_i - \bar{X}}{s}$$

$$X_n = \frac{2'5.875" - 2'6.0005"}{0.0467"}$$

$$X_n = -2.69$$

In effect, this means that the lower tolerance limit lies at 2.69 negative standard deviations from the mean point of our distribution curve.

The normalized value of the upper specification limit can be calculated in the same manner.

$$X_n = \frac{X_i - \bar{X}}{s}$$

$$X_n = \frac{2'6.125" - 2'6.0005"}{0.0467"}$$

$$X_n = 2.67$$

Similarly, this means that our upper tolerance limit lies at 2.67 positive standard deviations from the mean point of our distribution curve.

Now that we know where the upper and lower tolerance limits lie on our distribution curve, we can use the curve's mathematical properties to determine exactly what proportion of the distribution lies between them.

Table 6.4 gives the percent of the area under a normal distribution curve from given points on the X axis of the curve to the lowest negative point on the curve. (Since the mathematical model for a normal distribution curve assumes that it consists of an infinite number of data points, we should note that there actually is no single lowest negative point. The curve extends to negative infinity. The same is also true for the positive side of the curve.)

z	0.09	0.08	0.07	0.06	0.05	0.04	0.03	0.02	0.01	0.00
−3.5	0.00017	0.00017	0.00018	0.00019	0.00019	0.00020	0.00021	0.00022	0.00022	0.00023
−3.4	0.00024	0.00025	0.00026	0.00027	0.00028	0.00029	0.00030	0.00031	0.00033	0.00034
−3.3	0.00035	0.00036	0.00038	0.00039	0.00040	0.00042	0.00043	0.00045	0.00047	0.00048
−3.2	0.00050	0.00052	0.00054	0.00056	0.00058	0.00060	0.00062	0.00064	0.00066	0.00069
−3.1	0.00071	0.00074	0.00076	0.00079	0.00082	0.00085	0.00087	0.00090	0.00094	0.00097
−3.0	0.00100	0.00104	0.00107	0.00111	0.00114	0.00118	0.00122	0.00126	0.00131	0.00135
−2.9	0.0014	0.0014	0.0015	0.0015	0.0016	0.0016	0.0017	0.0017	0.0018	0.0019
−2.8	0.0019	0.0020	0.0021	0.0021	0.0022	0.0023	0.0023	0.0024	0.0025	0.0026
−2.7	0.0026	0.0027	0.0028	0.0029	0.0030	0.0031	0.0032	0.0033	0.0034	0.0035
−2.6	0.0036	0.0037	0.0038	0.0039	0.0040	0.0041	0.0043	0.0044	0.0045	0.0047
−2.5	0.0048	0.0049	0.0051	0.0052	0.0054	0.0055	0.0057	0.0059	0.0060	0.0062
−2.4	0.0064	0.0066	0.0068	0.0069	0.0071	0.0073	0.0075	0.0078	0.0080	0.0082
−2.3	0.0084	0.0087	0.0089	0.0091	0.0094	0.0096	0.0099	0.0102	0.0104	0.0107
−2.2	0.0110	0.0113	0.0116	0.0119	0.0122	0.0125	0.0129	0.0132	0.0136	0.0139
−2.1	0.0143	0.0146	0.0150	0.0154	0.0158	0.0162	0.0166	0.0170	0.0174	0.0179
−2.0	0.0183	0.0188	0.0192	0.0197	0.0202	0.0207	0.0212	0.0217	0.0222	0.0228
−1.9	0.0233	0.0239	0.0244	0.0250	0.0256	0.0262	0.0268	0.0274	0.0281	0.0287
−1.8	0.0294	0.0301	0.0307	0.0314	0.0322	0.0329	0.0336	0.0344	0.0351	0.0359
−1.7	0.0367	0.0375	0.0384	0.0392	0.0401	0.0409	0.0418	0.0427	0.0436	0.0446
−1.6	0.0455	0.0465	0.0475	0.0485	0.0495	0.0505	0.0516	0.0526	0.0537	0.0548
−1.5	0.0559	0.0571	0.0582	0.0594	0.0606	0.0618	0.0630	0.0643	0.0655	0.0668
−1.4	0.0681	0.0694	0.0708	0.0721	0.0735	0.0749	0.0764	0.0778	0.0793	0.0808
−1.3	0.0823	0.0838	0.0853	0.0869	0.0885	0.0901	0.0918	0.0934	0.0951	0.0968
−1.2	0.0985	0.1003	0.1020	0.1038	0.1057	0.1075	0.1093	0.1112	0.1131	0.1151
−1.1	0.1170	0.1190	0.1210	0.1230	0.1251	0.1271	0.1292	0.1314	0.1335	0.1357
−1.0	0.1379	0.1401	0.1423	0.1446	0.1469	0.1492	0.1515	0.1539	0.1562	0.1587
−0.9	0.1611	0.1635	0.1660	0.1685	0.1711	0.1736	0.1762	0.1788	0.1814	0.1841
−0.8	0.1867	0.1894	0.1922	0.1949	0.1977	0.2005	0.2033	0.2061	0.2090	0.2119
−0.7	0.2148	0.2177	0.2207	0.2236	0.2266	0.2297	0.2327	0.2358	0.2389	0.2420
−0.6	0.2451	0.2483	0.2514	0.2546	0.2578	0.2611	0.2643	0.2676	0.2709	0.2743
−0.5	0.2776	0.2810	0.2843	0.2877	0.2912	0.2946	0.2981	0.3015	0.3050	0.3085
−0.4	0.3121	0.3156	0.3192	0.3228	0.3264	0.3300	0.3336	0.3372	0.3409	0.3446
−0.3	0.3483	0.3520	0.3557	0.3594	0.3632	0.3669	0.3707	0.3745	0.3783	0.3821
−0.2	0.3859	0.3897	0.3936	0.3974	0.4013	0.4052	0.4090	0.4129	0.4168	0.4207
−0.1	0.4247	0.4286	0.4325	0.4364	0.4404	0.4443	0.4483	0.4522	0.4562	0.4602
−0.0	0.4641	0.4681	0.4721	0.4761	0.4801	0.4840	0.4880	0.4920	0.4960	0.5000

Table 6.4: Area Under the Normal Distribution Curve

z	0.00	0.01	0.02	0.03	0.04	0.05	0.06	0.07	0.08	0.09
+0.0	0.5000	0.5040	0.5080	0.5120	0.5160	0.5199	0.5239	0.5279	0.5319	0.5359
+0.1	0.5398	0.5438	0.5478	0.5517	0.5557	0.5596	0.5636	0.5675	0.5714	0.5753
+0.2	0.5793	0.5832	0.5871	0.5910	0.5948	0.5987	0.6026	0.6064	0.6103	0.6141
+0.3	0.6179	0.6217	0.6255	0.6293	0.6331	0.6368	0.6406	0.6443	0.6480	0.6517
+0.4	0.6554	0.6591	0.6628	0.6664	0.6700	0.6736	0.6772	0.6808	0.6844	0.6879
+0.5	0.6915	0.6950	0.6985	0.7019	0.7054	0.7088	0.7123	0.7157	0.7190	0.7224
+0.6	0.7257	0.7291	0.7324	0.7357	0.7389	0.7422	0.7454	0.7486	0.7517	0.7549
+0.7	0.7580	0.7611	0.7642	0.7673	0.7704	0.7734	0.7764	0.7794	0.7823	0.7852
+0.8	0.7881	0.7910	0.7939	0.7967	0.7995	0.8023	0.8051	0.8079	0.8106	0.8133
+0.9	0.8159	0.8186	0.8212	0.8238	0.8264	0.8289	0.8315	0.8340	0.8365	0.8389
+1.0	0.8413	0.8438	0.8461	0.8485	0.8508	0.8531	0.8554	0.8577	0.8599	0.8621
+1.1	0.8643	0.8665	0.8686	0.8708	0.8729	0.8749	0.8770	0.8790	0.8810	0.8830
+1.2	0.8849	0.8869	0.8888	0.8907	0.8925	0.8944	0.8962	0.8980	0.8997	0.9015
+1.3	0.9032	0.9049	0.9066	0.9082	0.9099	0.9115	0.9131	0.9147	0.9162	0.9177
+1.4	0.9192	0.9207	0.9222	0.9236	0.9251	0.9265	0.9279	0.9292	0.9306	0.9319
+1.5	0.9332	0.9345	0.9357	0.9370	0.9382	0.9394	0.9406	0.9418	0.9429	0.9441
+1.6	0.9452	0.9463	0.9474	0.9484	0.9495	0.9505	0.9515	0.9525	0.9535	0.9545
+1.7	0.9554	0.9564	0.9573	0.9582	0.9591	0.9599	0.9608	0.9616	0.9625	0.9633
+1.8	0.9641	0.9649	0.9656	0.9664	0.9671	0.9678	0.9686	0.9693	0.9699	0.9706
+1.9	0.9713	0.9719	0.9726	0.9732	0.9738	0.9744	0.9750	0.9756	0.9761	0.9767
+2.0	0.9773	0.9778	0.9783	0.9788	0.9793	0.9798	0.9803	0.9808	0.9812	0.9817
+2.1	0.9821	0.9826	0.9830	0.9834	0.9838	0.9842	0.9846	0.9850	0.9854	0.9857
+2.2	0.9861	0.9864	0.9868	0.9871	0.9875	0.9878	0.9881	0.9884	0.9887	0.9890
+2.3	0.9893	0.9896	0.9898	0.9901	0.9904	0.9906	0.9909	0.9911	0.9913	0.9916
+2.4	0.9918	0.9920	0.9922	0.9925	0.9927	0.9929	0.9931	0.9932	0.9934	0.9936
+2.5	0.9938	0.9940	0.9941	0.9943	0.9945	0.9946	0.9948	0.9949	0.9951	0.9952
+2.6	0.9953	0.9955	0.9956	0.9957	0.9959	0.9960	0.9961	0.9962	0.9963	0.9964
+2.7	0.9965	0.9966	0.9967	0.9968	0.9969	0.9970	0.9971	0.9972	0.9973	0.9974
+2.8	0.9974	0.9975	0.9976	0.9977	0.9977	0.9978	0.9979	0.9979	0.9980	0.9981
+2.9	0.9981	0.9982	0.9983	0.9983	0.9984	0.9984	0.9985	0.9985	0.9986	0.9986
+3.0	0.99865	0.99869	0.99874	0.99878	0.99882	0.99886	0.99889	0.99893	0.99896	0.99900
+3.1	0.99903	0.99906	0.99910	0.99913	0.99915	0.99918	0.99921	0.99924	0.99926	0.99929
+3.2	0.99931	0.99934	0.99936	0.99938	0.99940	0.99942	0.99944	0.99946	0.99948	0.99950
+3.3	0.99952	0.99953	0.99955	0.99957	0.99958	0.99960	0.99961	0.99962	0.99964	0.99965
+3.4	0.99966	0.99967	0.99969	0.99970	0.99971	0.99972	0.99973	0.99974	0.99975	0.99976
+3.5	0.99977	0.99978	0.99978	0.99979	0.99980	0.99981	0.99981	0.99982	0.99983	0.99983

(Table 6.4 continued)

First, let's determine the percentage of the population that falls between the specification's upper tolerance limit and the lowest point on the curve—negative infinity.

We can use Table 6.4 by taking the normalized value for our upper tolerance limit, +2.67, and breaking it into two pieces.

We look for the first two digits, +2.6, in the first column of the table. We find this 10 rows up from the bottom of the page. Next, we'll take the third digit, 0.07, and look for it in the table's first row. This time we'll find it in the eighth column of values. By going to the intersection of the row and column specified for our normalized value, we find that 99.62 percent of the population in our distribution will lie between this upper tolerance limit and negative infinity on the curve. The results of our calculation are shown graphically as Area A in Figure 6.5.

Now let's find the percentage of our distribution that will lie between our lower tolerance limit and negative infinity on the curve. Once again, we'll break up the normalized value for the lower limit, −2.69, into two pieces. This time we find the first two digits, −2.6, 10 rows down from the top of column one. The third digit, 0.09, is in the first row at the top of the first column of values. The intersection of the row and column indicated tells us that 0.36 percent of our population distribution lies between the lower tolerance limit of our panel specification and negative infinity on the curve. The results of this calculation are shown graphically as Area B in Figure 6.6.

Our final step in determining the percentage of population which lies between the upper and lower specification tolerances is to subtract Area B from Area A.

$$\text{Area A to B} = \text{Area A} - \text{Area B}$$
$$\text{Area A to B} = 0.9962 - 0.0036$$
$$\text{Area A to B} = 0.9926$$

Therefore, 99.26 percent of the curve is between upper and lower specification limits. The results are shown in Figure 6.7.

The door manufacturer now knows that 99.26 percent of his door panels are being cut to the correct width. The remaining 0.74 percent, or approximately 7 out of 1,000, are cut unacceptably. The process has an AQL capability of 0.7 percent defective. This is above the AQL level of 0.1 percent (or 1 board out of every 1,000) the manufacturer has specified for this process. Changes are needed to improve the quality capability of this process.

Before we examine the results of the door manufacturer's corrective action, let's review what we did.

First we took sample data which we would use to determine the process quality capabilities.

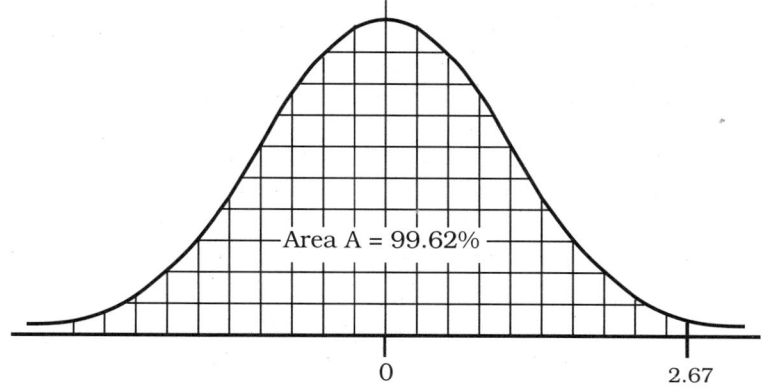

Figure 6.5: Area A of Population Distribution

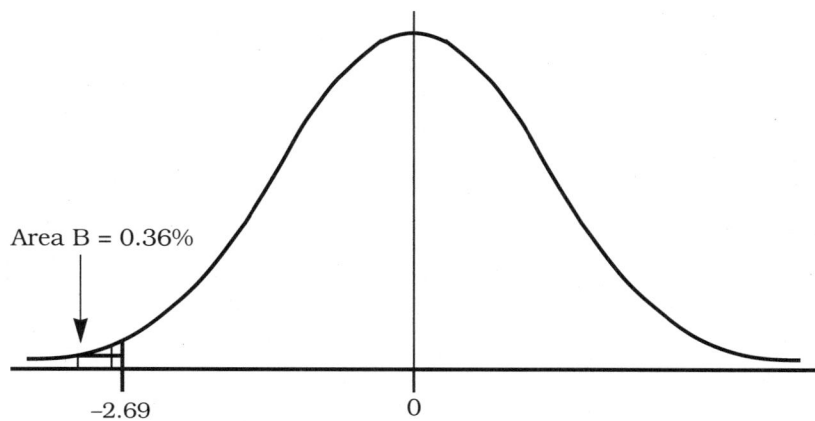

Figure 6.6: Area B of Population Distribution

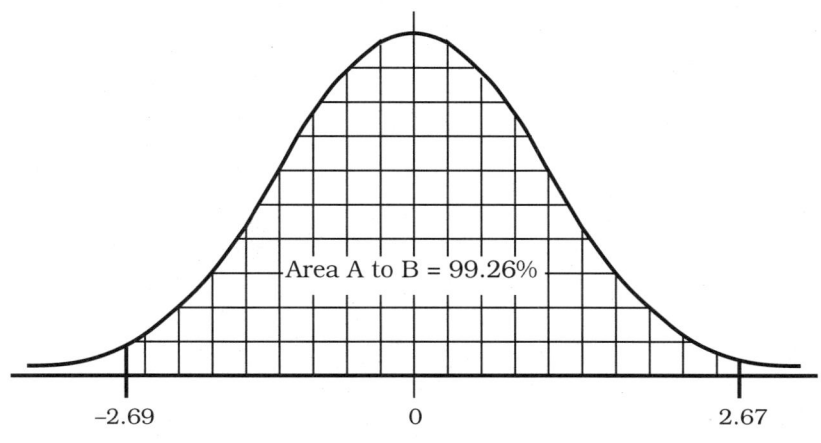

Figure 6.7: Area A to B of Population Distribution

A BEGINNER'S GUIDE TO QUALITY IN MANUFACTURING

Using this data, we drew a frequency distribution histogram. It showed us that the process looked reasonable, but it didn't give the numbers we need to make a final decision on the acceptability of the process step.

We then calculated the sample mean. It was very close to the target value, and we correctly considered that a positive indication.

Next we estimated the precise percentage of panels which would meet specifications and the corresponding percent defective. Our first step in this process was to calculate the standard deviation for the normal distribution curve suggested by our sample data. We then used the sample mean and the standard deviation to predict the percentage of doors that were not being made to specification tolerances. We found that approximately 0.74 percent were unacceptable. When we compared this to the AQL (0.1 percent), it was apparent that corrective measures had to be taken to bring the process up to the necessary quality level.

Increasing Process Capabilities

In response to his initial findings, the manufacturer reviewed the panel width cutting procedure and cutting equipment being used. The workers doing the cutting discussed the cutting task with their supervisors and the company's manufacturing engineer. Based on these discussions, changes in equipment and cutting procedures have been made to improve the accuracy of the cut. To check that the changes have corrected the problem, the company's quality control supervisor has been asked to take a sample of production and conduct an analysis. The data for the quality audit appears in Table 6.5.

2'6.04"	2'5.99"	2'6.05"	2'6.08"	2'6.02"
2'6.05"	2'6.04"	2'6.00"	2'6.07"	2'6.05"
2'6.10"	2'6.04"	2'6.02"	2'6.05"	2'6.13"
2'6.04"	2'6.05"	2'6.07"	2'6.02"	2'6.04"
2'6.05"	2'6.00"	2'6.05"	2'6.04"	2'6.07"
2'6.04"	2'6.05"	2'6.07"	2'6.02"	2'6.00"
2'5.96"	2'6.04"	2'6.08"	2'6.05"	2'6.02"
2'6.07"	2'6.04"	2'6.05"	2'6.02"	2'6.04"
2'6.07"	2'6.05"	2'6.04"	2'6.08"	2'6.07"
2'6.11"	2'6.02"	2'6.04"	2'6.07"	2'6.00"

Table 6.5: Panel Width Measurements for the Corrected Cutting Process

STATISTICAL QUALITY CONTROL

A sampling of 50 measurements was made. The largest value is 2'6.13" and the smallest value is 2'5.96". We find the *range* by subtracting 2'5.94" from 2'6.13".

Range = Largest Value − Smallest Value

Range = 2'6.13" − 2'5.96"

Range = 0.17"

The range equals 0.17". We must now decide how to group the data to make our histogram. If we divide the range into 12 parts, the cell interval would be 0.0142". This is very close to 1/64" (0.015625"). Because the specification limits and the target value are even multiples of 1/64", we will use 1/64" as our cell interval. Table 6.6 defines the cells and lists the frequencies of occurrence in each cell.

Cell Number	Lower Boundary	Upper Boundary	Frequency of Occurrence
1	2'5 61/64" (2'5.95313")	2'5 31/32" (2'5.96875")	1
2	2'5 31/32" (2'5.96875")	2'5 63/64" (2'5.98438")	0
3	2'5 63/64" (2'5.98438")	2'6" (2'6.0000")	1
4	2'6" (2'6.0000")	2'6 1/64" (2'6.01563")	4
5	2'6 1/64" (2'6.01563")	2'6 1/32" (2'6.03125")	7
6	2'6 1/32" (2'6.03125")	2'6 3/64" (2'6.04688")	12
7	2'6 3/64" (2'6.04688")	2'6 1/16" (2'6.0625")	11
8	2'6 1/16" (2'6.0625")	2'6 5/64" (2'6.07813")	8
9	2'6 5/64" (2'6.07813)	2'6 3/32" (2'6.09375")	3
10	2'6 3/32" (2'6.09375)	2'6 7/64" (2'6.10938")	1
11	2'6 7/64" (2'6.10938")	2'6 1/8" (2'6.125")	1
12	2'6 1/8" (2'6.125")	2'6 9/64" (2'6.14063")	1

Table 6.6: Cell Boundaries and Frequency of Occurrence

Figure 6.8 is the histogram of the frequency distribution of the panel widths for the revised process. If we compare this drawing to the original histogram in Figure 6.2, we notice two important differences.

The new distribution in Figure 6.8 is grouped much more closely around its center or mean. In fact, the range of variation has dropped to 0.17" in the new distribution compared to 0.27" for the first sample. This is a desirable result and tells us that there is less variation in the process step now that the changes in production methods have been made. Normally, this significant improvement would solve our problems. In this case, however, there has been another important change in our sample results.

While the distribution is grouped closely around the mean for the sample, the mean itself has shifted away from our target specification. As a result, despite the decreased variation in process results, there are still significant out-of-tolerance problems near the upper specification limit.

To determine if his conclusions about the revised process are correct, the manufacturer wants to make quantitative comparisons between the cutting process before and after the corrective measures. The first measure of quality he will calculate is the sample mean ($\bar{X}$). The sample mean is calculated

$$\bar{X} = \frac{\sum X_i}{n}$$

$$\bar{X} = \frac{125'2.27"}{50}$$

$$\bar{X} = 2'6.0454"$$

Comparing this mean value of 2'6.0454" with the original sample mean of 2'6.0005", we see that our first impressions were correct. The original process was more closely centered around the target specification. It seems that our corrective actions may have made things worse. Before we draw any conclusions, however, let's make the calculations for the standard deviation of the sample.

Calculating the standard deviation is a long process, especially when the sample size is as high as 50 samples. In general, a computer or calculator should assist in these calculations.

The door manufacturer's quality engineer calculated the standard deviation for the corrected cutting step. The standard deviation for the sample was 0.0303". The original sample had a standard deviation of 0.0467". A smaller standard deviation tells us that the panel widths are being cut more closely to the sample mean. This is a positive result and agrees with our initial conclusions after we compared the histograms for the two frequency distributions.

STATISTICAL QUALITY CONTROL

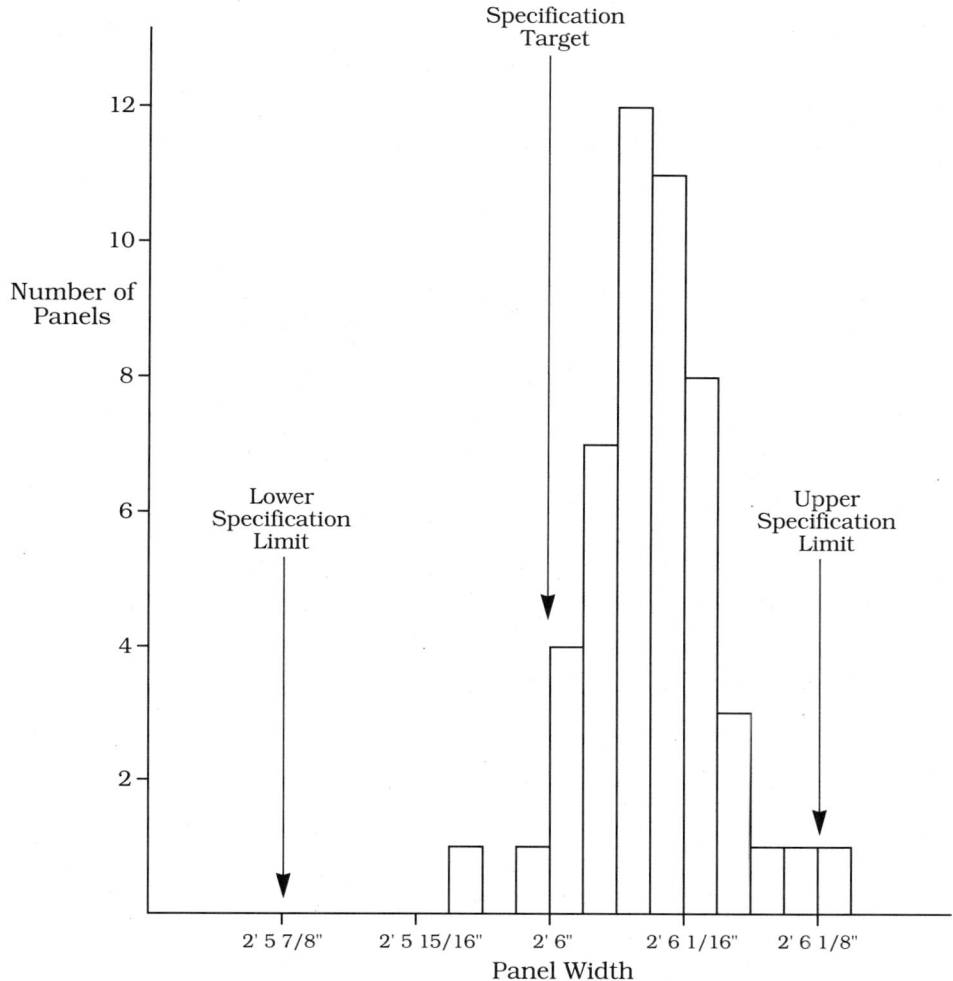

Figure 6.8: Door Panel Width Histogram for the Revised Process

Now we would like to know what percentage of the distribution is out of specification. If we look at the frequency distribution for the revised cutting process, we see that no samples are near the lower specification limit. However, because the mean is not close enough to the target specification, the right side of the distribution is too close to the upper specification limit.

Once again, let's calculate the area under the normal distribution curve between the lower specification limit and the upper specification limit. This will tell us the percentage of the distribution being made to specification. Subtracting this number from one gives us the percentage of production that is out of compliance. The percent defective value indicates whether the cutting process meets the manufacturer's AQL requirements.

A BEGINNER'S GUIDE TO QUALITY IN MANUFACTURING

First we must determine the area under the curve from negative infinity to the upper specification limit. To do this we must find the normalized value of our upper specification limit (X_n) for this distribution curve

$$X_n = \frac{X_i - \bar{X}}{s}$$

where X_i = 2'6.125" = 2'6 1/8" (the upper specification limit)
$\bar{X}$ = 2'6.0454" (sample mean)
s = 0.0303" (standard deviation)

$$X_n = \frac{2'6.125" - 2'6.0454"}{0.0303}$$
$$X_n = 2.63$$

Using Table 6.4 and the normalized value of the upper limit (X_n), we determine that the area under the curve from negative infinity to the upper specification limit (Area A) is 0.9957.

Our next step is to find the area under the curve from negative infinity to the lower specification limit. Again, we must find an X_n and use it in conjunction with Table 6.4. The calculation is

$$X_n = \frac{X_i - \bar{X}}{s}$$

where X_i = 2'5.875" = 2'5 7/8" (the lower specification limit)
$\bar{X}$ = 2'6.0454" (sample mean)
s = 0.0303" (standard deviation)

$$X_n = \frac{2'5.875" - 2'6.0454"}{0.0303}$$
$$X_n = -5.62$$

Because the X_n value is so low, it is not listed in Table 6.4. One source for this information is published by the National Institute of Standards and Technology (NIST), formerly the National Bureau of Standards. The publication is entitled "Tables of Normal Probability Functions," and it is Number 23 in the Applied Mathematics Series. Areas are listed from x to $-x$ as opposed to negative infinity to x. With that in mind, the area under the curve from negative infinity to −5.62, as calculated from the NIST tables, is 0.0000000095. This is such a small number that the area it represents between negative infinity and the lower specification limit (Area B) is effectively zero.

STATISTICAL QUALITY CONTROL

To determine the area between the lower specification limit and the upper specification limit, we simply subtract Area B from Area A:

$$\text{Area A to B} = \text{Area A} - \text{Area B}$$
$$\text{Area A to B} = 0.9957 - 0$$
$$\text{Area A to B} = 0.9957$$

This result tells the door manufacturer that 99.57 percent of the door panel widths are being cut within specifications. This means that approximately 0.4 percent of the panels are not cut to specifications. Again, the out-of-specification result is in excess of the AQL of 0.1 percent for the cutting step.

When the manufacturer looks at the frequency distribution, it is clear that his problem is now near the upper specification limit. Again he consults with cutting workers, supervisors, and the manufacturing engineer. The problem seems minor; a simple adjustment should correct the problem. The cutting equipment is readjusted, and 50 more samples are taken. The results of the sampling are the panel width measurements in Table 6.7.

2'5.99"	2'6.02"	2'6.01"	2'6.04"	2'5.99"
2'6.01"	2'5.97"	2'5.99"	2'6.01"	2'6.05"
2'6.01"	2'5.97"	2'5.99"	2'6.01"	2'5.97"
2'6.02"	2'5.99"	2'6.01"	2'5.97"	2'5.99"
2'6.01"	2'5.96"	2'6.02"	2'5.99"	2'5.93"
2'5.99"	2'5.97"	2'6.01"	2'6.02"	2'6.04"
2'5.99"	2'6.02"	2'6.01"	2'5.97"	2'5.96"
2'6.08"	2'5.99"	2'5.96"	2'6.01"	2'6.04"
2'6.02"	2'5.91"	2'6.05"	2'6.01"	2'5.96"
2'6.02"	2'5.97"	2'5.99"	2'6.01"	2'5.97"

Table 6.7: Panel Width Measurements for the Readjusted Panel

The largest value in the sampling is 2'6.08" and the smallest value is 2'5.91". We find the range by subtracting the smallest sampling value from the largest.

$$\text{Range} = \text{Largest Value} - \text{Smallest Value}$$
$$\text{Range} = 2'6.08" - 2'5.91"$$
$$\text{Range} = 0.17"$$

A BEGINNER'S GUIDE TO QUALITY IN MANUFACTURING

The range equals 0.17", the same as in the previous distribution. We must now decide how to group the data to make our histogram. If we divide the range into 12 parts, the cell interval would be 0.0142". Again, this is very close to 1/64" (0.015625"). Because the specification limits and the target value are even multiples of 1/64", we will use 1/64" as our cell interval. Table 6.8 defines the cells and lists the frequencies of occurrence in each cell.

Cell Number	Lower Boundary	Upper Boundary	Frequency of Occurrence
1	2'5 29/32" (2'5.90625")	2'5 59/64" (2'5.92188")	1
2	2'5 59/64" (2'5.92188")	2'5 15/16" (2'5.9375")	1
3	2'5 15/16" (2'5.9375")	2'5 61/64 (2'5.95373")	0
4	2'5 61/64" (2'5.95313")	2'5 31/32" (2'5.96875")	4
5	2'5 31/32" (2'5.96875")	2'5 63/64" (2'5.98438")	8
6	2'5 63/64" (2'5.98438")	2'6" (2'6.0000")	11
7	2'6" (2'6.0000")	2'6 1/64" (2'6.01563")	12
8	2'6 1/64" (2'6.01563")	2'6 1/32" (2'6.03125")	7
9	2'6 1/32" (2'6.03125")	2'6 3/64" (2'6.04688")	3
10	2'6 3/64" (2'6.04688")	2'6 1/16" (2'6.0625")	2
11	2'6 1/16" (2'6.0625")	2'6 5/64" (2'6.07813")	0
12	2'6 5/64" (2'6.07813")	2'6 3/32" (2'6.09375")	1

Table 6.8: Cell Boundaries and Frequency of Occurrence

Figure 6.9, is the histogram of the frequency distribution of the panel widths for our readjusted process. If we compare this histogram to our previous distribution in Figure 6.8, we notice that the readjusted process centers more closely around the specification target. When we compare our new histogram with the original frequency distribution histogram (Figure 6.2), we notice that the data is clustered nearer to the center. There are fewer data points near the specification limits.

STATISTICAL QUALITY CONTROL

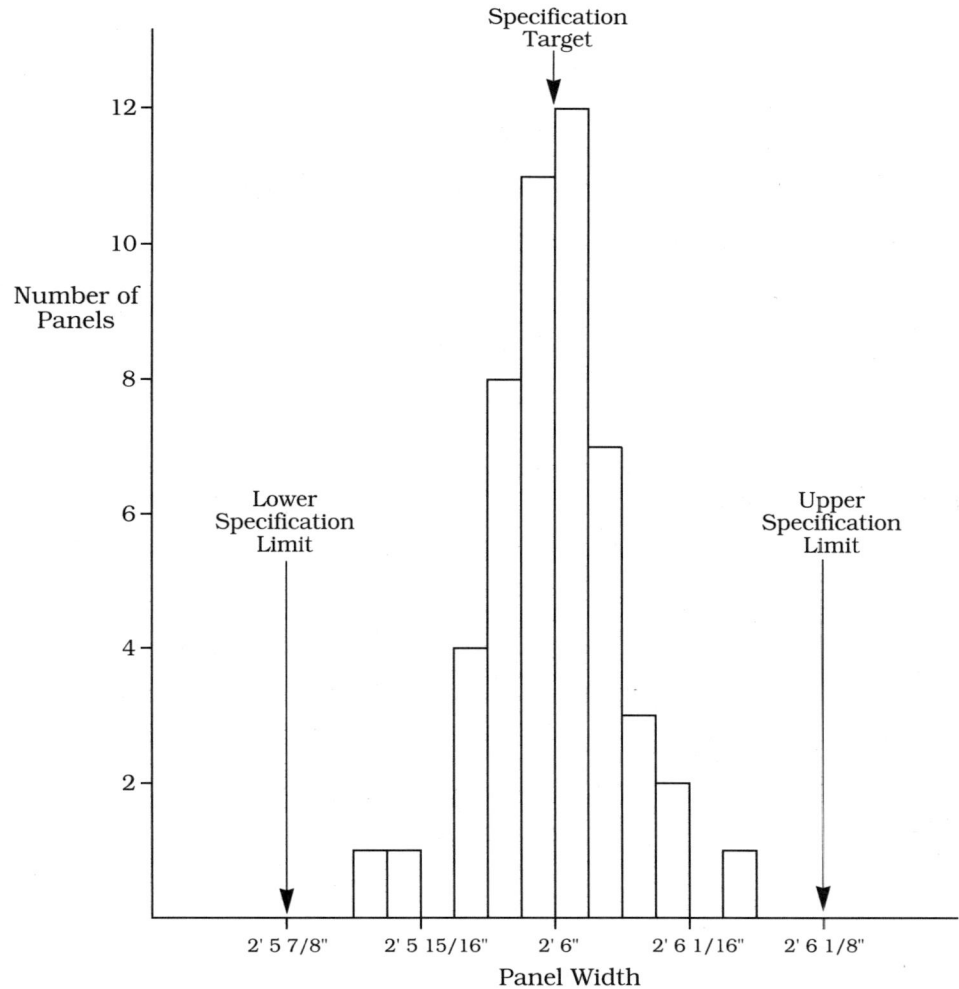

Figure 6.9: Door Panel Width Histogram for the Revised Process

The histogram for the revised and readjusted process seems to be saying that the process is well within specifications and is centered around the target specification. This is exactly the result the door manufacturer was hoping to achieve. To ensure that we have made the necessary corrections, we will calculate the sample mean, standard deviation, and percent of sample that is beyond the specification limit.

The first measure of quality to calculate is the sample mean ($\bar{X}$). The sample mean is calculated

$$\bar{X} = \frac{\Sigma X_i}{n}$$

$$\bar{X} = \frac{124'11.89"}{50}$$

$$\bar{X} = 2'5.9978"$$

This mean value of 2'5.9978" is extremely close to our target specification of 2'6". It seems that our readjustments have solved the most recent problem.

The standard deviation for the sample from the corrected cutting step is 0.0312". The original sample had a standard deviation of 0.0467". A smaller standard deviation tells us that there is less variation in the results, i.e., the panel widths are being cut consistently closer to the sample mean.

Last, we will determine the percentage of defective panels which the readjusted process is producing. If we look at the frequency distribution for the revised and readjusted cutting process, we see that no samples are near the lower or upper specification limit. As such, we expect to find the distribution well within the AQL.

Let's calculate the area under the normal distribution curve between the lower specification limit and the upper specification limit. This will tell us what percentage of the sampling is made to specification.

First we must determine the area under the curve from negative infinity to the upper specification limit. To do this we must use Table 6.4 and find X_n:

$$X_n = \frac{X_i - \bar{X}}{s}$$

where X_i = 2'6.125" = 2'6 1/8" (the upper specification limit)
$\bar{X}$ = 2'5.9978" (sample mean)
s = 0.0312" (standard deviation)

$$X_n = \frac{2'6.125" - 2'5.9978"}{0.0312}$$

$$X_n = 4.08$$

Using the NIST mathematical tables, we determine that the area under the curve from negative infinity to the upper specification limit (Area A) is 0.999955.

Our next step is to find the area under the curve from negative infinity to the lower specification limit. As was done above, an X_n must be found and used in conjunction with the NIST table. The calculation is

$$X_n = \frac{X_i - \bar{X}}{s}$$

where X_i = 2'5.875" = 2'5 7/8" (the lower specification limit)
        $\bar{X}$ = 2'5.9978" (sample mean)
        s = 0.0312" (standard deviation)

$$X_n = \frac{2'6.125" - 2'5.9978"}{0.0312}$$
$$X_n = -3.94$$

Once again, the X_n value is very low. The NIST tables are used to calculate that the area between negative infinity and the lower specification limit (Area B) is 0.000041.

To determine the area between the lower specification limit and the upper specification limit, we simply subtract Area B from Area A:

    Area A to B = Area A − Area B
    Area A to B = 0.999955 − 0.000041
    Area A to B = 0.999914

This result tells the door manufacturer that 99.9914 percent of the door panel widths are being cut within specification. This means that 0.0086 percent, or approximately 0.01 percent, of the panels are not cut to specification. The manufacturer has established that the panel cutting process now has a percent defective AQL of 0.01 percent. This surpasses his AQL target of 0.1 percent for the cutting step, and the manufacturer is ready to begin production.

6.7 Measuring Quality Level by Attribute

The closet door manufacturer was able to establish the quality level of the panel cutting process by tracking the actual measurements of the panels which were cut. As we have seen, these measurements ranged along a continuous scale from 2'5.86" to 2'6.13". Because these measurements could vary anywhere along this scale, they are called *variables*.

Seeing how the actual variable measurements were distributed around his target specification allowed the manufacturer to estimate the number of panels that were being cut to specification. The distribution of measurements even helped identify and correct problems with the process itself.

Sometimes, however, we may not be able to analyze the results of our production process in terms of variable measurements—inches of thickness, pounds and ounces of weight, and so on. Sometimes there can be only two possible outcomes: the product may be acceptable or it may be unacceptable; it may work or it may not.

We have already seen that the radio manufacturer solders various components to her printed circuit boards (PCBs). In this case, the solder either creates the needed electrical connection between the components or it doesn't. Similarly, the owner's manual is either included with the radio during final packaging or it isn't. When we evaluate the quality of a product simply by noting whether or not it is defective (rather than comparing its actual measurements against a target specification) we are analyzing quality based on *attributes*.

While it is preferable to use variable measurements to identify the quality level of a given production process, manufacturers can also use attributes to determine their process capabilities. Let's use the radio manufacturer's soldering operation as an example.

Every week, the manufacturer's soldering equipment processes 6,000 PCBs. Automatic inspections reveal that, on average, 60 of these boards will have defects in the electrical circuitry resulting from failures in the soldering process. To determine her quality level for soldered PCBs, the manufacturer will use the following formula:

$$\text{Percent Defective} = \frac{\text{Number of Defectives} \times 100}{\text{Number of Units Inspected}}$$

$$\text{Percent Defective} = \frac{60 \times 100}{6,000}$$

$$\text{Percent Defective} = 1.0\%$$

The manufacturer can now be satisfied that her soldering process has the measured capability of meeting her AQL of 1.0 percent defective.

As you can see, this calculation simply utilizes the formula for percent defective which we learned in chapter 5 to identify the quality capability of our process as it is currently configured.

The information available for analysis from statistics on product attributes—simply the number of defects—is obviously more limited than that provided by samples of product variables.

As a result, any effort to establish process quality capabilities through use of attribute data will require significantly larger sample sizes than for similar efforts using data on product variables. In our example, the AM radio manufacturer uses automatic equipment to test each of the PCBs as part of the normal production process. Consequently, her daily sample size is approximately 1,200.

6.8 Controlling the Variation

As our manufacturers begin operation, they know what quality level to expect from their production processes based on their assessment of process AQLs. They have recognized that there will be some normal variation in the actual measurements of their output of processed components and finished products. This variation, as we have seen, is based on the actual capabilities of the particular equipment in use, unavoidable inconsistencies in human performance over time, variability in material characteristics, and so on. By measuring and predicting the range and frequency of these normal variations, however, the manufacturer can ensure that the process will produce components and products which meet quality requirements. When a process consistently produces products which fall within this expected range of normal variations, it is said to be *in control*.

Often, however, a process will begin to produce products whose measurements fall outside this expected range of normal variations. The actual dimensions of some cut door panels, for example, may begin to fall further and further away from the target specification. Similarly, the percentage of door panels that are cut close to the target specification may also begin to drop, and more and more panels may begin to approach the upper or lower tolerance limits. When the actual output of our production process does not conform to the pattern of normal variations which we had originally projected, the process is said to be moving *out of control*.

There are many reasons why a process may begin to go out of control. Equipment settings may loosen and shift, leading to dramatic changes in actual cutting dimensions. Equipment tooling can become worn to the point that it is incapable of meeting specified cutting tolerances. Replacement tooling may be defective or improperly installed, leading to variations in process quality.

Similarly, human performance may begin to vary beyond the normal range which we have specified for the process. Variations in the care and attentiveness of workers, for example, can result from excessive fatigue at certain points during the workday or changes in work conditions. New workers, on the other hand, may not be able to meet performance goals due to inadequate training or lack of experience.

A BEGINNER'S GUIDE TO QUALITY IN MANUFACTURING

In each one of these situations, the manufacturer can easily reduce the range of variation and restore the process to its originally measured quality level. All that is needed is to correct the factor which has taken the process out of control. Equipment settings can be readjusted and worn or defective toolings can be replaced. Work schedules can be changed or breaks instituted to ensure that workers maintain peak efficiency. The manufacturer can also provide additional training for new operators.

These corrective actions will get the manufacturing process back under control. They will reduce the range of variations in finished product to the specified level and restore the process' ability to meet its AQL targets.

SPC provides the tools by which a manufacturer can monitor whether or not a process is in control. Even more important, SPC usually allows the firm to identify and correct process problems before they actually lead to the production of defective components or finished products.

6.9 Control Charts

One important tool for SPC is the *control chart*. To understand what control charts are and how they work, let's visit the baker and see how he identified and solved one of his quality problems.

The baker was told by customers that although the bread was very tasty, the sizes of the loaves varied noticeably. Some were too big and some were much too small. One of his best customers brought in some samples, and the baker had to admit that the variation was a real problem.

The first thing the baker did was review the bread-making process to determine where to focus attention. Weighing and cutting the dough was clearly the critical process.

Next, he needed to determine how much variation was acceptable at this inspection point. Based on the recipe, 1.8 pounds was the target specification for the cut dough.

He also needed to establish upper and lower tolerances for the process. After experimenting with different sizes, the baker decided that the cut dough could weigh anywhere between 1.6 and 2.0 pounds. If it did, there would be no noticeable difference in the finished loaf.

As a result, the baker formalized the specification for the cut loaf as 1.8 pounds ±0.2 pounds. The lower specification limit (LSL) would be 1.6 pounds and the upper specification limit (USL) would be 2.0 pounds.

Finally, the baker analyzed the dough cutting process itself and made changes necessary to ensure that it would meet the newly established specifications. He calculated that the sample mean was 1.8 pounds, which matched the target specification. The sample standard deviation was 0.07. Using this data and the statistical techniques we learned earlier in the chapter, he was satisfied that the process had achieved a quality level of 1.0 percent defective.

Now the baker needs to begin monitoring the process.

To do this, he will use a control chart showing data from a series of samplings to be taken on an ongoing basis. The baker produces approximately 800 loaves of bread daily. However, relying on statistical process control techniques, the baker will be able to monitor the quality level of production and save money on inspection costs by using a relatively limited number of inspections. Two samplings will be made daily. During each sampling, five samples of the cut dough will be weighed. For each sampling, the baker will calculate the mean.

Table 6.9 lists one week's data for monitoring the dough cutting process.

Date	Time	Data (pounds)					Mean
7/23	9:00	1.72	1.82	1.78	1.82	1.88	1.804
	13:00	1.82	1.72	1.88	1.72	1.78	1.784
7/24	10:00	1.88	1.88	1.72	1.78	1.62	1.776
	14:30	1.78	1.82	1.78	1.78	1.82	1.796
7/25	9:30	1.82	1.78	1.88	1.92	1.98	1.876
	15:45	1.88	1.82	1.88	1.78	1.78	1.828
7/26	8:15	1.72	1.82	1.78	1.78	1.72	1.764
	13:00	1.88	1.78	1.88	1.72	1.82	1.816
7/27	11:00	1.72	1.82	1.78	1.82	1.82	1.792
	14:15	1.68	1.82	1.78	1.82	1.88	1.796

Table 6.9 Daily Measurements of Cut Dough

The control chart used to record the data is shown in Figure 6.10. The baker records the mean weight for the various samplesthat run in sequence from left to right along the X axis of the chart. The baker has also drawn a line indicating the target specification of 1.8 pounds.

The control chart allows the baker to constantly compare the actual range of processing variation—as shown in mean weight in his daily samples—with the normal range of random variation he should expect for his current process.

The baker will use the control charts by establishing a series of warning points called control limits. The baker has included control points at one standard deviation (1s), two standard deviations (2s), and three standard deviations (3s) above and below the process mean. In this case, the process mean is the same as the target specification.

A BEGINNER'S GUIDE TO QUALITY IN MANUFACTURING

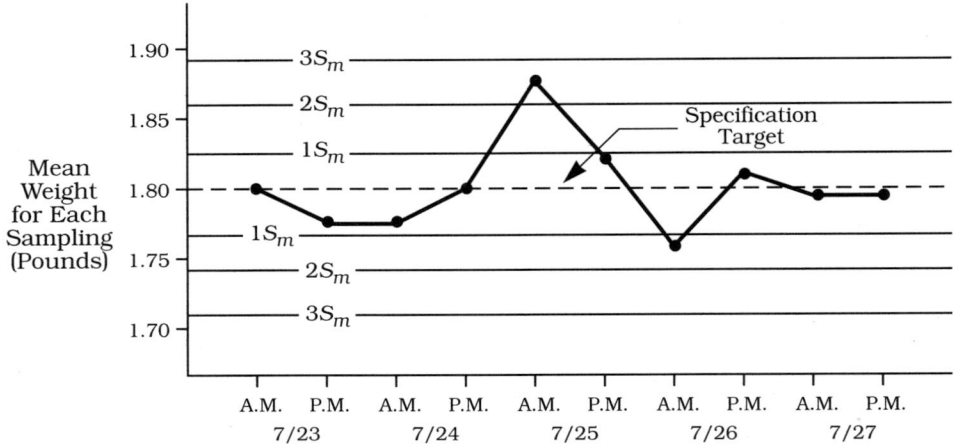

Figure 6.10: Control Chart for the Cut Bread Dough

We noted earlier that, when the baker assessed the quality capability of the dough cutting process, the sample distribution of dough weights approximated a normal distribution curve with a standard deviation of 0.07.

For control chart purposes, however, the baker will not track the individual measurements of each loaf found in the twice-daily samplings. Rather, he will track the mean weights of all five loaves tested in each of these samplings. The use of sample means as a control measurement allows the baker to record a single data point on his control chart for each sampling. At the same time, trends in these sample means will be more sensitive to changes in process capabilities than any of the individual loaf measurements which might be recorded.

The normal distribution curve for weights of individual doughs generated by the baker's cutting process is not the same as the distribution curve for mean weights of five-unit samples of doughs produced by the same process. (See Figure 6.11.) Sample means give us the average weight of all five individual doughs in a sample—cancelling out extremes at either end of the normal distribution. Consequently, we shouldn't be surprised to find that the normal distribution curve for mean weights of five-unit samples is substantially narrower than the distribution curve for weights of individual doughs.

Therefore, when constructing the control chart for sample means, the baker cannot use the standard deviation of 0.07 calculated for the distribution of individual dough weights. Instead, he must calculate a separate standard deviation for the narrower distribution of five-unit sample means.

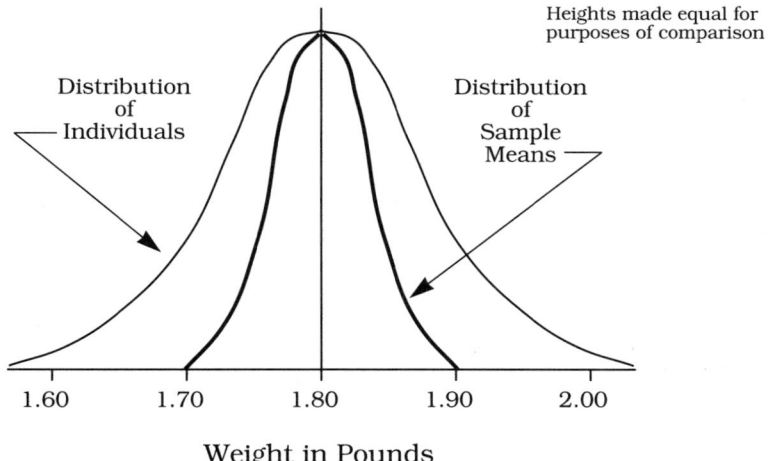

Figure 6.11: Cut Dough Weight Distribution by Individual and Sample Mean

One way to do this would be to take an extended series of five-unit samples, record the mean weights, compute the mean of the sample means, and then calculate the standard deviation for the distribution of sample means. The process simply repeats the process we outlined earlier in the chapter but uses the mean weights of our samples as the data points in our distribution.

Alternatively, the baker can mathematically calculate the standard deviation for mean weights of samples from his standard deviation for individual weights. For example, to calculate the standard deviation for our five-unit sample means, the baker will simply divide the standard deviation for individual weights—0.07—by the square root of five.

$$s_m = \frac{\text{Standard Deviation of Individuals}}{\sqrt{\text{Number of Units in the Sample}}}$$

$$s_m = \frac{s}{\sqrt{n}}$$

$$s_m = \frac{0.07}{\sqrt{5}}$$

where s_m = the standard deviation of the sample mean

$$s_m = 0.03$$

Based on these calculations and the target specification of 1.8 pounds, we can see that the baker's control chart shows $\pm 1 s_m$ points at 1.83 and 1.77 pounds respectively. The $\pm 2 s_m$ points are 1.86 and 1.74 pounds respectively. Finally, the $\pm 3 s_m$ points are 1.89 and 1.71 pounds respectively.

Now, let's look at the baker's chart and find out how to use these various control levels to assess the data from the twice-daily samplings.

The $3s_m$ Control Limits

The first thing that the baker will look for is any sample results which fall beyond the three standard deviation control limit.

Why? Let's answer this question by calculating the probability of finding a mean weight of more than 1.89 pounds if the dough cutting process is working correctly.

You will remember from earlier in the chapter that we expect 99.73 percent of the values in our normal distribution for the dough-cutting process to be within a $\pm 3s_m$ range. This, in turn, means that only 0.27 percent of our process' normal distribution will be beyond the $\pm 3s_m$ level. Consequently, half of these, or 0.135 percent of the total distribution, will fall beyond the $+3s_m$ level and have weights greater than 1.89 pounds. It is clear that the chance of any individual sample mean exceeding the 1.89-pound limit is quite small—135 in 100,000.

Since we have taken a series of 10 samplings, however, the probability of finding at least one sample mean beyond the $3s_m$ (1.89 pounds) limit is somewhat greater. Let's go through the calculations using some cumulative probability formulas that will be fully developed in chapter 7. It will be easier to compute the probability that no sample mean is larger and subtract from 1.0. We will use P to denote probability.

P (1 mean > 1.89) = 0.135% = 0.00135

P (1 mean is not > 1.89) = 1 − 0.00135 = 0.99865

P (no mean out of the 10 > 1.89) = $(0.99865)^{10}$ = 0.9866

P (1 or more mean > 1.89) = 1 − 0.9866 = 0.0134

There is only a 1.34 percent chance of finding a single sample mean weight of more than 1.89 pounds in our series of 10 samplings if our process is still functioning correctly. As you can see, the probabilities rise with a longer series of samplings. Nevertheless, the chances of getting a sample reading beyond the $3s_m$ level with a correctly functioning process remain quite small.

On the other hand, if the process has gone out of statistical control, the probability of finding sample measurements beyond the $3s_m$ control limit can rise dramatically.

Suppose, for example, that an equipment problem in our cutting process has shifted the actual mean weight of cut doughs to 1.83 pounds compared to the original target specification of 1.80 pounds. Now what are the chances of finding a sample mean beyond the $3s_m$ (1.89 pounds) control limit on our chart?

STATISTICAL QUALITY CONTROL

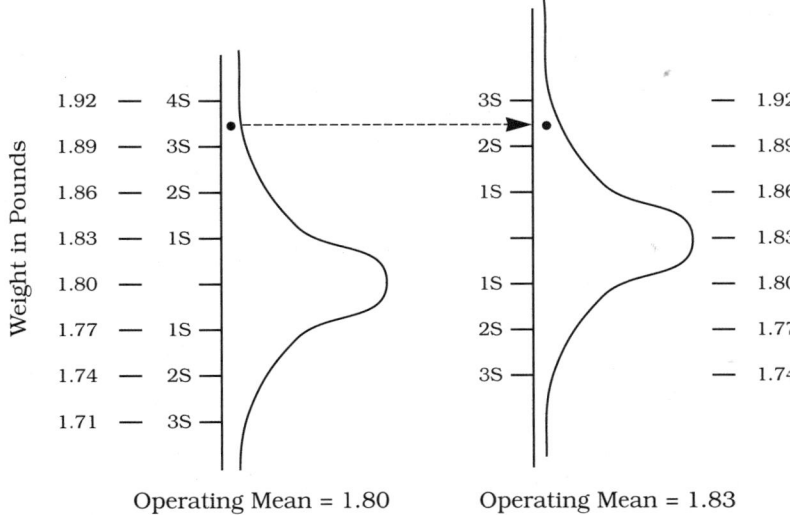

Figure 6.12: Comparison of Sample Mean > 1.89 for Operating Means of 1.80 and 1.83

In Figure 6.12, we notice that if our average loaf is 1.83 pounds, then values greater than 1.89 pounds are beyond $+2s_m$ of our mean. We know that 95.46 percent of the population is within $2s_m$, so 4.54 percent is beyond $2s_m$. To one side (4.54 percent/2) = 2.27 percent is above $+2s_m$. What is the probability that one or more of our 10 sample means is beyond 1.89 percent? Again, we compute the probability that no sample mean is larger, and subtract from 1.0.

P (1 mean > 1.89) = 2.27% = 0.0227

P (mean is not > 1.89) = 1.0 − 0.0227 = 0.9773

P (no mean out of 10 > 1.89) = $(0.9773)^{10}$ = 0.795

P (1 or more mean > 1.89) = 1.0 − 0.795 = 0.205 = 20.5%

Our chances of finding a mean weight beyond the $3s_m$ limit over the course of 10 samplings has increased to 20.5 percent due to the shift in the actual processing results from a mean weight of 1.80 pounds to a mean weight of 1.83 pounds.

Table 6.10 shows comparable probabilities of finding measurements beyond $3s_m$ in 10 samples if the actual process had shifted to other mean weights.

Current Operating Mean	1.80	1.81	1.82	1.83	1.84
P (1 or more mean >1.89)	0.013	0.037	0.095	0.205	0.385

Table 6.10: Probability of Measurements Beyond $3s_m$

A BEGINNER'S GUIDE TO QUALITY IN MANUFACTURING

We can conclude that the probabilities of finding control chart readings beyond the $\pm 3s_m$ limits are small if the process is still in control and functioning as originally specified. On the other hand, measurements beyond the $\pm 3s_m$ limits are more likely if the process has shifted out of control and is no longer operating as planned.

Therefore, the baker will use a control chart measurement beyond the $\pm 3s_m$ limit as a signal to shut down the operation and correct problems that have caused the process to go out of control.

The $2s_m$ Control Levels

Happily, none of the sample means exceeds the $3s_m$ control limits on the chart. This fact alone, however, cannot assure the baker that his process is still in control and meeting its original AQL targets. Therefore, he will also review the control chart for sample measurements which fall beyond the $\pm 2s_m$ control limit to help identify whether or not the process has shifted out of control.

One of the sample means is beyond the $2s_m$ mark of 1.86 pounds. Is this a cause for alarm?

Using the assumptions in our normal distribution curve model, we would expect only 2.135 percent of our values to be between 1.86 pounds and 1.89 pounds if our process is still producing the originally specified mean weight of 1.80 pounds. The basis for this estimate is:

Within	Lower Weight Limit	Upper Weight Limit	Percent of Sample Population
$3s_m$	1.71 pounds –	1.89 pounds	99.73%
$2s_m$	1.74 pounds –	1.86 pounds	95.46%

Between

$-2s_m$ and $-3s_m$ 1.71 pounds – 1.74 pounds
or
$+2s_m$ and $+3s_m$ 1.86 pounds – 1.89 pounds } 4.27%

(99.73% – 95.46%)

Between

1.86 pounds and 1.89 pounds   (4.27%/2) = 2.135%

Once again, however, the probabilities of finding a measurement between $+2s_m$ and $+3s_m$ will rise when we are taking a series of samples. Let's compute the chances of getting

STATISTICAL QUALITY CONTROL

our single "greater than $+2s_m$" control chart reading during the course of our 10 samplings. As noted, we will use a formula for probability that will be developed further in chapter 7.

$$\begin{aligned} \text{P (exactly one in ten samples)} &= 10 \times (0.02135)^1 \times (0.97865)^9 \\ &= 10 \times 0.02135 \times 0.8234 \\ &= 0.1758 = 17.58\% \end{aligned}$$

This 17.58 percent probability of getting a single "greater than $+2s_m$" measurement is reasonably large, so finding it does not give us a particularly strong indication that our process has moved out of control. Once again, the baker seems to be on safe ground.

On the other hand, how would we have interpreted two "greater than $2s_m$" control chart readings during the course of 10 samplings? Let's look at the odds of finding two such measurements if the process was still in control.

$$\begin{aligned} \text{P (exactly two in ten samples)} &= \frac{(10 \times 9)}{2} \times (0.02135)^2 \times (0.97865)^8 \\ &= 45 \times 0.00045 \times 0.84143 \\ &= 0.0172 = 1.72\% \end{aligned}$$

With only a 1.72 percent probability, these two "greater than $2s_m$" control chart readings give a stronger indication that our process has shifted out of control.

Now let's carry our analysis even further. If our process is functioning correctly, the chances of finding two "greater than $2s_m$" control chart readings in the course of three consecutive samplings are even more remote—only a 0.13 percent probability, or 13 out of 10,000. Based on these probabilities, finding two such measurements in the course of three samples can be interpreted as a powerful indication that the process is out of control.

The $1s_m$ Level

Our normal distribution curve model tells us that 13.6 percent of our sample results should fall in each of the two ranges between the $1s_m$ and $2s_m$ levels on either side of our target specification. Consequently, the baker is not at all surprised to get one measurement out of his 10 samples in the range between $-1s_m$ and $-2s_m$.

Within	Lower Weight Limit	Upper Weight Limit	Percent of Sample Population
$2s_m$	1.74 pounds –	1.86 pounds	95.46%
$1s_m$	1.77 pounds –	1.83 pounds	68.26%

Between

$-1s_m$ and $-2s_m$	1.77 pounds –	1.74 pounds	
or			27.20%
$+1s_m$ and $+2s_m$	1.86 pounds –	1.89 pounds	

(95.46% – 68.26%)

Between

1.77 pounds and 1.74 pounds   (27.20%/2) = 13.6%

Nevertheless, an extended number of measurements falling in the ranges between either $+1s_m$ and $+2s_m$ or $-1s_m$ and $-2s_m$ can signal trouble. For example, we can calculate that the probabilities are extremely remote that we would find four out of five consecutive control chart entries in one of these ranges if our process is functioning as originally specified.

$$P \text{ (exactly four in five samples)} = (5) \times (0.136)^4 \times (0.864)^1$$
$$= 5 \times 0.00034 \times 0.864$$
$$= 0.0014 = 0.14\%$$

With 0.14 percent odds, four out of five consecutive measurements in a range between $1s_m$ and $2s_m$ probably indicates that our process has moved out of control.

Other Non-Random Distributions

As we've seen, the baker has reason to be happy. So far the process appears to be in control. There is only one "greater than $\pm 2s_m$" reading during the course of 10 samplings and no measurements beyond the $3s_m$ control limit. Does this mean he can feel confident that the process remains in control and is meeting its originally specified quality targets? Not necessarily!

There are additional patterns of sampling results, other than points beyond the $\pm 1s_m$, $\pm 2s_m$ or $\pm 3s_m$ warning limits, which may indicate that a process is moving away from or is already out of statistical control. Essentially, these patterns are any distributions of sample means which are not consistent with the random, scattering of results we would expect from a normal process distribution.

One example of an apparently non-random distribution would be a control chart pattern showing sample means that consistently fall to only one side of the target specification. The baker, for example, might see a series of sample results that are all greater than 1.80 pounds. This would tend to indicate that the actual mean weight for the dough-cutting process had shifted to something higher than the 1.80-pounds target.

Another example of non-random distribution is a pattern in which sample results move steadily in a single direction. For example, the baker might record a series of sample means which steadily decrease in weight—1.82 pounds, 1.81 pounds, 1.80 pounds, 1.79 pounds, 1.77 pounds, and 1.74 pounds. This may indicate that the actual mean weight for the dough-cutting process has changed and is continuing to shift as the process continues.

Control Charts: Interpreting the Results

As you can see, control charts offer a means by which manufacturers can quickly and easily monitor the actual level of variation in process output. This can then be compared against the range of variation they would expect if the process was functioning as originally specified. At the same time, however, it is important to remember that control charts cannot offer a single control limit which will indicate, in any and all cases, that our processes have lost their ability to meet our quality targets. Use of control charts requires that we interpret patterns of sample results based on the probabilities of finding those results in a random normal distribution of process output. It also requires an accurate assessment of the risks which we are willing to sustain in interpreting the data.

Control Charts for Attribute Data

The baker monitored the quality of the cutting process with a control chart for the weight of the cut dough. Weight, as we learned earlier in the chapter, is a variable because it can have many different values. The cut dough ranged from 1.62 pounds to 1.92 pounds.

Variables, however, are not the only measurements that can be used for control charts. A control chart can also monitor attributes. Attributes, as we have seen, have only two values; they are either acceptable or defective.

The AM radio manufacturer uses a control chart for attributes to monitor the quality of the PCB assembly. After the components are automatically inserted onto the PCBs and soldered, they are automatically tested for a number of things. The auto-tester checks that the components are connected to each other and that they are within their tolerance values.

The manufacturer assembles and solders 1,200 PCBs in a day, and all are tested on the auto-tester. There are 55 components on the PCB. The manufacturer has set an AQL of 1.0 defect per hundred radios for the soldered PCBs.

The soldered PCBs are being tested as part of the normal manufacturing process by an auto-tester that is computer controlled. The computer automatically identifies defects and prints a ticket that is attached to the defective PCB so that the PCB can easily be fixed. It costs virtually nothing to use the computer to draw the control chart using the defect data. However, before the manufacturer programs the computer to draw the control chart, she needs to make some measurements and calculations.

First, the manufacturer takes data to determine the quality level of the process. She determines that the mean value for defects per hundred is approximately 1.0 percent. This meets the AQL target of 1.0 percent. She computes this value by finding the mean value of daily defect rates over a period of three months.

The manufacturer also uses this data to determine that the defect rate has a standard deviation of 0.08 from day to day during this period. She uses this data on the control chart. She will consider these values as benchmarks and hopes to improve on them as time goes on.

Now that all preliminary values have been calculated and the target AQL has been set, the manufacturer can begin taking data for the control chart. Table 6.11 contains the daily results of counting defects found on PCBs after auto-insertion and soldering.

At the end of each day, the computer posts another data point on the control chart. Figure 6.13 shows the attributes control chart prepared after 20 days of monitoring.

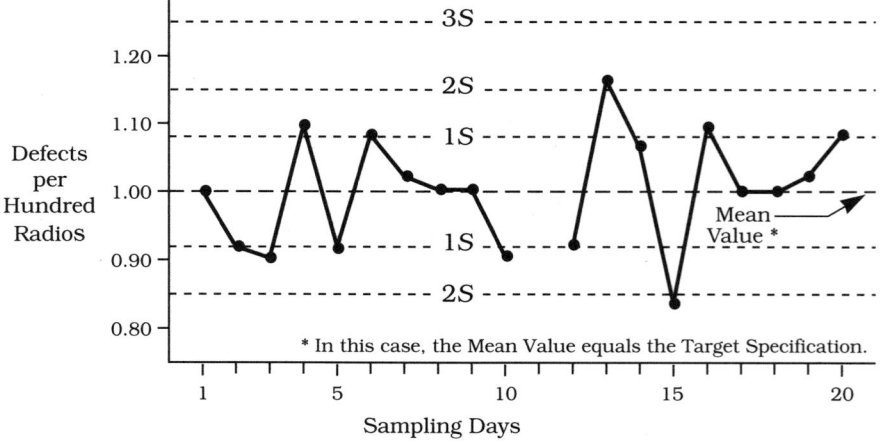

Figure 6.13: Control Chart for Defects per Hundred on PCBs after Soldering

Day	PCBs Made	Defects	Defects per Hundred Units
1	1,205	12	1.00
2	1,197	11	0.92
3	1,206	11	0.91
4	1,195	13	1.09
5	1,201	11	0.92
6	1,200	13	1.08
7	1,194	12	1.01
8	1,198	12	1.00
9	1,201	12	1.00
10	1,215	11	0.91
11	891	24	2.69
12	1,200	11	0.92
13	1,197	14	1.17
14	1,215	13	1.07
15	1,201	10	0.83
16	1,188	13	1.09
17	1,195	12	1.00
18	1,206	12	1.00
19	1,192	12	1.01
20	1,208	13	1.08

Table 6.11: Defects Found on Soldered PCBs

After reviewing this chart, we may make a number of observations. For the first 10 days, the process seems to be in control. The defects per hundred radios are approximately within one standard deviation of the target AQL. The data also oscillates above and below the target AQL. Both of these are positive signs.

Then on day 11 the defects went completely out of control. The production line supervisor stopped the line and notified the manufacturing engineer. The quality assurance engineer and the design engineer were called in to consult on the problem. An investigation discovered that a heater in the preheat chamber of the soldering machine was not working, so that components were not being soldered properly to the PCB. The soldering machine was corrected and the operation was restarted. No point was plotted on the control chart because it was beyond the limits of the chart.

On the 13th day, the defects per hundred radios reached two standard deviations of the AQL target. This was of concern to the line supervisor, but it did not persist on the next day of operation. In fact, on the 15th day the defects were so low the chart recorded a process improvement of almost two standard deviations. This was something the line supervisor investigated, in the hope of improving the AQL. But by the next day the process had settled back into its normal pattern.

A BEGINNER'S GUIDE TO QUALITY IN MANUFACTURING

The line supervisor holds monthly meetings with workers to discuss ways of improving quality. They want to reduce the defects per hundred radios below the 1.0 level. They are constantly devising new ways to improve their quality, and with the help of these control charts, they have a means to measure their success.

As we have seen earlier in this chapter, the information available for analysis from statistics on product attributes is obviously more limited than that provided by samples of product variables. Furthermore, with decreasing AQL targets, the number of defects which we would expect to find in most production lots is quite small. Consequently, the use of control charts which monitor attribute data will require significantly larger sample sizes than for similar efforts using data on product variables. Once again, the AM radio manufacturer uses automatic equipment to test each of the PCBs as part of the normal production process. Consequently, her daily sample size is approximately 1,200.

6.10 First Piece Inspection

Control charts provide ongoing detailed information on the status of our manufacturing process. We should note, however, that the simplest and most basic form of process control is first piece inspection. Data are collected on the first product to undergo a particular step in the manufacturing process. First piece inspection is usually done when a product run starts for the day, when a piece of equipment is adjusted, or during any startup situation.

The AM radio manufacturer, for example, carefully sets the temperature and flow speed of the automated soldering machine. She then inspects the first PCB to go through the process. If the inspection reveals any defects, the machine will be reset and another first piece inspection will be conducted on the next PCB to go through the process. If no defects are found, the day's production can begin.

Similarly, first piece inspection is an important process control technique in the closet door factory. At the beginning of each day, the saw operator sets the equipment to cut the components of the door frame. The operator then cuts the first piece of wood and measures it to check that it is as close to the stated specification as possible. If it is not, the operator will adjust the saw.

It is important to note that the saw operators will not accept any first piece inspection that simply meets the component's normally "acceptable" specification. Nor will the operators simply accept a measurement that falls anywhere

STATISTICAL QUALITY CONTROL

within the process' normal range of variation. On first piece inspection, we should expect a measurement which closely conforms to the target specification, since the equipment has been freshly adjusted and the operators will naturally be making their cuts with particular care.

First piece inspection is a simple, effective technique for ensuring that a process starts off correctly. The data determine what action is needed. The process can be corrected immediately, before many nonconforming parts are made.

Chapter Summary

1. Process control sites are placed along the manufacturing process to monitor the process and ensure an AQL.

2. The actual output of any manufacturing process will vary somewhat from one unit of production to another. These normal variations result from equipment capabilities, variances in material and component specifications, employee performance, and processing procedures. Manufacturers can assess their process' capability or current quality level based on current equipment, employee performance, procedures, purchased materials, and so on. Manufacturers can increase the capability or quality level of their process by use of improved equipment, higher levels of employee training or motivation, higher quality component parts, and other techniques.

3. Frequency distribution is data that has been gathered and grouped according to its occurrence. Range is the difference between the largest observed value and the smallest observed value in the frequency distribution. Cells divide the range into equal parts so that the frequency distribution can be graphed. A histogram is the graph of a frequency distribution.

4. A normal distribution curve can be used as a mathematical model for the results of many manufacturing processes. The normal distribution curve model is helpful because it allows us to estimate the percentage of a process' output which meets the manufacturing specifications.

5. One useful measurement of the output's distribution for any process is the population mean or average. This is a measure of central tendency and can be used in judging if the sample or population is at or near the target specification. The formula for population mean or average is as follows:

A BEGINNER'S GUIDE TO QUALITY IN MANUFACTURING

$$\text{Population Mean} = \frac{\text{Sum of measurements}}{\text{Number of measurements}}$$

$$\mu = \frac{\sum X_i}{n}$$

where $\sum X_i = X_1 + X_2 + X_3 + X_4 + X_5 + \ldots\ldots X_n$

The total number of data points in the sampling is represented by n.

6. A second useful measurement of our process output is called standard deviation. This is a measure of variance. The population standard deviation is defined by the formula

$$\sigma = \left\{ \frac{1}{n-1} \sum (X_i - \mu)^2 \right\}^{1/2}$$

where X_i = the observed values
μ = the population mean
n = number of observations made on the population

The standard deviation of a sample is written s and can be calculated by the formula

$$s = \left\{ \frac{1}{n-1} \sum (X_i - \bar{X})^2 \right\}^{1/2}$$

where X_i = the observed values
$\bar{X}$ = the sample mean
n = number of observations made on the sample

7. A control chart is a graph used for monitoring a process to determine if its output continues to fall within the normal range of variation. If it does, the process is said to be in control. If the process output falls outside the normal range of variation, the process is out of control. Control charts can measure variables such as length, weight, or resistance. The control chart that measures variables might plot sample mean, range, or standard deviation. Attributes (defects) can also be monitored. An attribute control chart could plot percent defective or defects per hundred units.

8. First piece inspection checks the quality of the first product made when a new product line is started, when production starts for the day, or when production starts after any shutdown period.

STATISTICAL QUALITY CONTROL

Questions for Chapter 6

Use the following table of values for question 1.

8.877	8.243	8.150	8.740	8.549
8.886	8.784	8.983	8.331	8.611
8.545	8.616	8.824	8.407	8.207
8.502	8.475	8.454	8.304	8.294
8.716	8.890	8.442	8.867	8.845

Table 6.12: Table of Values

1. a. Find the range of this sample.

   b. Find the mean of this sample and round off to the thousandths place.

   c. Subtract the mean from each number in the sample and square the result.

   d. Add your results from part c, and divide the result by one less than the number of values in the table.

   e. Take the square root of the result in part d; this is the standard deviation of the sample.

   f. Find the values that are one standard deviation from the mean. Find the values that are two standard deviations from the mean.

   g. Draw a histogram of the sample. Use a target of 8.500, and use cell widths of 0.100.

A BEGINNER'S GUIDE TO QUALITY IN MANUFACTURING

2. Use Table 6.4 to find the area between negative infinity and each normalized value.

   a. −0.76

   b. +2.34

   c. +1.00

   d. −0.29

   e. −1.18

3. For each pair of normalized values, find the area between the values.

   a. −2.05, +3.12

   b. −3.43, +3.19

   c. −3.04, +2.88

   d. −2.60, +3.11

STATISTICAL QUALITY CONTROL

Use the following sample data for questions 4–7. All measures are given in inches.

4.01	3.87	4.09	4.04	3.89	4.05	4.01	3.87	3.92	4.00
4.07	3.88	3.90	4.02	4.01	3.94	4.02	4.04	3.95	4.03
3.93	4.03	3.91	3.96	3.96	4.01	4.03	4.06	4.02	3.95
3.99	4.01	4.03	4.06	3.94	3.98	4.01	4.06	4.02	3.94
4.06	4.00	4.05	3.97	3.98	4.04	3.97	3.98	4.00	3.95

4.   a. Find the range. Draw a histogram using a specification target of 4.00 inches and a cell width of .02 inches.

      b. Find the mean to the nearest hundredths place, and the standard deviation to the nearest thousandths place. Compute the values for 1, 2, and 3 standard deviations. Place these values and the mean on your histogram.

      c. The tolerance for this sample is 1/8. Place the upper and lower specification limits on your histogram.

5.   a. When determining our cell width, we wish the cell width to be a factor of the tolerance. It is simple to compute the factors of a tolerance such as 1/8; we multiply the denominator by the integers 1, 2, 3 .... Therefore, 1/8, 1/16, 1/24, etc., are factors of 1/8. Compute the first 15 factors of 1/8; also, change each to a decimal.

      b. The approximate cell width is obtained by dividing the range by the number of cells desired. For the range found in question 4, determine the approximate cell width if we desire the following number of cells: 10, 11, 12, 13, 14, and 15.

      c. For each cell width found in part b, choose the factor of 1/8 that will be closest.

A BEGINNER'S GUIDE TO QUALITY IN MANUFACTURING

6. We have decided to use 14 cells. Using the closest factor of 1/8, draw a new histogram. On the histogram, note your specification target, your sample mean, your lower and upper specification limits, and 1, 2, and 3 standard deviations.

7. We are going to find the percentage of production that is within specification.

    a. Normalize the lower specification limit. Normalize the upper specification limit.

    b. Using Table 6.4, find the area from negative infinity to the upper specification limit. Find the area from negative infinity to the lower specification limit. Subtract these two values.

    c. What percentage of our sample is within specifications?

Use the following table for questions 8 and 9.

Day	PCBs Made	Defects	Defects Per Hundred Units
1	1314	13	
2	1206	8	
3	1189	12	
4	1167	10	
5	987	7	
6	1005	14	
7	1145	13	
8	1075	14	
9	1100	11	
10	1179	11	
11	1206	11	
12	1159	13	
13	1200	12	
14	1202	13	
15	1199	12	
16	1201	11	
17	1188	11	
18	1234	16	
19	1123	12	
20	1000	11	

Table 6.13: Defects Found on Soldered PCBs

STATISTICAL QUALITY CONTROL

8. Complete the table by computing the number of defects per hundred units. Round off to the nearest hundredth.

9. Draw a control chart for this data.

Chapter 6 Project

Refer to the flowchart that was drawn in chapter 4 for your project. Indicate what process variations could occur at each process step. At the AM radio plant, a failure in the preheating chamber of the soldering machine prevented the components from being properly soldered to the PCB. What would be the effect of the variations you've identified on the subassemblies or assemblies at each process step at your factory?

THE MATHEMATICS OF QUALITY CONTROL

7.1 Introduction

In chapter 5, we wrote incoming inspection plans based on MIL-STD-105E. This allowed us to avoid 100 percent inspection, a procedure that might well be more expensive than the raw materials themselves. A question that arises is: Will a sampling plan guarantee that each lot we accept actually conforms to our AQL? It would be simplistic to think that a sample size smaller than 1 percent of the total lot would guarantee an AQL for the entire batch. In this chapter, we will discuss what is meant by our confidence level when we apply MIL-STD-105E or any other sampling technique. We will also look at some elementary probability theory needed to construct and interpret a sampling program such as MIL-STD-105E.

7.2 True Quality Level vs. Measured Quality Level

Every lot or batch has a true quality level. If we were to do a 100 percent inspection of a lot of 1,900 boards and found that 19 were defective, the true quality level (percent defective) would be 1.0 percent.

$$\text{Percent Defective} = \frac{\text{Number of Defectives}}{\text{Number of Units Inspected}} \times 100$$

$$\text{Percent Defective} = \frac{19}{1,900} \times 100 = 1.0$$

To ensure an AQL of 0.65, a single sampling plan as outlined in MIL-STD-105E would use a sample size of 125 boards for a lot size of 1,900. It would accept the lot if two or fewer defective boards are found and reject the lot otherwise.

Since there are 19 bad boards in the lot, we could find any number of defectives—from zero to 19—in our sample of 125.

Our sample could yield zero defectives if all 19 actual defectives were in the group of 1,775 boards not inspected. This lot would then be accepted by our plan, even though the true quality level of 1.0 does not meet our AQL target of 0.65. Likewise, we might find up to two defectives in our sample of 125 boards, with the remaining 17 defective boards being in the group of 1,775 boards not inspected. Once again, we would be accepting a lot that does not meet our AQL. This is a risk the consumer takes when initiating acceptance sampling.

On the other hand, the lot of 1,900 boards might only have twelve actual defectives. In this case, the true quality level would be 0.63.

$$\text{Percent Defective} = \frac{12}{1,900} \times 100 = 0.63$$

This value is within the AQL of 0.65 that we have set.

As we inspect the sample of 125 boards, we might find three of the defective boards in this group. The 1,775 remaining uninspected boards would contain the nine other defectives. In this case, our sampling plan would reject the lot, even though the supplier has met our AQL target. Moreover, even if there were only three defective boards in the entire lot of 1,900, there is the possibility that all three might be in our 125-board sample. Once again, we would be rejecting a lot that clearly meets our standards. A supplier who has met our AQL will have the lot returned. This is the risk the supplier takes when we use an acceptance sampling plan.

7.3 Probability and Expectation

Now let's look at the mathematics used in MIL-STD-105E to help us feel confident that accepted lots meet our AQL and rejected lots do not.

Suppose we were to take a fair coin (one with an equal probability of heads and tails) and flip it four times. How many heads would we expect?

It seems reasonable that, since it is a fair coin, we would expect two heads and two tails. Yet, we have experienced that often this is not the case. We could get no heads, one head, two heads, three heads, or four heads. However, since the coin is fair, two heads seems to be the most reasonable result.

THE MATHEMATICS OF QUALITY CONTROL

Probability tells us that if we flip the coin an infinite number of times, half the tosses will result in heads and half in tails. We can't actually flip coins an infinite number of times. However, the same basic rules apply. If we were to flip the coin a very large number of times, maybe 100,000 or one million times, approximately half the tosses will result in heads. As we increase the number of tosses, the proportion of heads will be closer and closer to one-half.

Let's go back to our example of tossing the coin four times. If we were to repeat this series of four tosses over and over, we would expect to get two heads in most cases, one head or three heads less frequently, and zero or four heads least often.

There is a formula for this expectation. We let p stand for the probability of success on each individual toss. So in this case, $p = 1/2$.

$$p = \frac{\text{Number of Possible Successful Outcomes}}{\text{Total Number of Possible Outcomes}}$$

$$p = \frac{\text{One Chance of Getting a Head}}{\text{Two Possible Outcomes, Heads or Tails}}$$

$$p = \frac{1}{2} = 0.5$$

As we've said, with a fair coin, we expect to get heads half of the time.

Conversely, we will let q stand for the probability of failure on each toss: $q = 1 - p$.

$$q = 1 - 0.5 = 0.5$$

We also expect to get tails half of the time.

These basic formulas calculate the probability of getting a certain outcome in a single attempt. We can expand them to give us the probability of getting certain specified outcomes in a series of attempts. For example, we can calculate the probability of getting exactly two heads on four tosses of our coin. Let's look at how we construct our formula.

We will let the number of times we repeat a process be represented by n. In this case n equals four tosses. We will let r represent the number of results that we consider to be a success. In our example r equals two heads. The probability of getting exactly r successes in n repetitions is

$$P_n(r) = \frac{(n)*(n-1)*(n-2)*(n-3)*\ldots(3)*(2)*(1)}{[(r)*(r-1)*(r-2)*\ldots(2)*(1)]*[(n-r)*(n-r-1)*\ldots(2)*(1)]} * p^r * q^{n-r}$$

Now let's calculate the probability of getting exactly two heads on four tosses:

$$P_4(2) = P_4(2 \text{ heads}) = \frac{4 * 3 * 2 * 1}{(2 * 1) * (2 * 1)} * p^2 * q^2$$

$$P_4(2) = \frac{4 * 3 * \cancel{2 * 1}}{(2 * 1) * \cancel{(2 * 1)}} * 0.5^2 * 0.5^2$$

$$P_4(2) = \frac{12}{2} * 0.25 * 0.25$$

$$P_4(2) = \frac{0.75}{2} = 0.375 = \frac{375}{1000}$$

This means that if we do 1,000 repetitions of tossing a coin four times, we would expect to get exactly two heads 375 times. We usually represent this as a decimal (0.375), but occasionally we will refer to it as a percent, 37.5 percent (0.375 × 100 percent = 37.5 percent).

There is a notation that will make writing and using this formula easier. We define *n-factorial*, written *n!*, for positive integers

$$n! = (n) * (n - 1) * (n - 2) * ...(3) * (2) * (1)$$

For example:
$$4! = 4 * 3 * 2 * 1 = 24$$
$$7! = 7 * 6 * 5 * 4 * 3 * 2 * 1 = 5{,}040$$
$$2! = 2 * 1 = 2$$
$$1! = 1 = 1$$

Also, we define 0! = 1.

We can now rewrite our formula as

$$P_n(r) = \frac{n!}{r! * (n - r)!} * p^r * q^{n-r}$$

Before giving a few more examples of applying this formula, we will give a simplified overview of how we might apply it to our incoming inspection plan. If the true quality level of our lot of 1,900 boards is 1.0 percent (19 defective boards), then the probability of each board being defective is 1.0/100 = 0.01. The probability of each board not being defective is 0.99, (1 − 0.01). So, in this case, $p = 0.01$ and $q = 0.99$. If we were to sample four boards, then the probability of finding exactly two defective boards would be

THE MATHEMATICS OF QUALITY CONTROL

$$P_4(2) = \frac{4!}{2! * (4-2)!} * (0.01)^2 * (0.99)^{4-2}$$

$$P_4(2) = \frac{4!}{2! \times 2!} * (0.01)^2 * (0.99)^2$$

$$P_4(2) = \frac{24}{2 \times 2} * (0.0001) * (0.9801)$$

$$P_4(2) = \frac{24}{4} * 0.00009801$$

$$P_4(2) = 0.00058806$$

This is a very small probability. Since so few boards are defective, we would not expect to find two out of four defective.

On the other hand, if we were to sample 125 boards, the probability of finding two defective boards would be

$$P_{125}(2) = \frac{125!}{2! * (125-2)!} * (0.01)^2 * (0.99)^{125-2}$$

$$P_{125}(2) = \frac{125!}{2! * 123!} * (0.01)^2 * (0.99)^{123}$$

$$P_{125}(2) = \frac{125 * 124 * \cancel{123 * 122 * \ldots 3 * 2 * 1}}{2 * \cancel{123 * 122 * \ldots 3 * 2 * 1}} * (0.0001) * (0.29)$$

$$P_{125}(2) = \frac{15{,}500}{2} * 0.000029$$

$$P_{125}(2) = 7{,}750 * 0.000029 = 0.225$$

If the defectives were in the same proportion in our sample as they are in the entire batch, we would expect 1.25 defectives in the sample ($125 \times 0.01 = 1.25$). Of course, we must have an integer number of defectives. Therefore, the probability of finding two defectives should be reasonably high, and it is: the probability is 0.225. The probability of finding one defective should be higher, since there should be slightly more than one defective found in each sample of 125 boards. The probability of finding one defective board is

$$P_{125}(1) = \frac{125!}{1! * 124!} * (0.01)^1 * (0.99)^{124}$$

$$P_{125}(1) = \frac{125 * \cancel{124 * 123 * \ldots 3 * 2 * 1}}{1 * \cancel{124 * 123 * \ldots 3 * 2 * 1}} * 0.01 * 0.288$$

$$P_{125}(1) = 0.359$$

A BEGINNER'S GUIDE TO QUALITY IN MANUFACTURING

As expected, the probability of exactly one defective board is greater than the probability of exactly two defective boards.

7.4 The Binomial Distribution

We will complete computing the probabilities of achieving exactly zero, one, two, three, and four heads on four tosses of a coin.

Zero heads: $P_4(0) = \dfrac{4!}{0! * 4!} * 0.5^0 * 0.5^4$

$= \dfrac{4*3*2*1}{1*4*3*2*1} * 1 * 0.0625$

$P_4(0) = 0.0625$

One head: $P_4(1) = \dfrac{4!}{1! * 3!} * 0.5^1 * 0.5^3$

$= \dfrac{4*3*2*1}{1*3*2*1} * .05 * 0.125$

$P_4(1) = 0.25$

Two heads: $P_4(2) = 0.375$

Three heads: $P_4(3) = \dfrac{4!}{3! * 1!} * 0.5^3 * 0.5^1$

$P_4(3) = \dfrac{4*3*2*1}{3*2*1*1} * 0.125 * 0.5$

$P_4(3) = 0.25$

Four heads: $P_4(4) = \dfrac{4!}{4! * 0!} * 0.5^4 * 0.5^0$

$P_4(4) = \dfrac{4*3*2*1}{4*3*2*1*1} * 0.0625 * 1$

$P_4(4) = 0.0625$

Note the sum of

$P_4(0) + P_4(1) + P_4(2) + P_4(3) + P_4(4)$
$= 0.0625 + 0.25 + 0.375 + 0.25 + 0.0625 = 1$

The sum of the probabilities of all possible outcomes will always equal 1.

Let us graph r vs. $P_4(r)$.

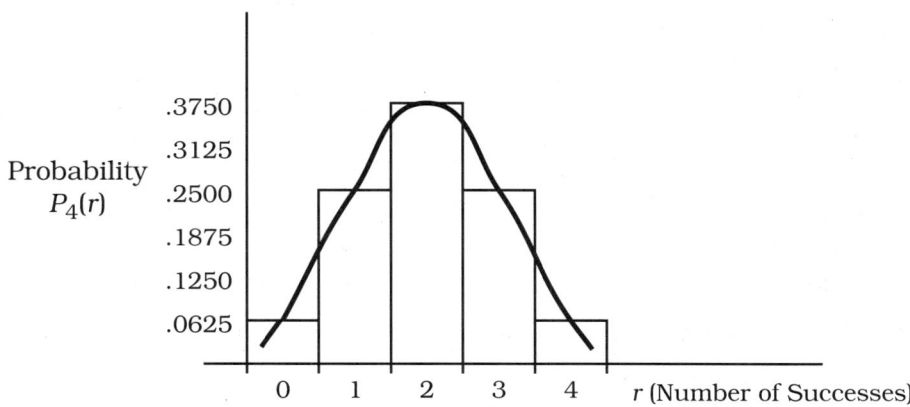

Figure 7.1: Probability of Achieving Various Numbers of Successes in Four Trials

It should not surprise us that the frequency distribution curve looks similar to the normal curve in chapter 6. If we were to increase the number of repetitions from four tosses to ten or 20 tosses or more, we would expect this distribution to more closely resemble the normal curve. This distribution is called the *binomial distribution*. It is one of two distributions used in MIL-STD-105E.

Without showing the computation, Table 7.1 gives the binomial distribution for 20 tosses of a coin. Decimals have been rounded off to four places. Remember that $p = 0.5$ and $q = 1 - 0.5 = 0.5$.

r	$P_{20}(r)$	r	$P_{20}(r)$	r	$P_{20}(r)$
0	.0000	7	.0739	14	.0370
1	.0000	8	.1201	15	.0148
2	.0002	9	.1602	16	.0046
3	.0011	10	.1762	17	.0011
4	.0046	11	.1602	18	.0002
5	.0148	12	.1201	19	.0000
6	.0370	13	.0739	20	.0000

Table 7.1: Binomial Distribution for Twenty Coin Tosses

As expected, the highest probability is for 10 heads, half the number of tosses. Also, the sum of the probabilities is one. Figure 7.2 shows a graph of the frequency distribution.

A BEGINNER'S GUIDE TO QUALITY IN MANUFACTURING

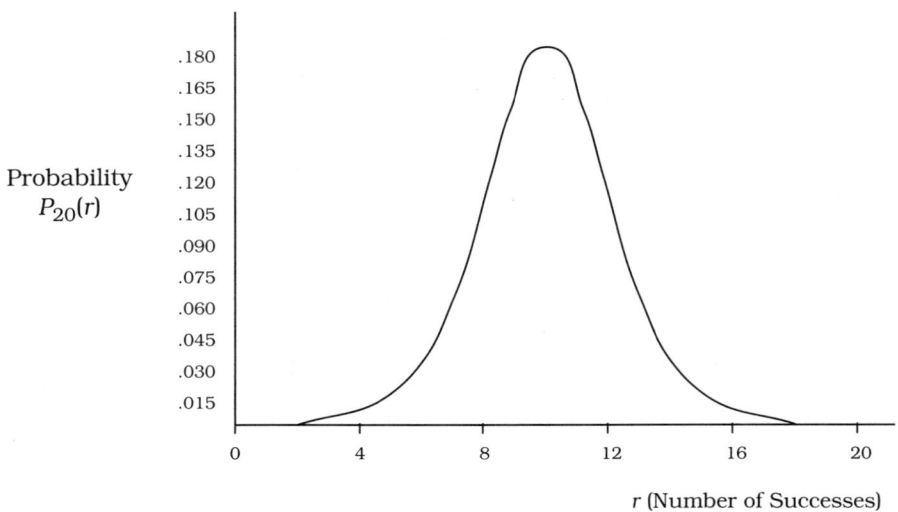

Figure 7.2: Frequency Distribution for Coin Toss (20 Trials)

7.5 Cumulative Probability

When we analyze MIL-STD-105E, we need to apply cumulative probability, that is, cumulative terms of the binomial distribution. For example, what is the probability of obtaining one or more heads on our four tosses? To achieve this, we add

$$P_4(1) + P_4(2) + P_4(3) + P_4(4)$$
$$= 0.25 + 0.3750 + 0.2500 + 0.0625$$
$$= 0.9375$$

Sometimes it is easier to compute the opposite of what we want, and subtract this value from one. In this case, the probability of zero heads, $P_4(0) = 0.0625$, can be subtracted from 1 to obtain the probability of one or more heads.

$$P_4(1 \text{ or more heads}) = 1 - P_4(0)$$
$$= 1 - 0.0625$$
$$= 0.9375$$

7.6 Levels of Confidence

As we outlined earlier, we can only be 100 percent confident that our inspection plan is giving us lots meeting our AQL if we do a 100 percent sampling plan. Since in our sampling plans we will be using a small fraction of our lot, we cannot have 100 percent confidence.

THE MATHEMATICS OF QUALITY CONTROL

Statisticians usually accept confidence levels of 0.90 or 0.95. MIL-STD-105E, in general, aims at a confidence level of 0.95.

What, exactly, does a 0.95 confidence level mean? It does not mean that we are 95 percent confident that our accepted lot meets our AQL. Being 95 percent confident is as meaningless as being 95 percent sad or 95 percent tired. We cannot assign numbers to sadness, tiredness, or confidence. Nor does it mean that if a sample passes our acceptance plan, then 95 percent of the lot meets our AQL.

A 95 percent confidence level means that if a supplier consistently provides us with a product that meets our required AQL then we will accept approximately 95 percent of the batches. As with our coin tossing experiments, the statistical model unrealistically assumes that we will be inspecting an infinite number of batches. Nevertheless, as the number of batches increases, we will get closer and closer to the 95 percent mark. This is why MIL-STD-105E gives sampling plans designed for use where the units of the product are produced in a continuous series of lots or batches over a period of time. We should also note that the model presumes the manufacturer provides us with the product in approximately equal size batches and that we use the same inspection plan on all deliveries.

Let us continue analyzing our batch of 1,900 boards, which has an actual quality level of 0.65. MIL-STD-105E tells us to accept the lots if two or fewer defectives are found in a sample of 125 boards. Suppose the supplier meets our standards; that is, he consistently submits lots whose true AQL is 0.65. Let us compute the probability of finding two or fewer defectives in the sample. We need to compute $P_{125}(2) + P_{125}(1) + P_{125}(0)$. Since the true AQL is 0.65, we see $p = 0.65/100$, since it is the percent defective.

$$p = \frac{0.65}{100} = 0.0065; \quad q = 1 - p = 1 - 0.0065 = 0.9935$$

We use: $$P_n(r) = \frac{n!}{r! * (n-r)!} * p^r * q^{n-r}$$

So: $$P_{125}(2) = \frac{125!}{2! * 123!} * 0.0065^2 * 0.9935^{123}$$

$$= \frac{125 * 124}{2} * 0.00004225 * 0.448382018$$

$$P_{125}(2) = 0.14681$$

And: $$P_{125}(1) = \frac{125!}{1! * 124!} * 0.0065^1 * 0.9935^{124}$$

A BEGINNER'S GUIDE TO QUALITY IN MANUFACTURING

$$= \frac{125}{1} * 0.0065 * 0.445467535$$

$$P_{125}(1) = 0.36194$$

And:
$$P_{125}(0) = \frac{125!}{0! * 125!} * 0.0065^0 * 0.9935^{125}$$

$$= 1 * 1 * 0.442571996$$

$$= 0.44257$$

Summing: $P_{125}(2) + P_{125}(1) + P_{125}(0)$

$$= 0.14681 + 0.36194 + 0.44257$$

$$= 0.95132$$

This is our desired level of confidence. Note that we have rounded off; also, since we must use integers instead of fractions for our acceptance number, we could not achieve the number 0.95 exactly. This number is called the *probability of acceptance*, and is denoted as P_a. $P_a = 0.95132$.

Producer's Risk

The *producer's risk* is the probability that even though the producer is providing a product that meets our AQL, we will reject the lot. The producer's risk is $1 - P_a$. In the above example, the producer has met our AQL of 0.65, yet some lots will be rejected. This risk is equal to $1 - P_a = 1 - 0.95132 = 0.04868$.

If the producer delivers a product with a quality level better than our target of 0.65, say 0.50, we would expect that our probability of acceptance would be larger. This, in turn, will reduce the producer's risk. In this case, $p = 0.0050$ and $q = 0.995$.

$$P_a = P_{125}(2) + P_{125}(1) + P_{125}(0) = 0.1045 + 0.3357 + 0.5344$$

$P_a = 0.9746$; and the producer's risk, $1 - P_a = 0.0254$.

Consumer's Risk

The use of acceptance sampling plans also leads to a *consumer's risk* that lots which do not meet our AQL target will be accepted.

We can also calculate these risks using cumulative probability.

THE MATHEMATICS OF QUALITY CONTROL

Earlier, we computed $P_{125}(2)$ and $P_{125}(1)$ when the producer's actual quality level was 1.00. The probability of accepting these lots, despite the fact that they fail to meet our AQL target of 0.65, would be

$$P_a = P_{125}(2) + P_{125}(1) + P_{125}(0)$$
$$= 0.225 + 0.359 + 0.285$$
$$P_a = 0.869$$

The probability of acceptance is still relatively high at 87 percent. We can see, therefore, that consumers can face considerable risks in using acceptance sampling plans. Later in the chapter, we will discuss how the tightened levels of MIL-STD-105E compensate for these risks.

7.7 Operating Characteristic Curves

Obviously, there is significant complexity in computing the probability of acceptance for all of the sampling plans, all of the AQL targets, and all of the actual producer quality levels which a manufacturer could confront. MIL-STD-105E provides this information in a series of *operating characteristic curves* and their associated tabulated values. Let's look at how these diagrams and tables apply to the door manufacturer's incoming inspection plan.

We have been evaluating our delivery of 1,900 boards using General Inspection Level II on a 125-board sample. MIL-STD-105E assigns a sample size code letter of K for this sampling plan. Using this code letter, we will turn to the operating characteristic curves shown in Figure 7.3.

First, we'll locate the curve with 0.65 marked on it. This is the AQL target of 0.65 that we have been using in our example.

Along the bottom of the chart, we have the true quality level of the lots submitted. We've already indicated that the actual quality level of our delivery is 1.0. Therefore, we should go to the point marked 1.0 on the horizontal axis. Now let's travel upward from this point until we reach the curve marked 0.65 for our AQL. If we move to the left from this intersection, we will find that the percentage of lots we will expect to accept under this sampling plan will be just slightly greater than 85 percent. This is the 87 percent consumer's risk we calculated in the previous section.

Now, let's locate an actual quality level of 0.65 on the horizontal axis. The axis is marked at 0.60 and 0.80, so 0.65 will be one fourth of the distance from 0.60 to 0.80. You might wish to put a ruler here to help you find the percent of lots expected to be accepted. The intersection with our 0.65 AQL curve shows a

A BEGINNER'S GUIDE TO QUALITY IN MANUFACTURING

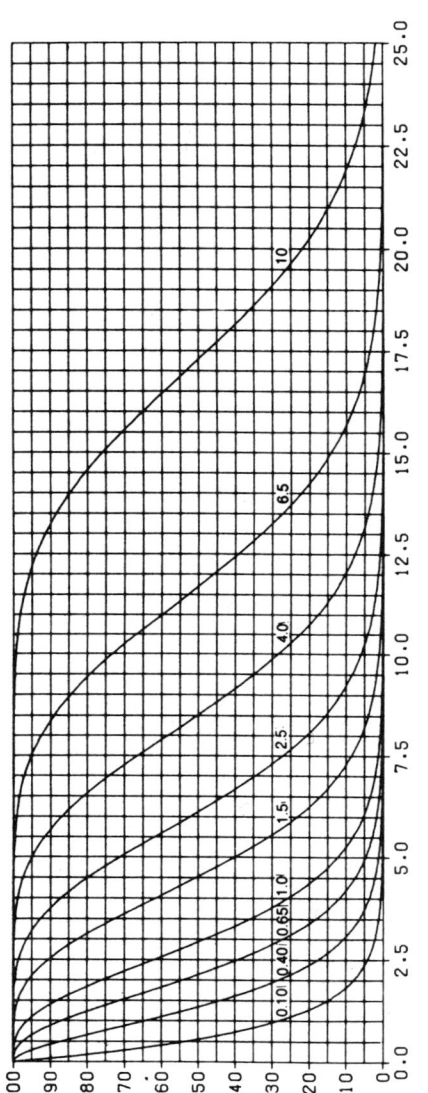

Figure 7.3: Operating Characteristic Curves for Single Sampling Plans Using Sample Size Code Letter K

THE MATHEMATICS OF QUALITY CONTROL

probability of acceptance which is slightly above 95 percent. Earlier, we had calculated that $P_a = 0.95132$ when both the AQL and the actual quality level of a shipment equaled 0.65. Once again, the 95 percent acceptance level shown on the operating characteristics curve chart agrees with our prior calculations.

Let's look at other cases where the actual quality level equals our AQL target.

Locate the curve for an AQL of 1.0 and find the true quality level of 1.0 along the horizontal axis. The percentage of lots expected to be accepted is approximately 95 percent. Do the same for both an AQL of 0.40 and a true quality level of 0.40. In each case the $P_a = 95$ percent.

As we've indicated, our level of confidence in using a sampling plan from MIL-STD-105E is 0.95 (95 percent). That is, if a supplier manufactures a product which consistently meets our required AQL target, we will accept approximately 95 percent of the batches. Once again this assumes that the deliveries will be of equal size and evaluated using the same inspection plan.

We should also note that as the producer's quality level improves, the probability of acceptance is greater. Conversely, when the producer's quality level drops and he begins delivering more defective boards, the probability of acceptance dwindles. If his quality level is 2.0, the probability of acceptance is only about 50 percent.

If the sampling plan worked to perfection, the operating characteristic curve would look significantly different. For an AQL of 0.65, the graph appears in Figure 7.4.

This curve would give 100 percent acceptance if the producer's quality level was 0.65 or better and 0 percent acceptance if the quality level was worse than 0.65.

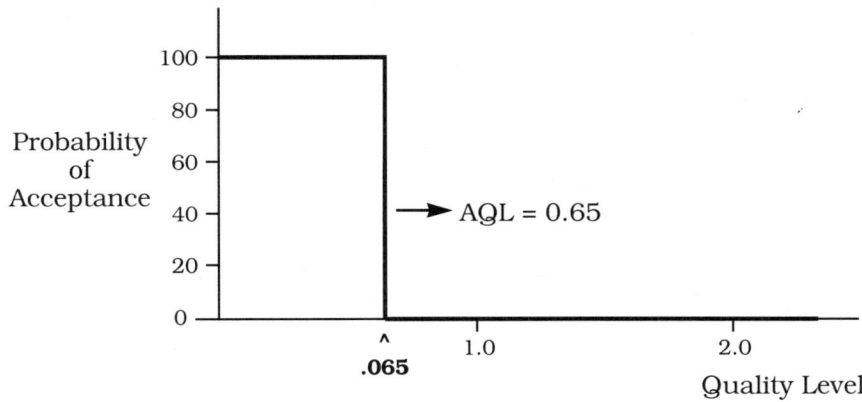

Figure 7.4: Operating Characteristics Curve for Perfect Sampling Plan

MIL-STD-105E provides tabulated values for the operating characteristic curves in Table 7.2. Although the table should be based on the binomial distribution, it is easier for the statistician to use a formula based on another distribution called the Poisson distribution. Within the range of values used in our sampling plans, the two distributions give values that are very close, so the table has been constructed using the Poisson distribution as an approximation to the binomial. The mathematics for the Poisson distribution are beyond the scope of this book.

The values given in this table are the same as those graphed on the operating characteristics curve, but are presented in a form that may be easier to read. Again, locating an AQL of 0.65 along the top, and a P_a of 95.0 on the left, we find that this probability of acceptance occurs when the quality level (percent defective) is 0.65.

7.8 Tightened Inspection

As we've seen, if our AQL target is 0.65 and the manufacturer's quality level is 1.0, we will still be accepting 87 percent of the lots, an unacceptably high rate. MIL-STD-105E adjusts for this by having us move to a tightened inspection plan. We make this change when two out of five consecutive lots have been rejected on original inspection. Since inspection is an ongoing process, the calculation of instituting tightened inspection is quite complicated, but we will provide a model to give a feeling for when this happens.

Let us assume that we have accepted quite a few consecutive lots and have just rejected one lot. Since the probability of rejection is 13 percent (1 − 0.87), this was inevitable. Now, if we accept the next four lots, we would stay on normal inspection. On the other hand, if we reject even one of the next four lots, we will have rejected at least two out of five consecutive lots and will institute tightened inspection.

In our model, what will be the probability of rejecting one or more of the next four lots? It will be easier to compute the probability of accepting the next four lots and subtracting from 1. With $p = 0.87$ and $q = 0.13$,

$$P_4(4) = \frac{4!}{4! * (4-4)!} * (0.87)^4 * (0.13)^0$$

$$= \frac{4!}{4! * 0!} * 0.573 * 1$$

$$= 1 * 0.573 * 1$$

$$P_4(4) = 0.573 \qquad 1 - P_4(4) = 0.427$$

P_a	Acceptable Quality Levels (normal inspection)											
	0.10	0.40	0.65	1.0	1.5	2.5	X	4.0	X	6.5	X	10
	p (in percent defective or defects per hundred units)											
99.0	0.00804	0.119	0.349	0.659	1.43	2.32	2.81	3.82	4.88	5.98	8.28	10.1
95.0	0.0410	0.284	0.654	1.09	2.09	3.18	3.76	4.94	6.15	7.40	9.95	11.9
90.0	0.0843	0.425	0.882	1.40	2.52	3.72	4.35	5.62	6.92	8.24	10.9	13.0
75.0	0.230	0.769	1.382	2.03	3.38	4.76	5.47	6.90	8.34	9.79	12.7	14.9
50.0	0.555	1.34	2.14	2.94	4.54	6.14	6.94	8.53	10.1	11.7	14.9	17.3
25.0	1.11	2.15	3.14	4.09	5.94	7.75	8.64	10.4	12.2	13.9	17.4	20.0
10.0	1.84	3.11	4.26	5.34	7.42	9.42	10.4	12.3	14.2	16.1	19.8	22.5
5.0	2.40	3.80	5.04	6.20	8.41	10.5	11.5	13.6	15.6	17.5	21.4	24.2
1.0	3.68	5.31	6.72	8.04	10.5	12.8	18.3	16.1	18.3	20.4	24.5	27.5
	0.15	0.65	1.0	1.5	2.5	X	4.0	X	6.5	X	10	X
	Acceptable Quality Levels (tightened inspection)											

Note: All values given in above table based on Poisson distribution as an approximation to the Binomial.

Table 7.2: Tabulated Values for Operating Characteristic Curves for Single Sampling Plans

Summarizing, the probability of accepting four consecutive lots is 57 percent; the probability of rejecting at least one lot is 43 percent. This is a very high probability. It means that if the manufacturer provides us with a quality level of 1.0, we will soon be on tightened inspection.

Once we've made our switch to a tightened inspection plan, we can refer to Table 7.2 for the tabulated values showing probabilities of acceptance at various AQL targets and true producer quality levels. Along the bottom, find our AQL of 0.65. Look up the column. If the quality level is 1.0 (somewhere between 0.769 and 1.34), the probability of acceptance is between 75 percent and 50 percent. To calculate the probability of acceptance exactly, we can once again use our formula for cumulative probability. On tightened inspection, we keep our sample size at 125 but accept a lot only if there is one or zero defects. Therefore, the value of P_a is

$$P_a = P_{125}(1) + P_{125}(0)$$

Since: $P_{125}(1) = \dfrac{125!}{1! * (125-1)!} * (0.01)^1 * (0.99)^{124} = 0.359$

and: $P_{125}(0) = \dfrac{125!}{0! * (125-0)!} * (0.01)^0 * (0.99)^{125} = 0.285$

we have $P_a = 0.644$ or 64%

This 64 percent probability of accepting a bad lot while using a tightened inspection plan is significantly lower than the 87 percent probability we found with normal inspection.

To return to normal inspection, we must accept five consecutive lots. Since the probability of accepting a single bad batch is so low, the probability of accepting five consecutive lots on tightened inspection is very low unless the provider substantially improves the true quality level. MIL-STD-105E terminates all deliveries from suppliers who remain on a tightened inspection plan for 10 consecutive lots due to an inability to improve their quality.

THE MATHEMATICS OF QUALITY CONTROL

Chapter Summary

1. Every acceptance sampling plan involves a consumer's risk of accepting a batch that does not meet AQL targets. Similarly, sampling plans involve a producer's risk that batches that meet AQL targets will be rejected.

2. The probability that an event that has a probability of occurring of p (and a probability of not occurring of $q = 1 - p$) will happen exactly r times in n repetitions of an event is given

$$P_n(r) = \frac{n!}{r! \times (n-r)!} * p^r * q^{n-r}$$

3. The binomial distribution is a mathematical formula that closely resembles the normal curve. It tabulates the values for exactly r successes in n repetitions of an event.

4. Cumulative probability allows us to compute the probability of either r or fewer successes, or r or more successes, in n repetitions of an event.

5. An acceptance sampling plan's level of confidence represents the percentage of shipments we will accept if a supplier consistently supplies a product which exactly meets our required AQL. MIL-STD-105E is based on a 95 percent confidence level. This assumes that the supplier delivers batches of approximately the same size which are evaluated using the same inspection plan.

6. The probability of acceptance is denoted as P_a. The producer's risk is $1 - P_a$.

7. Operating characteristic curves and the associated tabulated values provide us with the probability of acceptance based on various AQLs and true producer quality levels.

8. Tightened inspection allows us to reduce the consumer's risk of accepting shipments that do not meet our required AQLs.

A BEGINNER'S GUIDE TO QUALITY IN MANUFACTURING

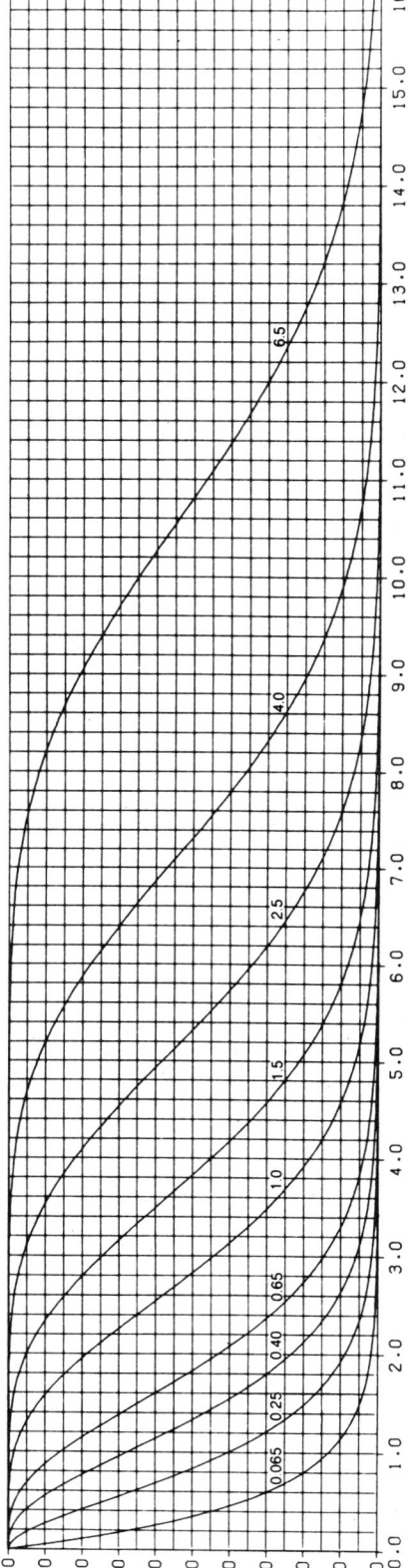

Figure 7.5: Operating Characteristic Curves for Single Sampling Plans for Sample Size Code Letter L

THE MATHEMATICS OF QUALITY CONTROL

Questions for Chapter 7

1. For a batch size of 4,000 units and General Inspection Level II, the corresponding operating characteristics curves appear in Figure 7.5. Using the graph and an AQL of 0.65, find the percentage of lots expected to be accepted if the quality of the submitted lot is

    a. 4.0

    b. 3.0

    c. 2.6

    d. 2.0

    e. 1.5

    f. 1.0

    g. 0.8

    h. 0.65

    i. 0.6

    j. 0.2

2. Repeat problem 1 for an AQL of 1.0 and an AQL of 0.40.

3. Using the same graph as in problem 1, give the corresponding quality of submitted lots if 75 percent of the lots are expected to be accepted and the AQL is

    a. 0.065

    b. 0.25

    c. 0.40

    d. 0.65

    e. 1.0

    f. 1.5

    g. 2.5

    h. 4.0

    i. 6.5

A BEGINNER'S GUIDE TO QUALITY IN MANUFACTURING

P_a	0.065	0.25	0.40	0.65	1.0	1.5		2.5		4.0		6.5
							Acceptable Quality Levels (normal inspection)					
		p (in percent defective or defects per hundred units)										
99.0	0.00503	0.075	0.218	0.412	0.893	1.45	×	2.39	3.05	3.74	5.17	6.29
95.0	0.0256	0.178	0.409	0.683	1.31	1.99	2.35	3.08	3.84	4.62	6.22	7.45
90.0	0.0527	0.266	0.551	0.872	1.58	2.33	2.72	3.51	4.32	5.15	6.84	8.12
75.0	0.144	0.481	0.864	1.27	2.11	2.98	3.42	4.31	5.21	6.12	7.95	9.34
50.0	0.347	0.839	1.34	1.84	2.84	3.84	4.33	5.33	6.33	7.33	9.33	10.8
25.0	0.693	1.35	1.96	2.55	3.71	4.83	5.40	6.51	7.61	8.70	10.9	12.5
10.0	1.15	1.94	2.66	3.34	4.64	5.89	6.50	7.70	8.89	10.1	12.4	14.1
5.0	1.50	2.37	3.15	3.88	5.26	6.57	7.22	8.48	9.72	10.9	13.3	15.1
1.0	2.30	3.32	4.20	5.02	6.55	8.00	8.70	10.1	11.4	12.7	15.3	17.2
	0.10	0.40	0.65	1.0	1.5	×	2.5		4.0		6.5	×
							Acceptable Quality Levels (tightened inspection)					

Note: All values given in above table based on Poisson distribution as an approximation to the Binomial.

Table 7.3: Tabulated Values for Operating Characteristic Curves for Single Sampling Plans

THE MATHEMATICS OF QUALITY CONTROL

4. Repeat problem 3 if 95 percent of the lots are expected to be accepted.

5. Using Table 7.3, and a probability of acceptance of 75 percent, read the percent defective for an AQL of

    a. 0.065

    b. 0.25

    c. 0.40

    d. 0.65

    e. 1.0

    f. 1.5

    g. 2.5

    h. 4.0

    i. 6.5

    Compare these values with your answers to problem 3.

6. Repeat problem 5 if tightened inspection has been instituted.

7. Assume that the probability of rolling a 5 on one die is 0.16. Suppose this die is rolled six times. Compute the expectation of rolling exactly these numbers of fives on these six rolls:

    a. 3

    b. 2

    c. 1

    d. 0

    What is the probability of rolling two or fewer fives?

A BEGINNER'S GUIDE TO QUALITY IN MANUFACTURING

8. Compute the following:

   a. $P_{10}(3)$ if $p = 0.9$

   b. $P_8(2)$ if $p = 0.7$

9. What is the meaning of a 0.90 level of confidence?

FINAL INSPECTION

8.1 Introduction

In chapter 1, we discussed the customer's expectations for the product. The manufacturer's goal was to meet or exceed those demands. To do this, the manufacturer had to clearly define the customer's needs and requirements. The manufacturer did this by establishing specifications. Wherever possible, these specifications were defined in quantitative terms so the manufacturer could determine whether the product was acceptable.

The manufacturer soon found that not every product was made exactly to its specification. However, the manufacturer also learned that a product might be acceptable to the customer even if it did not meet the target specification exactly. These acceptable variations in a product's specifications are called tolerances.

Despite our efforts to ensure the quality of our purchased materials and control the quality of our own production efforts, our manufacturing process will still generate some defective finished products.

Final inspection is the last point in the manufacturing process where we can verify that the product is acceptable for the customer. In this chapter, we will discuss how manufacturers can use the techniques of 100 percent inspection, visual inspection, and quality audits to verify the quality of their finished products.

We will also examine the "fitness for use" decision which manufacturers must make when they find products which do not conform to specifications.

8.2 Need for Final Inspection

As we have seen in prior chapters, our manufacturers have devoted considerable effort to ensuring the production of goods which meet their specifications. The companies have carefully specified and inspected their raw materials and purchased component parts. They have also identified the quality levels of their own production processes and instituted controls to ensure that they consistently perform at these specified standards.

Unfortunately, despite these efforts, each of our manufacturers will continue to produce a certain number of finished products which fail to meet specifications. We must remember that our AQL targets for both incoming inspections and statistical process controls presume the production of at least some defects. These quality tools enable us to limit the numbers of our defective products and continually improve our product quality. Nevertheless, most manufacturers will continue to generate some finished products with defects.

Final inspection offers the manufacturer with his last opportunity to catch these defective products before they are shipped to the customer. As a result, final inspection is the manufacturer's tool for avoiding additional financial expenses of product replacement, field service, and other warranty costs. Even more important, it allows the manufacturer to avoid serious damage to customer satisfaction and the firm's reputation for quality.

The Radio Manufacturer and 100 Percent Inspection

Let's begin our review of the final inspection process by examining the procedures used by the AM radio manufacturer.

The company begins its final inspection process after all the electronic components have been assembled and connected. At this point in production, every unit should be functional. The radio is only lacking its case and product literature. The advantage of testing at this point is that the radio can be easily placed in a test fixture, powered up, and connected to a radio signal. The operator can easily tune the radio and determine if it plays.

The manufacturer has decided to use 100 percent inspection at this point. She will test each and every radio produced.

The use of 100 percent inspection must certainly be a source of mixed emotions for most manufacturers. On one hand, testing each and every product virtually guarantees that the customer will receive no products which do not meet specifications. On the other hand, since inspections have their own costs in time and money, we would like to do as few as possible. Despite these costs, 100 percent inspection is frequently used during the final inspection process. This is particularly true for complex products like the radio where an ability to function must be tested.

Another consideration in the use of 100 percent inspection is the time, trouble, and resulting cost associated with each individual product test. As we've noted, the radio manufacturer uses an automated test fixture which allows the operator to rapidly inspect each radio. The increasing availability of computerized test equipment makes 100 percent inspection more practical and less expensive for a wide variety of products. The use of this computerized equipment reduces the time and manpower requirements for inspection programs and increases the amount of data on product performance which can be stored and analyzed.

The radio manufacturer has balanced her ability to do a rapid test of each radio at this stage against the disadvantage that not all the parameters of the radio, like sensitivity and output power, are quantitatively tested. The manufacturer knows this and uses other techniques during the final inspection process to make these evaluations. They will be discussed at the end of this section.

The Radio Manufacturer and Visual Inspection

The next step in the final inspection process begins after the radios have been put in their cases. An employee conducts a visual inspection of the finished product.

Once again, the manufacturer uses visual inspections on a 100 percent basis since the inspection can be done quickly and at low cost.

Visual inspection relies on a precise sensor and a highly sophisticated computer—the human eye and the human mind. These inspections are primarily used to judge the aesthetic acceptability of the product: Does the product have any cosmetic defects, e.g., streaks, chips, or smudges? Is it the right color? The advantage of the visual inspection is that it does a complicated inspection quickly.

While it sounds simple and straightforward, a visual inspection program actually poses some interesting problems.

The first challenge in setting up a visual inspection program is making sure that the inspector knows what to look for. The AM radio manufacturer, for example, has written the following specification:

Visual Inspection of AM Radios

1. *Case color* The color of the case shall be consistent over the surface of the entire case. There shall be no lines or other discolorations.

2. *Scratches and other case disfigurations* There shall be no scratches or other case disfigurations on the radio.

3. *Case printing* Printing on dial settings, volume settings, and label information shall be readable and without defect.

A written specification is a good start. Unfortunately, it still leaves a lot of room for individual interpretation on the part of inspectors. For example, they may have some doubt as to the types of lines or discoloration which would make the radio unacceptable.

Since one picture is worth a thousand words, the manufacturer can offer further guidance to her inspectors by providing a series of photographs which help define unacceptable discoloration, unacceptable scratch marks, or unreadable print.

A second concern in visual inspection programs is making certain that inspectors always look at things the same way. Such factors as light intensity, the viewing angle, the background, and the distance between the product and the inspector must be kept constant for each inspection. To ensure consistent results, the inspector has constructed a test fixture. This fixture is open on both sides so that the radio can be easily placed on the fixture floor, which is marked so that radios are placed in the same spot every time. A light in the fixture ensures the radio is viewed under the same conditions every time. Finally, there is a glass cover to ensure each radio is viewed from the same distance and viewing angle every time.

The final problems to be overcome in visual inspection programs are inconsistencies in employee performance and the monotony of the task itself. The ability to consistently identify defects through visual inspections will vary from individual to individual. Consequently, careful selection of employees for these programs is important. Similarly, there is generally a need to break up the tedium associated with repeated visual inspections over an extended period of time. This tedium can easily numb an inspector's reaction to product defects and limit the effectiveness of the inspection process itself.

The radio manufacturer attempts to avoid this problem by periodically requiring her inspectors to perform an alternate task. A buzzer sounds every hour to indicate that the inspector should conduct a test. The inspector puts a battery in one of the radios to test whether the radio plays. This functional test relieves the tedium of the visual inspection and provides additional monitoring of the manufacturing process.

The Radio Manufacturer and Product Quality Audits

Once daily, a *product quality audit* is performed by a quality control inspector. This is the last step in the final inspection of the AM radio. The primary aim of the product quality audit is to determine whether quality controls applied earlier in the process are identifying and eliminating defects on a systematic basis.

During the audit, five radios are taken from stock that has been packaged for shipment. As the radio is carefully unpacked, the inspector checks that the radio was properly packaged with the user's manual and the warranty information. The inspector carefully examines the case for any discoloration or scratches. Printing on the radio is checked for readability. The case is then measured for height, width, and depth, and all values are checked for compliance to the specification tolerances.

After these initial inspections, the radio is subjected to electrical testing. It's sensitivity, selectivity, power output, harmonic distortion, and frequency range are checked to ensure they are within tolerance limits.

The inspector keeps track of all these values by using a data page similar to the one in Figure 8.1. Notice that, for acceptable samples, the answers to the first six questions will be *Yes*. This simplifies reviewing the data page. Any *No* answer would be reason for action.

Model number: _____ Revision level: _____
Inspector: _____ Inspection date: _____

Packaging and Case Inspection

1. All packaging material present: Yes ___ No ___
2. User's manual present: Yes ___ No ___
3. Warranty information present: Yes ___ No ___
4. Case free from discoloration: Yes ___ No ___
5. Case free from scratches: Yes ___ No ___
6. Case printing is readable: Yes ___ No ___
7. Case height = _____ (inches)
8. Case width   = _____ (inches)
9. Case depth   = _____ (inches)

Electrical Characteristics

1. Frequency range: _____ (KHz) to _____ (KHz)
2. Sensitivity: _____ (micro-volts)
3. Selectivity: _____ (dB)
4. Harmonic distortion: ____ (%) at rated power into 8 ohms
5. Power output: _____ (milliwatts)
Corrective action (if required):_____
_____

Figure 8.1: Quality Control Audit Final Inspection for AM Radio

All electrical measurements—frequency range, sensitivity, selectivity, harmonic distortion, and power output—are logged onto control charts. Trends are watched carefully by quality control engineers. Any tendencies that may lead to out-of-tolerance measurements are investigated.

The product quality audit is most useful for inspections and tests that require significant time to perform. When tests cannot be done quickly and cost effectively, they must be done as part of a sampling program. As we have seen, the radio manufacturer finds that it is too complicated and expensive to fully test all of the radio's electrical measurements during 100 percent testing of the radio prior to packaging. Consequently, she uses the product quality audit to test these measurements on a sample basis.

The audit is also useful for identifying problems which result after final product inspections. It can identify damage done to the product during the packaging or problems with the packaging process itself. The radio manufacturer's product quality audit, for example, identified a problem with missing user manuals and warranty cards that were not being included during packaging.

However, the product quality audit does not focus only on quality problems arising at the end of the process. Rather, it allows a quality assessment of the finished product and the production process as a whole. The control charts which are maintained on all specification measurements—size, electrical readings, etc.—can help to uncover problems in any phase of the manufacturing process.

Based on final inspection efforts, the radio manufacturer is hopeful that customers will receive only products that meet their specifications. She cannot be certain, however, that they will be fully satisfied. In chapter 9, we will see how the manufacturer uses customer feedback and field data to continue evaluating the quality of her product even after it has left the factory.

8.3 Final Inspection and Testing at the Closet Door Manufacturer

The closet door manufacturer must also use the final inspection process to ensure that no defective products reach his customers. Although the specific inspection and testing procedures will differ, he will employ the same quality control tools as the radio manufacturer.

The company will use 100 percent inspection to ensure that the doors are the correct height, width, and depth. Once again, automated test equipment will allow the door manufacturer to minimize the time and trouble involved in the inspection process. As the door moves off the sanding equipment, gauges measure the width and thickness. Optical equipment measures the height. All this information is automatically fed into a computer. The computer checks the measured values against the tolerance limits and uses the data to make control charts that monitor production. If any dimension is beyond tolerance limits, an alarm sounds and the monitor on the computer indicates the dimension that is in error.

Like the radio manufacturer, the door company uses 100 percent visual inspection to ensure that each of the doors is free from cosmetic imperfections. After the door is sanded and measured, inspectors examine the surface of the door for scratches, cracks, and knotholes. The manufacturer has combined the visual inspection process with the task of moving the doors into position for bulk packaging. This combined function allows the use of two inspectors who share responsibility for the inspection and the physical work of transporting the finished doors. This dual inspection/packaging activity also helps alleviate the boredom associated with the visual inspection process.

Finally, the door manufacturer also utilizes a product quality audit. Every four hours, the quality control department takes a door just before it is bulk packaged. The sample door is examined in detail. The height, width, and depth measurements are checked against specifications. Although we have conducted a 100 percent inspection of these measurements, the product quality audit checks the accuracy of the automated measuring equipment. The location and dimensions of the hinge mortises and doorknob holes are compared to the specifications. The door inspector does the inspection with the aid of a computer. The computer asks specific questions. The inspector makes the measurements or answers the questions by inputting the information into the computer via the computer keyboard. The computer uses this data to generate control charts for all the measurements that are made. If any measurement is found to be out of tolerance or if an unacceptable trend is detected, the computer sounds a buzzer and indicates the problem on the screen. Automatically, the appropriate control chart appears on the computer monitor. The inspector can make an analysis and take whatever corrective actions are necessary.

8.4 Final Inspection and Testing at the Bakery

The baker must also follow a plan for final inspection to ensure that his bread is of the highest quality. The loaves are sold mainly to restaurants, and the appearance of the bread is very important to the customer. The bread also must taste good and have the necessary vitamins and nutrients.

The baker has designated one employee to do most of the analysis on the incoming ingredients, and this staff member will also do a nutritional analysis of the baked bread. This test procedure is time-consuming and will be done once a week. Records are kept and compared to specification guidelines.

The baker will use a visual inspection to check the color, shape, and size of the finished loaf. To assist staff in making this judgment, the baker has made plaster models of two loaves. One is the lightest acceptable color and the smallest acceptable size. The other model is the darkest color and largest size that is permitted to be shipped.

Finally, the taste of the bread must be ensured. A master baker employed to oversee the bread-baking process is responsible for tasting a slice from every lot of bread made. The master baker suggested that the bread be offered to the employees during their break time. They were instructed to alert the master baker if the bread did not taste just right.

Even though the bakery is a small operation, it still follows quality control principles and practices. A 100 percent visual inspection is done for color, size, and shape. Vitamin and nutrient content analysis are done on a sampling basis as part of what could be called a quality control audit. Taste testing is also done on a sampling basis. Since taste is so important, the baker encourages the entire staff to participate in the process.

8.5 The "Fitness for Use" Decision

Once our manufacturers have identified certain finished products which do not meet specifications, another question arises: What should be done with them?

In chapter 1, we defined quality as conformance to specifications. Our door manufacturer, as you will remember, originally estimated that four of every 10 doors failed to meet specifications. At that time, he was simply disposing of the defective products at a cost of $22.29 each. The losses associated with this lack of quality were quickly driving the company out of business.

Since then, the manufacturer has substantially improved product quality. Nevertheless, he is still producing at least some doors which fail to meet specifications, and there are still costs associated with these defective products.

Despite their lack of "quality," these defective doors may actually be perfectly acceptable to the customer—or at least to certain customers under certain conditions. By finding appropriate uses for these nonconforming products, the manufacturer can avoid losing some or all of the money involved in their production. The process by which manufacturers evaluate defective finished products and identify the most cost-effective disposition of them is known as the *"fitness for use" decision.* To understand this process better, let's take a closer look at the closet door manufacturer.

As part of the final inspection process, the manufacturer removes all doors which fail to meet specifications to a holding area adjacent to the bulk packaging station. Here, the nonconforming doors are sorted according to defect. Doors that are too long or too wide go on one pile. Doors that are too short or too narrow go on another. Doors that have minor cosmetic defects are placed in a third stack. Doors that have serious cracks or major damage on the face panels are set aside.

The manufacturer has established a formal process for evaluating these defective products and determining what to do with each one. Twice weekly, a meeting is held with representatives of the company's quality control, manufacturing engineering, and sales departments. These representatives examine the defective doors and make their decisions.

Doors with minor cosmetic defects are carefully examined by the sales department and, where appropriate, routed into shipments destined for a customer who uses them for industrial construction projects. The sales staff's experience indicates that this customer rarely worries about the decorative quality of the doors and will accept delivery of officially "defective" products with a modest reduction in price.

Doors with more serious cosmetic problems are set aside to be offered at a discount through salvage sales at the company's factory outlet.

Doors that are too tall or too wide are carefully evaluated by the manufacturing engineer and, where economically feasible, sent back to special rework stations for repair and reassembly.

Doors that have been cut too short or too narrow are examined by the quality control representative. Those that exceed the minimum tolerance by less than 1/8" are also assigned to the factory outlet's salvage sale. Those that exceed the minimum tolerance by more than 1/8" are simply scrapped.

By formalizing these standards for disposing of defective finished products, the door manufacturer has maximized profits without endangering his reputation for product quality. Customers receive only products that have been evaluated as fit for their use. Where applicable, defective products are marked as such and sold at a discount to customers who understand what they are getting. Finally, nonconforming doors cannot be scrapped until they are reviewed to ensure that they cannot be economically reworked and sold.

Chapter Summary

1. 100 percent inspection and testing is a quality check done on every product. It must be done cost effectively: quickly, with little labor involvement, and without damaging or altering the product.

2. Visual inspection utilizes plant personnel to identify unacceptable characteristics. This type of inspection does a complicated function quickly. Photographs, models, or samples should be used to help inspectors decide on the acceptability of the product. This inspection can become tedious. To avoid this problem, the tedium of the visual inspection should be broken with other tasks, or inspectors should be relieved on a periodic basis.

3. The quality control audit is a sampling process done by the quality control department to monitor quality levels. During the final inspection process, it should probe all the characteristics of the product.

4. The "fitness for use" decision determines what is to be done with products that do not meet specifications. Some units will be reworked; alternate markets will be found for others; and some will be scrapped.

FINAL INSPECTION

Questions for Chapter 8

1. What are three techniques that verify the quality of a finished product?

2. List the items that an inspector will be looking for during a visual inspection of the closet door. Then create a specification for the "Visual Inspection of the Closet Door" that the inspec-tor would refer to during visual inspection.

3. During the quality control audit, the closet door is thoroughly inspected. List all the items that the inspector will inspect and measure. Design a data sheet to be used for the "Quality Control Audit, Final Inspection for Closet Door." Use the data sheet for the "quality control audit for AM Radio" as a model.

4. List the items that an inspector will be looking for during a visual inspection of a loaf of bread. Then create a specification for the "Visual Inspection of a Loaf of Bread" that the inspector would refer to during visual inspection.

5. During the quality control audit, the loaf of bread is thoroughly inspected. List all of the items the inspector will inspect and measure. (Refer to the packaging on a purchased loaf of bread for nutrient and vitamin content.) Design a data sheet for the "Quality Control Audit, Final Inspection for Loaf of Bread." Use the data sheet for the "Quality Control Audit for AM Radio" as a model.

6. Although loaves of bread that do not meet our color, size, shape, nutrient, and even taste specifications cannot be delivered to our usual customers, they do have "fitness for use" salvageable value. For each defect, or combination of defects, list customers who would be interested in purchasing our bread, probably at a reduced price.

FINAL INSPECTION

Chapter 8 Project

1. For the product that you have chosen to manufacture, decide where in the flowchart you would insert 100 percent inspection. At each place that you are going to insert 100 percent inspection, list which items you are going to inspect and how you are going to inspect them. At each of these inspection points, consider whether it is cost-effective to have 100 percent inspection. Would sampling be more cost-effective?

2. Where would you insert visual inspection? What will your inspector be looking for? How will you set up the process so that there is consistency in your inspection? Prepare a specification for the inspector to use during this visual inspection.

3. List the items that the inspector will inspect and measure during the product quality audit. Design a data sheet for a product quality audit of your product.

4. Is there a "fitness for use" of your defective units? Give prospective consumers for units that have each type, or combination of types, of defects.

QUALITY CONTROL AND FIELD DATA

9.1 Introduction

We have spent the preceding eight chapters learning about ways to ensure that the product leaves the factory complying with our specifications. If all of our efforts have proved effective and our product arrives at its destination without any perceptible defects, we might expect that the only customer comments would be praise. Unfortunately, this is not always the case.

There are other factors that affect our product. Components malfunction in the field and cause the product to degrade or stop working altogether. Environmental stress, like severe temperatures, can cause the product to fail. The customer may not understand how to use the product or may abuse it. The customer may not be satisfied with the way the product works, even though it meets specifications. All these problems occur at the customer's location. They are known as *field failures*.

The manufacturer must be concerned with all these quality-related issues. They directly affect its reputation and therefore its ability to sell and stay in business. In this chapter we will discuss these problems and their solutions. In addition, we will discuss ways the manufacturer can reach out to customers to ensure that its reputation for quality is at a high level.

9.2 Reasons for Field Returns

Component failures and *component malfunctions* are one source of field failures and field returns. The component, like a resistor in a radio, may be fine during the inspection at the factory. The product travels to the customer site, and after a period of time the component malfunctions and brings the product out of specification. The customer cannot use the radio and returns it to the manufacturer for replacement or refund.

In addition to component failures, there are also *manufacturing defects* that can test acceptably in the factory but cause the product to fail in the field. A manufacturing defect is a defect that is a result of an unsuccessful manufacturing process. Soldering is an example of a manufacturing process that can lead to field returns. During the auto insertion process at the radio manufacturing plant, components were attached mechanically to the PCB and then soldered to ensure an electrical connection. Even if one of these components were not soldered properly, the unit could conceivably pass factory inspection. However, once the radio was out in the field, normal handling could lead to a broken connection and cause the radio to fail. Field returns, when properly analyzed, can uncover manufacturing process problems.

Customer abuse can also lead to field returns. People drop things; they don't always follow installation instructions properly; they exert too much force on the product. People make mistakes. The manufacturer must protect against these recurring mistakes by designing the product to withstand the punishment customers will dish out.

A hammer, for example, is a tool that is sometimes used on a ladder. It is not unusual for a hammer to fall two stories to the ground. A manufacturer who wants to avoid potential field returns will design the hammer to survive this drop. Similarly, our closet door manufacturer has constructed the door to withstand being kicked shut and yanked open. The radio manufacturer has built the radio so that it can survive a fall from a 30"-high table.

On the other hand, a manufacturer cannot design the product to withstand every possible form of abuse. While a hammer must withstand a two-story drop, an AM radio need not. The radio is not intended for use on tall ladders, and it would be rare indeed for it to fall such a distance. Therefore, there is no reason to increase its cost by designing it to survive such an extraordinary event.

Environmental stress is another source of field returns. A product made for outside use must survive in rain, snow, and wind. Products used in unventilated attics must withstand extremely high temperatures. Lightning creates problems for sensitive electronic products. For perishable products, like bread, time is the enemy. A manufacturer must know where the product is going to be used to protect it against the hazards of the environment.

Field returns that are a result of environmental stress are usually analyzed by the quality engineer familiar with environmental testing. When failures due to environmental stress reoccur frequently, one solution is to redesign the product. Another alternative is to provide warnings to the customer so that the product will not be exposed to stresses that will cause failure.

Electrical products like receptacles and extension cords are clearly marked for use either outdoors or indoors.

Some products will be returned when there are actually no defects. Sometimes the customer will not know how to use the product or understand when it is functioning correctly. A sophisticated videocassette recorder, for example, may be capable of recording up to 32 different programs on 88 separate channels. However, consumers who do not understand how to correctly adjust the picture quality will feel that the product is defective. A well-written user's manual can spell the difference between a satisfied customer and a service call. The computer software industry quickly became aware of the importance of this concept and coined the phrase "user-friendly."

Customers may also find that the product does not meet their original requirements. Sales staff must guard against the urge to "oversell" by creating expectations which exceed their product's actual capabilities. The dissatisfaction that results will only lead to unwanted field returns.

9.3 Field Returns and Customer Complaints

Field returns and customer complaints offer the manufacturer an opportunity to judge exactly how fit for use the product really is. When a customer complains about a product, it is important to retrieve the failed product for analysis. It is also important to question the customer regarding the complaint and to be sure the product was being used for its intended purpose. Customer complaint information should be carefully recorded. Armed with the returned product and the customer complaint, the quality department can take steps to avoid similar field failures in future production.

Field return analysis will follow the same basic steps we have outlined in previous chapters. First, we will make observations on the field returns, then analyze the data to identify causes of the problems and possible solutions. Finally, the manufacturer will revise the production process and make additional observations to determine whether the revisions have solved the problem.

The radio manufacturer, for example, has organized a repair department to receive field returns. The repair department is responsible for determining the reason for failure, fixing the returns, reporting the problem, and reporting how long the unit has been in the field. These data are sent to the quality control department for analysis and recommendations. In some companies the quality assurance department performs this function. Table 9.1 is a monthly summary report of the field return data that was supplied to the Quality Control Department.

A BEGINNER'S GUIDE TO QUALITY IN MANUFACTURING

Defective Part	Frequency	Service Life (months)	Defect Description
R1	4	1, 3, 2, 1	Resistor open
C2	10	1, 1, 3, 2, 2 3, 1, 4, 2, 2	Shorted capacitor
Speaker	5	1, 2, 1, 1, 2	Open at solder connection
D2	1	2	Shorted diode
Earphone jack	1	14	Broken internally
T5	3	24, 27, 26	Open base to collector junction in transistor
Switch/volume control	2	30, 35	Broken knob
CND	2	1, 1	CND (Cannot determine any cause of failure)

Table 9.1: Field Return Data from the Repair Department

After receiving the data from the Repair Department, the quality engineer will start the analysis.

First, the engineer calculates the *rate of return* for the month. The rate of return is defined as the percentage of returned units for the month divided by the average number of units produced in a month. The formula for rate of return is

$$\text{Rate of Return} = \frac{\text{Number of Returns}}{\text{Average Number of Devices Made}} * 100\%$$

Using this equation, let's calculate the monthly rate of return reported in Table 9.1. The total number of returns was 28. This is determined by totaling the frequency column. The average number of radios produced in a month is 26,400. The monthly return rate is calculated

$$\text{Rate of Return} = \frac{\text{Number of Returns}}{\text{Average Number of Devices Made}} * 100\%$$

$$\text{Rate of Return} = \frac{28}{26,400} * 100\%$$

$$\text{Rate of Return} = 0.11\%$$

QUALITY CONTROL AND FIELD DATA

This means that approximately one out of 1,000 radios is returned from the field. As with defects during production, the manufacturer is always looking for ways to reduce her rate of return.

Next, the engineer calculates the new defective rate. The radio manufacturer defines a new defective as any defective unit that is returned within three months of the date it was made. This measure indicates the number of units that have suffered from *product infant mortality*. Product infant mortality occurs when a component in a field unit has malfunctioned very early in its life. Each industry or manufacturer may wish to define the product infant mortality period differently. The new defective rate is determined by dividing the number of new defectives by the average number of products made for a particular period and then multiplying by 100 percent. The formula for calculating the new defective rate is

$$\text{New Defective Rate} = \frac{\text{Number of New Defectives}}{\text{Average Number of Devices Made}} * 100\%$$

Let's calculate the new defective rate for the field return data in Table 9.1. Since we are defining our new product period as three months, we'll count only those defectives that were returned during their first three months in service. To do this, we check the "Service Life" column in Table 9.1 to see how long the units were in the field before they were returned. We find that of the 28 units returned, 19 were new defectives. We calculate the new defective rate as

$$\text{New Defective Rate} = \frac{\text{Number of New Defectives}}{\text{Average Number of Devices Made}} * 100\%$$

$$\text{Rate of Return} = \frac{19}{26{,}400} * 100\%$$

$$\text{Rate of Return} = 0.072\%$$

The quality engineer has completed the initial calculations and will now analyze the data from these observations. It is clear that the manufacturer's most serious problem is new defectives. They accounted for 19 of the 28 field returns.

The radio manufacturer's new defective problem is not unusual. Many products experience a high failure rate during the early stage of their useful life.

One approach to correcting a new defectives problem is to *burn-in* final products before they go into the field. The burn-in process, in its simplest form, requires that the product be operated at the manufacturer's location for a period of time to determine whether it will fail early in its life cycle. The radio, for example, might be powered up for 48 hours. Any units that fail during the burn-in period are analyzed to determine why they failed and are reworked.

Some manufacturers may place their product under extreme environmental stress to accelerate the burn-in process. The radio manufacturer, for example, operates her radios in an oven at approximately 86°F for five days.

A successful burn-in plan should yield approximately the same new defective rate as the manufacturer had previously found in field failures. If it doesn't, the burn-in procedure must be modified. The use of the testing oven, for example, helped the radio manufacturer bring the burn-in defect rate approximately in line with the original 0.072 percent new defective rate. Once the rates match, the manufacturer can feel relatively confident that the burn-in plan is eliminating new defective products before they reach the customer.

Although it is effective, the burn-in process is also an extremely expensive way to solve a new defective problem. By carefully analyzing field returns and customer complaints, manufacturers can identify ways of improving their products through changes in the production process and use of better materials and components.

The AM radio manufacturer, for example, reviewed the field return data in Table 9.1 to identify the exact source of the new defectives problem:

- The resistor R1 was found defective in four different units (its frequency was = 4). The first unit was returned after being in the field for one month. The second unit was returned after being in the field for three months, the third after two months, and the fourth after one month.

- C2 accounted for nine new defectives, since one of the 10 returned units was in the field for longer than three months.

- The diode accounted for one new defective.

- The speaker problem was the result of a manufacturing defect and accounted for five new defectives.

- The only other units that were returned within three months were the CND (Cannot Determine) units. These units were not found defective when returned and therefore do not fit our definition of new defective.

QUALITY CONTROL AND FIELD DATA

The manufacturer will identify the most serious problems and greatest opportunities for improvement. The winner by far is the shorted capacitor C2. The quality engineer will work with the supplier to find a solution.

The soldering problem at the speaker connection is the next most serious problem. The quality engineer will work with the manufacturing engineer and the design engineer to find a solution.

Once the solutions have been determined, action will be taken to make the changes. The burn-in process will be carefully monitored to determine if the solutions employed actually solve the problem. When the quality engineer sees a significant reduction in defects during burn-in, the engineer will drop the process.

All the while, the repair department will continue to generate new data from field returns, uncovering new problems, and, hopefully, demonstrating that old ones have been corrected.

To some extent, the problems which the manufacturer has identified through field return data involve issues of *reliability*, that is, the length of time a product is expected to function normally in the field. Reliability engineering has developed into a sophisticated discipline and goes beyond our definition of quality control. In chapter 12, we will briefly discuss reliability engineering as part of the development of a broader quality assurance effort.

9.4 Reaching Out to the Customer

In many cases, dissatisfied customers don't bother to return the defective product or even to lodge a complaint. Recent surveys have found that as many as 70 percent of unhappy consumers choose not to inform manufacturers of their dissatisfaction. For purchases costing $5 or less, the number of unhappy customers who simply go away mad rises to 98 percent.

This silent majority does voice its disapproval in the marketplace, however. These customers simply stop buying the offending company's product and take their business elsewhere. For major appliances, surveys find that 90 percent of non-complainers make a conscious decision to avoid repeat purchases from the same company. Unhappy customers also routinely spread the word of their negative experiences. Dissatisfied consumers tell twice as many people about problems as satisfied customers do for positive experiences.

In light of these findings, it is important for manufacturers to actively seek out information about customer dissatisfaction. This becomes the only way by which companies can collect and accurately assess information on field failures. It also becomes a mechanism for retaining customer loyalty by allowing consumers to express this dissatisfaction and gain a resolution to their complaints.

There are a variety of ways in which manufacturers can actively solicit customer reactions to product quality.

One effective method is to get the *sales staff* involved. Sales personnel represent a company's first and most important link to the customer. By actively seeking out reactions to product quality, salespeople can obtain valuable field intelligence as to their product's performance while strengthening their relationships with the consumer. Once these channels of communication have been established, customers are more likely to express their dissatisfaction before moving to another supplier.

The door manufacturer, for example, has sales staff question personnel in retail outlets. The manufacturer wants to know whether his doors are selling well compared to the competition. Are there any quality issues involved? These discussions uncovered a problem in the way the doors were packaged. Some of the doors were not properly protected and were being slightly damaged during shipment. The information was fed back to the factory for review, and a solution was found and implemented.

Customer surveys are another good way of polling consumers to determine product satisfaction. The survey can be conducted through mailed questionnaires or through direct telephone contact. Did the customer have any problems with the product? Which features did the customer find most useful? What additional features are needed? Was the customer satisfied with the product? If not, what could have been done to make them satisfied? Would the customer recommend this product to a friend? If not, why not?

The AM radio manufacturer, for example, sent a survey to customers who returned their warranty card information. In general, the responses were positive, and the manufacturer felt that customers were satisfied. A few quality problems were identified, however. The station numbers were small and hard to read. The volume control was too recessed, making access inconvenient. These types of complaints may not drive customers to return the product. On the other hand, they might lead them to look elsewhere for their next purchase. In this case, the manufacturer incorporated the comments into the next design change to ensure that she would be even more competitive in the future.

To be effective, customer surveys, either by mail or phone, must be convenient for the consumer. Forms should be short and easy to fill out. They should be self-addressed and include postage for the return mailing. Telephone surveys should be brief, courteous, and scheduled for maximum customer convenience. Any obstacle, no matter how trivial, that hinders customers from rapidly expressing their level of satisfaction must be eliminated. Otherwise, the manufacturer's access to accurate information on the acceptability and competitiveness of the product will be limited.

Complaint hotlines allow manufacturers to let customers express dissatisfaction. The use of toll-free, often 24-hour telephone numbers for the expression of complaints has grown dramatically in recent years as many manufacturers have recognized the value of actively soliciting information on customer reactions. The hotline phone numbers and instructions on when to use them are clearly indicated on product packaging, in product literature, and often on the product itself. The numbers allow customers to vent their frustrations over product problems. In many cases, the complaint calls allow manufacturers to immediately resolve problems resulting from customer misunderstanding regarding the use and performance of products. In other cases, the hotline allows the manufacturer to regain customer loyalty through the scheduling of service calls or other corrective actions. Sometimes, the calls are totally unrelated to product problems but become a means of providing information to customers who are interested in purchases of additional products.

Customer focus groups can be another important source of information for some industries. These groups bring together customers and company representatives for a face-to-face discussion of product quality and performance. A primary objective of these groups is to determine how the product can be improved to better meet customer needs.

9.5 Publications and Independent Market Research Organizations

Manufacturers can also obtain information regarding the comparative field performance of their products from consumer magazines and trade publications. Publications such as these will frequently conduct product reviews which compare product specifications, features, reliability, and performance. *Consumer Reports*, for example, which is published monthly by Consumers Union, provides in-depth product reviews and comparisons on a wide range of consumer products. Trade publications frequently offer similar comparisons on industry products and equipment used by industry manufacturers.

Independent market research surveys also can provide manufacturers with objective assessments of their product's field performance. JD Powers, Inc., for example, collects data on customer satisfaction in the automotive industry. The company will provide this data, at a price, to interested manufacturers. Similar independent marketing surveys provide comparable information on other industries.

9.6 Competitive Analysis

Another popular method for determining how well your product compares with the competition's is to go out and buy their product. Then start testing both devices. Does the competition's product do the job better than yours? If it does, and the price is comparable, you can expect to lose market share.

The baker constantly buys bread from other bakeries to compare taste. The AM radio manufacturer periodically purchases radios from competitors, then compares all the specification parameters that define the product: power output, sensitivity, selectivity, etc. The AM radio manufacturer is always checking to ensure she offers the best product.

9.7 The Bottom Line

Perhaps the most basic field information on the quality and competitiveness of any product is the level of sales and profits. A decrease in either area can indicate that there is a quality problem.

As we've indicated, dissatisfied customers frequently will "vote with their feet." Rather than expressing their complaints, they will simply begin buying from the competition. A drop in total sales or relative market share may result from a decline in customer satisfaction with product quality. On one hand, this may mean that a product's quality level has dropped in absolute terms, i.e., more defective products are getting through to the customer. On the other hand, the product's quality may have declined in relative terms, i.e., competitive products may include fewer defects or have higher standards of performance. In either case, the product's decreased quality competitiveness is leading to lost sales and revenues.

Declining profits can also indicate newfound quality problems. The door manufacturer, for example, noted that his profits were inching downward despite rising sales. An investigation determined that defect rates at the factory had increased, resulting in higher scrap costs that were eroding profits.

However, there is a problem with using sales and profits to indicate changing quality levels. By the time they reflect a problem, it may be too late. To avoid reaching this point, it is important to actively seek out and monitor information on field failures and customer satisfaction. The company that doesn't remain vigilant in satisfying the customer will probably be replaced by one that does.

QUALITY CONTROL AND FIELD DATA

Chapter Summary

1. Field returns are products that have been sent back to the manufacturer because the customer was not satisfied. Field returns are a result of component failures, component malfunctions, manufacturing defects, customer abuse, environmental stress, and customer dissatisfaction.

2. The rate of returns over a predetermined period of time may be calculated

$$\text{Rate of Return} = \frac{\text{Number of Returns}}{\text{Average Number of Devices Made}} * 100\%$$

3. One type of field return is the new defective. This is a return that occurs early in the product's life cycle. New defectives are caused by "product infant mortality." The new defective rate, calculated for products which have been returned during a specified length of service, is:

$$\text{New Defective Rate} = \frac{\text{Number of New Defectives}}{\text{Average Number of Devices Made}} * 100\%$$

4. Manufacturers should actively seek out customer reactions to product performance. Sales personnel, customer surveys, and customer focus groups are ways to accomplish this.

5. Publications, such as trade journals and consumer magazines, and independent market research organizations offer alternative assessments on a product's comparative field performance.

6. Competitive analysis is done by purchasing the competition's product and comparing it with your own. Does it work better than yours? Is it designed better? Does it look better? Does it last longer? If the answer to any of these questions is Yes, then you have some work to do.

7. Declining profits and sales may indicate a quality problem.

Questions for Chapter 9

1. What are the six reasons for field returns listed in this chapter?

2. Consider the closet door. Give specific examples of why the closet door could be returned for each of the six reasons that result in field returns.

3. Give specific examples of manufacturing defects, customer abuses, environmental stress, and customer dissatisfaction for a loaf of bread.

4. List the three basic steps of field return analysis.

5. How could the closet door manufacturer set up a system to observe field returns? How could the bread manufacturer accomplish the same objective?

6. What are ways of soliciting customer reaction as listed in the chapter? Specifically, which approach or approaches would be most applicable to each of our three manufacturers? Give reasons.

7. Why is it unwise to rely on sales and profits to indicate the quality of a product?

QUALITY CONTROL AND FIELD DATA

Chapter 9 Project

1. For the product that you have chosen to produce, give specific examples of possible component failures, component malfunctions, manufacturing defects, customer abuses, environmental stresses, and customer dissatisfaction.

2. Design an insert for your product that warns the consumer to avoid possible stresses that might result in product failure.

3. What procedure would you implement to make observations on field returns and collect data?

4. Set up a mock field return data sheet, similar to Table 9.1, for your product. Using the values in your table, compute the rate of return. Select those items that could have malfunctioned in the first three months, and compute the new defective rate.

5. What would be the best ways for you to solicit customer reactions?

CHAPTER 10

THE QUALITY IMPROVEMENT LOOP

10.1 Introduction

The goal of the quality control department is zero defects. We do not want defects in the raw materials, components, or parts we receive from our vendors. We do not want defects in the processed components or subassemblies that are produced on our factory floor. Last, and most important, we do not want any defects in our final product. If it sounds like we are striving for perfection, we are! Can we achieve it? Yes, we can!

In our discussions of incoming inspection, statistical process control, and final inspection we have learned techniques to help us achieve our goal of zero defects. These techniques should be applied as part of a process which strives for ongoing and continuous improvement in product quality. This improvement process, which we will call the *quality improvement loop*, involves continuous repetition of (1) observations, (2) analysis, and (3) action.

By repeating the steps of the quality improvement loop, our manufacturers can eliminate various problems which prevent our processes from meeting our originally specified quality level targets. Once our manufacturing processes have been stabilized at our target AQLs, the quality improvement loop will allow us to eliminate additional sources of defects and continuously increase the quality capability of our manufacturing process.

10.2 Observation

All of our efforts to improve product quality have started with information obtained through observation of the manufacturing process. In chapter 1, we began by seeing that four out of every ten closet doors failed to meet our manufacturer's specifications. The incoming inspection procedures that we established measured and tested the purchased materials and component parts that would go into our finished products. Our statistical process control techniques recorded data obtained through an ongoing series of sample inspections. Finally, we have observed, through 100 percent final inspections and sample audits, the overall quality level of our finished products.

Making observations and collecting data constitute the first step toward improving quality. We must know our quality starting point clearly and precisely to judge our eventual progress.

If we are to proceed, however, our observations must provide us with information that can actually guide us toward our goal. To do this, the information we collect must be detailed and unambiguous. We must be able to work with it. Our initial observation in chapter 1 regarding the closet door manufacturer's 40 percent defect rate dramatically proclaimed the company's overall quality problem. It was useless, however, in identifying the specific problems which led to lack of quality. Consequently, it could not tell us how to proceed in improving the situation. Only when we began gathering inspection information on defective materials and tracking variations in the cutting process did we have information on why these doors failed to meet specifications and what we could do about it.

10.3 Analysis

Once we are equipped with the information obtained from our observations, we can begin to analyze our situation. The analysis is a four-part process.

First, we must determine the specific problems we wish to solve. Second, we must identify the actual source of the problem. Third, we must develop a plan for corrective action. Fourth, we must determine if the corrective action is cost-effective.

Step One: Finding the Problems—Troubleshooting vs. Quality Improvement

Quality problems generally fall into two main categories. Both types of problems relate directly to the current quality level of our manufacturing systems, which we learned to calculate in chapter 6.

The first type is sporadic disturbances that can prevent us from producing at the quality levels our production processes are capable of achieving. For example, our panel cutting system may be routinely capable of meeting an AQL target of 0.65 percent defective, ±0.10 percent. The day it jumps to 1.0 percent defective, we know we have a new and major problem. These occasional problems can result from such factors as sudden changes in employee performance as a result of staff turnover, radical decreases in equipment performance due to improper adjust-ments, changes in the quality level or design of component materials, and so on.

When we deal with these sporadic problems, we are *troubleshooting*. Our response must be to quickly identify and correct the source of our problem to restore our manufacturing process to its original quality level.

The second type of problems are those that we confront when our system is already consistently meeting its current AQL targets. These are problems that prevent us from improving our process quality level and establishing new and higher quality targets. For example, we have already identified the current quality capability of our panel cutting process as 0.65 percent defective. The only way we can improve the results of this process to a consistent 0.25 percent defective is by confronting a number of obstacles inherent in the process itself. These systemic problems can result from such sources as defect-prone product designs, weaknesses in our processing techniques or procedures, inadequate equipment capabilities, current component and material AQLs, existing standards of employee performance based on current levels of training and experience, and other factors.

When we identify and confront these obstacles, we are engaged in *quality improvement*. Performing quality improvement is the only way we can increase the quality level of our products on an ongoing basis.

It is important to remember that troubleshooting must come before quality improvement. If we cannot consistently meet our current 0.65 percent defective targets, we shouldn't try to raise our sights to a level of 0.25 percent defective. The simplest reason for not doing so is that we will be unable to identify process-related obstacles due to the number of one-time quality problems. We must first stabilize the process at our current quality target. Then, and only then, should we attempt to systematically correct limitations in our process and increase our quality capabilities to new levels of performance.

Pareto Analysis

Identifying which quality problems to address is not always easy. As we have seen, the range of processing variation and the resulting quality level of any manufacturing operation result from many factors. We have already noted that these include equipment capabilities, staff performance, variations in material specifications, and biases in production procedures. Usually these factors contribute to the problem in different degrees.

Pareto analysis is one method for identifying a wide range of quality problems and selecting those which we should tackle first. Pareto analysis does this by determining the various problems affecting our production process *and* their relative impact on our product quality. We list the sources of quality problems in order of their importance—contributors that are responsible for most of the problems first and the lesser contributors last.

A BEGINNER'S GUIDE TO QUALITY IN MANUFACTURING

Once we've identified our major trouble spots, we can focus our attention and resources on solutions which offer the largest rewards in terms of quality and profit.

Let's look, for example, at how the AM radio manufacturer can use Pareto analysis to improve the quality of her product. As we've seen, the manufacturer auto-tests all assembled PCBs to determine if there are any problems. The test equipment identifies defects in individual electronic components and in the soldered circuitry. The computer prints out a ticket for each PCB to indicate needed repairs and also records data on all defects in a central database.

This record of PCB defects allows the manufacturer to print out all the defects and how many times they occurred. In addition, the computer sorts the defects in order, starting with the defect that occurred most often and finishing with the least of our problems. The results after three months of operation appear in Table 10.1.

Description of Defect	Number of Defects	Percent of Total
1. Shorted connection to capacitor C7	318	40%
2. Broken diode (D1)	190	24%
3. Open connection on resistor R10	116	15%
4. Shorted connection on transistor U3	71	9%
5. Resistor R2 missing from PCB	41	5%
6. Open connection on transistor U4	24	3%
7. Capacitor C12 missing from PCB	16	2%
8. Resistor R13 is incorrect value	8	1%
9. All other defects	8	1%

Table 10.1: Pareto Analysis of AM Radio Defects at Auto-Testing

The first column of Table 10.1 lists the nine types of defects we have found in our testing. The second column shows the number of times we have found each defect during the three-month period. The final column indicates the resulting percentage of total defects.

For presentations, it is often effective to graph the Pareto analysis. Figure 10.1 is a graph of the Pareto analysis done on the defect rates for the PCBs after they completed the soldering process.

THE QUALITY IMPROVEMENT LOOP

The results of the manufacturer's Pareto analysis are clear. The biggest quality problem, representing 40 percent of all defects, is the shorted connections to Capacitor C7. Two other problems, the broken Diode D1 and the open connection at Resistor R10, account for another 39 percent of all defects. In total, therefore, approximately four of every five defects result from these top three quality problems.

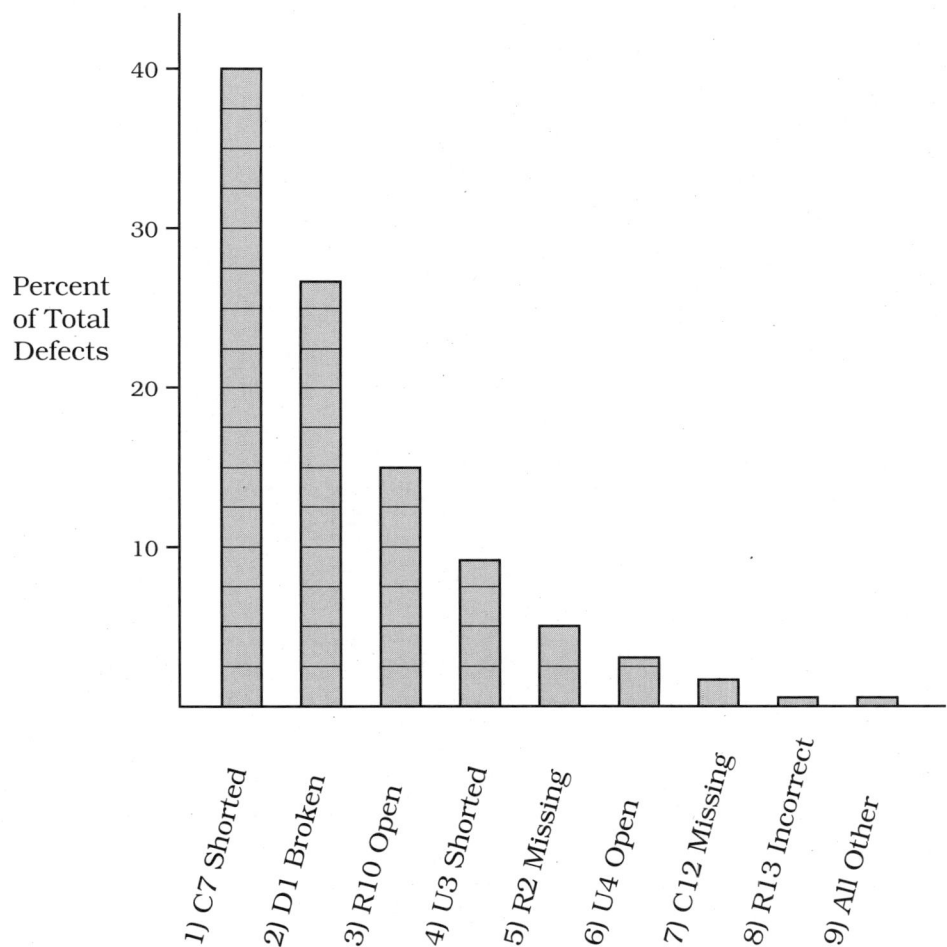

Figure 10.1: Pareto Analysis of AM Radio Defects at Auto-Testing

Step Two: Finding the Source of the Problem

Now that the manufacturer knows what her biggest problems are, she must find out why they exist in the first place. The defects are only results of deeper problems in the process. To correct them, the manufacturer must trace the problem back to its source.

The manufacturer did this by assigning a task force to review its major quality problems. The team consisted of representatives of the quality control department, manufacturing engineering, and design engineering. Let's see what they learned.

First, the task force agreed that the shorted connections at Capacitor C7 and Transistor U3 were probably being caused by problems in the design of the PCB. Their locations on the board led to frequent problems during the soldering process which could not be remedied by adjustments to the equipment.

Secondly, the team determined that Diode D1 is being broken during the auto-insertion process. Further analysis indicated that the defect stemmed from the material quality of the purchased diode rather than any problem with the insertion process.

Sometimes a manufacturer will find a number of possible sources for a single quality problem. The closet door company, for example, has found that its doors were being damaged during the cutting of mortises for hinges; sections of wood around the mortise were chipping.

The manufacturing engineer in the door factory started the investigation by talking to the workers who operated the cutting equipment. One reaction was that the hardness of the wood could vary, and at certain hardnesses the cutting tool started to rip the wood. Another possibility was that the cutting tool was running at too high a speed. A third possibility was that the cutting tool might begin to damage the wood as it grew dull from continued use.

The door manufacturer's problem with chipping might result from any or all of the sources identified. To determine which of these factors may be creating the problem, the manufacturer may have to observe the process in greater detail and collect additional information.

Step Three: Identify Corrective Actions

Once the manufacturer has identified the specific source of the quality problem, a solution is usually easy to find. The AM radio manufacturer's design engineer, for example, quickly indicated that a change in the design of the PCB could solve the problems with Capacitor C7 and Transistor U3. A change in location would allow improved soldering and eliminate the shorts which were appearing so regularly. Similarly, the firm's quality control engineer determined that the purchase of a Diode D1 with a slightly different material construction would avoid the breakage problem during auto-insertion.

Sometimes the manufacturer may be able to identify several alternative remedies to the problem. As we've seen, the door company has found several possible causes of the problem with chipping. Consequently, the manufacturer has also identified three potential plans to correct the problem. One alternative was that the machine could be run at a slower speed. A second was to increase maintenance on the tool to ensure that it was sharp enough to cut without problems. Finally, the door manufacturer could buy a more expensive cutting tool that would stay sharper longer.

Step Four: Determine if Corrective Action is Cost-Effective

Even when solutions to quality problems are easy to identify, they still can be difficult and expensive to implement. Before selecting any course of corrective action, manufacturers must determine whether their actions will reduce overall costs as well as increasing the quality of their product. If, as in the case of the door manufacturer, there is more than one solution, we must determine not only whether the solutions are cost effective but also which one is the most cost-effective.

If the manufacturing process has been properly monitored, determining whether a solution is cost-effective is easy. Our decision will be based on a comparison of the cost of improvement vs. savings in defects over the life of the product. The costs of improving the process are subtracted from the savings the manufacturer achieves through higher product quality; the result is the net savings. If the subtraction results in a positive number, then the solution should be implemented. If the subtraction results in a net savings that is negative (a loss), then further consideration is necessary. The formula for net savings for a quality solution is

Net Savings = Savings Due to Decreased Defects
 − Cost of Implementing Solution

The cost of improvements should include such items as:

- Costs of purchasing new equipment for ongoing production

- One-time costs of implementing the solutions, including design costs, labor expenses, and lost production as a result of process downtime

- Recurring costs of operating the improved system, including increased costs for higher quality materials, additional labor expenses, and lost revenues resulting from decreases in process productivity

Savings are a product of decreased defects. They include the selling price of the products that would otherwise have been scrapped because of defects and other costs which would have been incurred as a result of poor quality.

Let's go back to the door manufacturer and do some cost analysis on the solutions proposed for the cutting damage problem.

First, let's determine the savings the manufacturer would see if he could eliminate the defects created by this problem. On average, three doors are scrapped every week because of this problem. The selling price of the door is $22.00. The manufacturer will calculate his savings over a 10-year period since he believes that it will take that long for style and technology to make the product obsolete. Based on these assumptions, the manufacturer will calculate the total savings over the life of the product:

$$\text{Savings} = \text{Selling Price} * \text{Number of Doors Saved}$$

where Number of Doors Saved = Number of Defects per Week
* 52 Weeks per Year
* Life of the Product in Years

$$\text{Savings} = \$22.00 * 3 * 52 * 10$$

$$\text{Savings} = \$34{,}320.00$$

Now that the manufacturer knows the value of solving the problem, let's look at the various costs he might face in doing so.

The first proposed solution required that the cutting process be slowed to avoid chipping. There were no material costs or additional maintenance costs. However, the slower cutting speed would reduce the factory's total output. The manufacturing engineer estimated that, on average, two fewer doors would be produced each day.

The manufacturer's cost structure for the door is:

Selling Price		$22.00
Costs:		
Material Costs	$12.29	
Fixed Costs	$ 6.00	
Total	$ 18.29	$18.29
Profit		$ 3.71

Based on these assumptions, each door which the manufacturer fails to produce costs approximately $9.71. This consists of the $3.71 profit that he has lost plus the $6.00 in fixed costs which must now be absorbed by the other doors.

THE QUALITY IMPROVEMENT LOOP

If the manufacturer made two fewer doors per day, therefore, his total daily loss would be as follows:

Daily Loss = 2 * ($3.71 + $6.00)
Daily Loss = $19.42

Over the 10-year life of the door, the cost of solution one, due to a decrease in productivity, would be

Cost = Daily Loss * 5 days per week * 52 weeks * 10 Years
Cost = $19.42 * 5 * 52 * 10
Cost = $50,492.00

Now let's compare the savings from eliminating the problem with the costs of implementing solution one. The formula, as we've seen is,

Net Savings = Savings Due to Decreased Defects
              − Cost of Implementing Solution
Net Savings = $34,320.00 − $50,492.00
Net Savings = −$16,172.00

The use of a slower cutting speed to eliminate the chipping defect will lead to a net additional cost of $16,172. The higher quality level, in this case, appears to cost us money. Now let's look at our second alternative—an increased maintenance program to keep the cutting tool sharper and eliminate the damage.

Presently the tools are sharpened every month. Sharpening the tools requires a half-day's work (4 hours) by a skilled machinist. The tools are sharpened on a Saturday so that production is not interrupted. It costs the manufacturer $20.00/hour in overtime pay to keep the cutting tools sharp. Now, the manufacturer will want to sharpen the tools twice as often to avoid the damage problem. The cost involved in additional overtime pay is four hours per month for 10 years at $20.00/hour. The resulting cost is

Cost = Wage/Hour * Hours/Month * 12 Months/ year * 10 Years
Cost = $20.00 * 4 * 12 * 10
Cost = $9,600

Comparing this cost with a savings of $34,320.00, our net savings would be

Net Savings = Savings Due to Decreased Defects
              − Cost of Implementing Solution
Net Savings = $34,320.00 − $9,600.00
Net Savings = $24,720

This alternate plan is certainly acceptable. It improves the quality of the product and saves the company money.

Before we make our final decision, however, let's analyze the costs of our third alternative. The equipment supplier sells a higher-grade cutting tool which requires less maintenance. In fact, the door manufacturer would not have to increase his maintenance if he used the higher grade tool.

The higher-quality tool costs $130.00. It would have to be replaced every year, just like the tool now in use. The cost difference between the two tools is $70.00.

The cost of implementing this solution would be the initial one-time expense of switching to the new tool ($130) plus the added expense of replacing the tool annually ($70). Total costs for this solution are

Costs = Initial Equipment Costs
        + Increased Tool Replacement Costs for the Next Nine Years
Costs = $130.00 + (9 * $70.00)
Costs = $760.00

The net savings for this plan is

Net Savings = Savings Due to Decreased Defects
              − Cost of Implementing Solution
Net Savings = $34,320.00 − $760.00
Net Savings = $33,560.00

Obviously, this third alternative appears most attractive. It requires relatively little change in the manufacturer's process and offers the biggest financial rewards for increasing his quality level.

10.4 Action

Our manufacturer has observed the process and collected data on the quality level of his products. An analysis of this data has identified problems to be solved, traced the problems to their source, and determined the most cost-effective method of correcting the situation. The only thing which remains is to implement the solution.

Oddly enough, this is sometimes the hardest part of the loop to accomplish. Quality improvement requires change—something that all organizations find hard to accept. Organizations, however, are only people, and people do learn to adapt to new situations. In a later chapter, we will talk about the ways manufacturers can help their employees make quality, and continuous quality improvement, a natural way of life.

10.5 Repeating the Cycle

Once we've implemented our solutions, the time has come to begin the quality improvement loop again. We must make new observations to learn whether our solutions have corrected the problem we originally identified. If they haven't, we must analyze the data, find new solutions, and take action again. If we have solved our initial quality problem, we can select a new problem which stands as an obstacle to a higher quality level. By continuously repeating the cycle of our quality improvement loop, we can gradually but inevitably raise the quality of our product toward our goal of zero defects.

Chapter Summary

1. The quality control loop consists of observation, analysis, and action.

2. The observation results in the data necessary to make our evaluations. Data must be accurately taken and recorded.

3. Analysis includes all the techniques we have studied to determine product and process acceptability. It also includes the prioritizing of quality problems, called Pareto analysis. Developing plans to solve the problems is the next phase of the analysis process. Deciding which plan to follow is done with careful cost vs. savings analysis. Final decisions on the best directions to follow are mindful of the customer perception of the product. Decisions to improve quality at the expense of profit, though not popular, are sometimes critical to the product's survival.

4. Action is the implementation of the solution that is the most cost-effective way to improve product quality.

5. The quality loop completes itself with more observations. First we must learn whether quality improvements have accomplished their goals of decreased defects and improved savings. When this has been determined, more observations are necessary to begin the quality improvement process once again.

A BEGINNER'S GUIDE TO QUALITY IN MANUFACTURING

Questions for Chapter 10

1. List the four steps in the analysis of a problem.

2. One of the defects found on the AM radio is a resistor missing from the PCB. What are some of the possible causes of this problem? For each cause, state what corrective actions could be taken.

3. One of the defects of our AM radio is a resistor that has an incorrect value. What would be one or two of the most likely reasons for this problem? What corrective action would you take?

4. For the following defects in the production of a loaf of bread, identify some possible sources of the problem. Give some corrective actions that could be taken for each defect.

    a. the bread is too dark

    b. the bread is underweight

    c. the dough rises too much

    d. the bread is too salty

THE QUALITY IMPROVEMENT LOOP

Use the following situation for questions 5–9.

The baker finds that staleness, or hardening, of the bread occurs in 5.0 percent of the samples. After investigation, he finds that the problem is lack of an airtight seal on the package (the baker uses a poly bag with a twist tie at one end). The material cost for each loaf of bread is $0.68 and the fixed cost is $0.60. The selling price is $1.49, and the bakery produces 1,000 loaves per day. Compute the profit per loaf and daily loss. The baker has a few options: (1) use a poly bag which has a small amount of adhesive in the area were the twist tie is applied; (2) readjust more frequently the part of the packaging machine that applies the tie; and (3) purchase a machine that will give an extra twist when closing the bag. Since the packaging machine requires a major overhaul every five years, the baker calculates his savings (loss) under each course of action over a five-year period.

5. If the defects were eliminated, what would be the savings for a 52-week year and a 5-day work week over the course of the five years?

6. The baker currently pays $0.07 for a poly bag. Poly bags with adhesive cost $0.10 per bag. What would be the daily loss and cost over five years of buying these bags? What is the net savings?

7. If the machines are adjusted more often, the baker will produce 50 fewer loaves of bread per day. What will be the daily loss and cost over five years?

8. It costs $5,000 to overhaul the current machine each year. The new machine comes with a warranty and a service contract that includes the cost of the overhaul every five years. The annual premium for the contract is $1,200. The machine costs $70,000. What is the cost of this option (assume the old machine is scrapped)? What is the net savings?

9. Which option does the baker choose?

Refer to Table 10.1 and the following to answer questions 10–12.

For the radio manufacturer, the shortened connections to Capacitors C7 and U3 account for the greatest number of defects, 49 percent. The company's design engineer indicates that the problem could be avoided if the components were relocated slightly on the PCB. The costs of making this change amount to approximately $2,000 in engineering time. On the other hand, repairing the improperly soldered PCBs costs $5.00 each.

10. How many defective PCBs are there in a three-month period?

11. What is the cost of repairing the PCBs every three months?

THE QUALITY IMPROVEMENT LOOP

12. Is it cost-effective to implement the design engineer's plan? If so, what would be the first year's savings if the plan is implemented, and what would be the savings in subsequent years?

Use Table 10.1 and the following to answer questions 13–15.

Broken Diode D1 is the cause of 24 percent of the defects in the PCBs. Each defective board costs $5.00 to repair. A higher quality diode which is not susceptible to breakage was identified at a cost of $0.015 compared to the current cost of $0.01. Base your answers on the manufacturer's production target of 26,400 radios per month.

13. What is the increased cost per month, and every three months, if the manufacturer uses the higher quality diode?

14. What is the three-month repair cost of the PCBs if we continue to use the lower quality diode?

15. Will there be a net savings or a net loss if we use the higher quality diode? What will be the net savings (loss) in a three-month period?

241

Chapter 10 Project

Choose a defect that might occur in your product. Determine possible courses of action that you might take to correct the problem.

11 CHAPTER

TEST PROCEDURES, REPORTS, EQUIPMENT, AND CALIBRATION

11.1 Introduction

During all phases of incoming inspection, statistical process control, and final inspection, we make observations on the product or the process. These observations are then recorded in the form of data. Some observations are simple, like weighing dough or measuring the length of a door panel. At other times, taking data can be a complicated process.

It is very important that the data be accurate, since our analysis of process and product quality depends on it. If the data are not correct, we cannot accurately assess our quality level. For this reason, well-defined test procedures are necessary to assist our staff in making the measurements.

Additionally, the data must be collected using equipment with the required accuracy and range of measurement. The equipment must also be checked regularly to ensure that its accuracy does not degrade.

Once the data is taken, it must be reported in a clear and concise way. Test reports are one of the primary ways to direct staff to solve quality problems.

11.2 Test Procedures

A test procedure is a document that contains all the information and instructions needed to take a specific measurement or do an inspection. A test procedure should include the following:

Title page	Procedure
Scope	Test set-up diagrams
Definitions	Acceptability criteria
Test equipment	References

The *title page* uniquely identifies the test procedure in question. It will indicate the test procedure number, test procedure revision level and/or revision date, test procedure title and company name. Additionally, the title page may contain the department name, the release date and other pertinent information. The title page from MIL-STD-105E is a good example and is displayed in Figure 11.1.

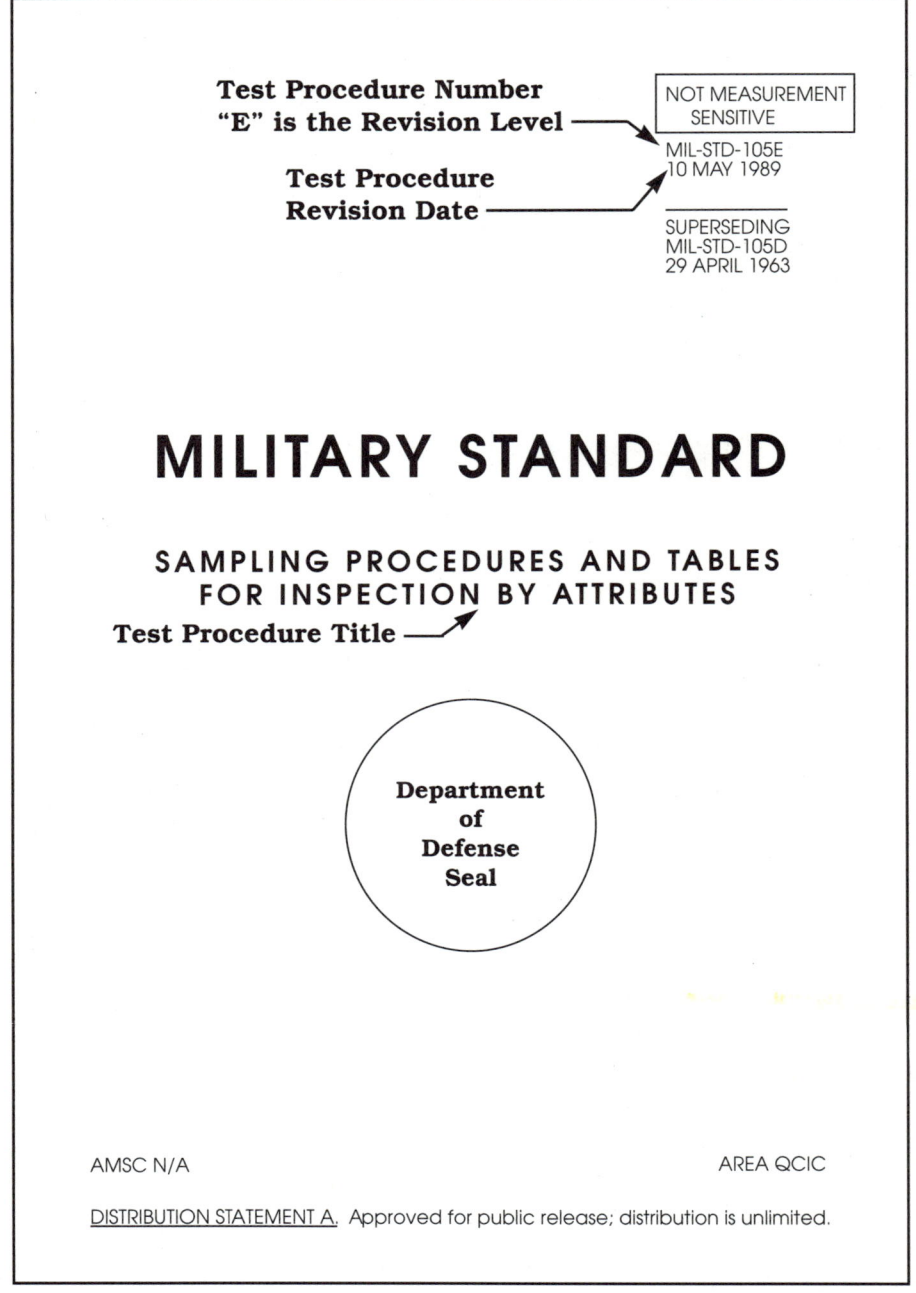

Figure 11.1: Test Procedure Title Page—MIL-STD-105E

TEST PROCEDURES, REPORTS, EQUIPMENT, AND CALIBRATION

The *scope* of the test procedure informs the inspector of the extent of the test to be accomplished. This part of the test procedure brings the purpose of the testing into focus. In some test procedures, the scope has other names, like the purpose or the introduction. The scope may also include the type of product for which the test procedure is applicable.

An example of a scope is the one in the procedure for measuring the output power of the AM radio. It reads

1. Scope

This procedure is intended to outline the steps necessary to measure output power of an AM or AM/FM radio. The Device Under Test (DUT) will be tested with a standard 8-ohm load. The DUT will be energized with a signal generator.

Another example of a scope is the one contained in MIL-STD-105E:

1. Scope

1.1 Purpose. This publication establishes lot or batch sampling plans and procedures for inspection by attributes. This publication shall not be interpreted to supersede or conflict with any contractual agreements. The words "accept," "acceptance," "acceptable," etc., refer only to the contractor's use of the sampling plans contained in this standard and do not imply an agreement by the Government to accept the product. Determination of acceptability by the Government shall be as described in contractual documents. The sampling plans described in this standard are applicable to AQLs of .01 percent or higher and are therefore not suitable for application where quality levels in the defective parts per million range can be realized.

1.2 Application. Sampling plans designated in this publication are applicable, but not limited, to inspection of the following:

   a. End item
   b. Components and raw materials
   c. Operations or services
   d. Materials in process
   e. Supplies in storage
   f. Maintenance operations
   g. Data or records
   h. Administrative procedures

These plans are intended primarily to be used for continuing series of lots or batches. The plan may also be used for the inspection of isolated lots or batches, but, in this latter case, the user is cautioned to consult the operating characteristic curves to find a plan which will yield the desired protection.

In both examples, the scope focuses on exactly what the test procedure intends to do. Additionally, information about test application was included. The scope sets the direction the test will take.

Definitions are an important part of the test procedure. The definitions clarify the special meaning of words that are used in the test procedure. For example, terms like "major defect" and "minor defect" have special meaning for MIL-STD-105E, and they are included in the list of definitions. Any word that has a special meaning or needs to be highlighted should be included in the list of definitions.

Test equipment must be specified in the test procedure. Equipment with the correct range of measurement and degree of accuracy must be used to do the testing. This is why the equipment list must include the name of the equipment (e.g., ruler, micrometer, voltmeter), the manufacturer, and the model number. Including this information will ensure that the test will be done with accurate equipment and will help the inspector locate the equipment needed for the test. Later in this chapter we will discuss how to determine the required precision of the equipment.

The *procedure* contains step-by-step instructions of how to conduct the test. The steps must be easily understandable. They must follow the actual sequence of the test. Special attention should be paid to meter settings, adjustments on the Device Under Test (DUT), and settings on equipment used to exercise the DUT. For example, during the testing of the AM radio, the wattmeter must be set to the 20-watt scale and the volume control on the radio must be turned up full.

Always be precise about what is to be done to the DUT. For example, if the DUT is to be heated in an oven, don't say "warm the DUT." Specify the temperature setting of the oven and how long the DUT should stay in the oven.

To determine whether our quality has improved, we must be sure that measurements have been taken in exactly the same way both before and after our corrective actions have been implemented. The procedure must be written so that the test is done correctly every time.

Diagrams are very useful in making the test procedure clear for the reader. The power output test for the AM radio includes a wiring diagram. This shows the inspector how to

test equipment to the DUT. The door manufacturer has included a mechanical drawing of the door which shows all the dimensions. It allows the inspector to check the location of the doorknob holes and the mortises for the hinges. These diagrams should be referred to in the text of the procedure.

Acceptability criteria tell the inspector if a DUT is acceptable or unacceptable. This information will indicate an acceptable range of values for each measurement or test.

References are included in a test procedure to direct the reader to additional information related to the test. These references give the inspector a better understanding of why the test is being done in a certain way. When the test procedure is being revised, these references can be used to make constructive changes.

Test procedures are documents that will require change from time to time. The design and specifications of our product will change; quality improvements may lead us to more stringent acceptability criteria; and new test equipment purchases may require a change in the test equipment list or changes in test procedures. It is important that when the test procedure is revised, the new revision level be marked on the test procedure. It is advisable that the revision date also be marked on the test procedure.

11.3 Test Reports

Test reports should be brief, yet contain all the information collected in the test. The test report includes, but is not limited to, a report summary, test data, test procedure, and recommendations. The quality control department will issue reports on individual units (*data pages*) and summaries of testing over a period of time or for a particular lot. The guidelines presented here are applicable to both situations.

The *report summary* should contain the model number of the unit or units tested, its revision level, its serial number (if applicable), the inspector's name or code number or the name of the report writer, the date of the report, and the results of the testing.

It is important to indicate the results of the test early in the report. Data pages on individual units should clearly state whether the sample was acceptable or unacceptable. This information is presented first to alert staff to problems. Similarly, reports covering an entire lot, such as incoming inspection reports, should say at the beginning if the lot was accepted or rejected.

The *test data* should show the actual values which were found through tests or measurements. The data presentation should state clearly the values being measured (e.g., "door height") and units of measure (inches, feet, volts, etc.). Data are often presented in tabular form. However, graphs such as histograms or control charts help make the data more easily understandable and should be used regularly.

The test report should also make reference to the *test procedure* that was used to do the inspection. If there was any deviation from the test procedure or if the test procedure does not completely describe the test, this information must be part of the test report.

Recommendations are typically needed when unacceptable data has been reported. In such cases, recommendations complete your test report. If the lot does not comply with the acceptability criteria, direct the purchasing department to return the lot. If a process is out of control, i.e., it is performing beyond its AQL, make suggestions for improving performance. If you have no recommendations for improving quality, recommend a test plan to determine possible solutions.

Recommendations may also be part of a report where no unacceptable data have been found.

If there is some analysis required, it can be included in this part of the report. Again, graphs are useful in presenting the numbers that are computed during analysis.

Reports are very important to quality's goal of an ever-improving product. Reports are one of the primary vehicles to present quality issues to upper management and other company departments. It is important that your message be clearly stated and well documented. If you want a production line to stop, this will cost the company money in lost production. It is therefore critical that the quality control report and recommendations be based on correct measurements and that the decision to stop production be an outcome of faultless analysis. When a report makes recommendations on lowering defect rates, include a cost vs. savings analysis to prove your point. As was stated before, any change is usually resisted. Your quality report is a lever to overcome this inertia.

11.4 Test Equipment

Thermometers measure temperature, scales measure weight, rulers measure distance. Thermometers, scales, and rulers are all types of measuring equipment. Like any product, measuring devices have their own specifications and tolerances.

The first specification we will consider for measuring equipment is the *range of measurement*. Some thermometers measure cold temperatures, some measure hot temperatures. A thermometer for an oven in the bakery must measure hot temperatures. The bread must bake at temperatures between 395° to 415°F. Therefore, the thermometer for the baking oven must include these temperatures. The baker has chosen a thermometer that has a range of 390°–420°F.

The baker must also weigh the finished loaf of bread. The specified weight of these loaves is 1 pound ±2 ounces. Therefore, the baker has chosen a scale which has a range of 2–24 ounces.

The next specification to be considered for the measuring equipment is *degree of accuracy.*

To determine the accuracy which we will require of our test equipment, we must first determine the smallest unit of measurement in our product specification. The baker, for example, wants to bake his bread at 405°F, ±10°. The smallest unit of measurement in the specification is 1°F.

We then identify the required degree of accuracy for our test equipment by dividing this unit of measurement by two. Since the baker's smallest unit of measurement was 1°F, he needs a thermometer that will measure temperatures to at least 0.5°F. The baker chose a thermometer with an accuracy of 0.1°F, well above the required degree of accuracy for this test.

Consider the plastic wrapper for the loaf of bread. The thickness of the wrapper was specified as 0.015", ±0.001". The smallest measurement in this specification is one one-thousandth of an inch, or 0.001". Divide this by two; the accuracy of the measuring device (a micrometer) required to measure the thickness of the plastic wrapper must be better than 0.0005".

Sometimes, test equipment may be required to perform specific functions in addition to measuring at a certain range and accuracy. For example, both the timer and the thermometers at the bakery must make a sound if the process being monitored goes beyond specified limits. At the radio factory, an auto-tester will check the components on the soldered printed circuit board. Then it must print out a list of components that are not in compliance with specifications. This is done so that workers at the repair area will know which components to replace to make the board acceptable

Different equipment, though measuring the same dimension, may have dramatically different ranges and accuracies. A ruler and a micrometer both measure length. The ruler may have an accuracy of 1/8" (0.125") and measure from 0"–12"; a micrometer may have an accuracy of 0.0005" and measure from 0"–2". It is therefore very important that, for each test, the inspector know which equipment is to be used. As we discussed in the preceding section, test procedures should specify the equipment to be used by manufacturer's name, model number, and, in some cases, serial number.

Because different equipment has different specifications and tolerances, it is important that each piece of equipment be supplied by the manufacturer with a specification data page or user's manual. This material must be kept in a file so that any

A BEGINNER'S GUIDE TO QUALITY IN MANUFACTURING

questions about accuracy, range, or function can be easily answered. The more complicated the equipment, the more important such a file becomes. The trend toward increased use of computer-controlled and/or computer-monitored test equipment only magnifies this need for appropriate documentation. The test equipment used to determine the sensitivity of the AM radio or the auto-test equipment used to check components on the soldered PCBs at the radio factory are good examples of such complex test equipment.

11.5 Calibration

Your customer, a restaurant owner, calls and complains that you are sending bread that weighs 12 ounces. It should be 16 ounces. The customer sends the loaf back and wants an explanation.

You have purchased weighing equipment. It measures what you need it to measure with the accuracy you require. You measure the returned loaf of baked bread and find it weighs 16 ounces. This is precisely the weight called for in the product specification. So why is your customer complaining?

You call the customer, who invites you to bring the bread to the restaurant and weigh it there. You accept the invitation. The customer has the same scale you do; it measures the same range of weights with the same accuracy. You put the loaf of bread on this scale, and it measures 12 ounces.

How do you determine whose scale is correct? You need a *standard*, something that everyone agrees weighs one pound. Then you could weigh the standard on both scales. If either scale was in error it could be adjusted. Once both scales were adjusted to read the correct value (based on the standard), you could determine whether or not the loaf of bread was the correct weight.

This process of comparing test equipment to a standard and adjusting the equipment so that it provides the correct values is called *calibration*.

But who has this standard that everyone agrees on?

The National Institute of Standards and Technology (NIST) provides the highest order calibration service in the United States. NIST is part of the Department of Commerce and has laboratories in Gaithersburg, MD and Boulder, CO.

NIST will check, adjust, or characterize particular instruments, devices, and sets of standards on a one-time pre-request basis. To begin the process, the customer will contact NIST to determine what the calibration fee will be and where to send the item for calibration. Usually the customer will send the item to be calibrated to NIST. The item is then calibrated and returned to the customer. Under separate cover, NIST provides a test report for the calibrated item that includes test procedures and results.

NIST provides a wide range of calibration services. Length measurements, flow rate measurements, mass standards, acoustic measurements, laser power and energy meter calibration, resistance measurements, characterization of atomic time, and frequency standards are among the many services provided by NIST.

However, NIST is not the only source of calibration services. There are private laboratories which will calibrate test equipment for a fee. Usually these laboratories will advertise that they are "traceable" to NIST. They are saying that the test equipment they use for calibration was calibrated at NIST or was calibrated with equipment whose ultimate standard was NIST. In other words, if you followed records of the equipment used to do the calibrations, the original standard used would be that of NIST. It should be noted that NIST says it "does not define nor enforce traceability." If both the customer and supplier can agree on a laboratory other than NIST, there are some advantages. For example, it may be more convenient to use a laboratory closer to your location.

Another option is to institute a calibration laboratory at your own location. For some measures, like weight, standards can be purchased and, since they will not change with time, can be used to calibrate the scales in your plant. In fact, the baker has done this by purchasing a weight set with calibration documentation "traceable" to NIST. Now, if there is any question about his scale, the baker simply places a 1-pound weight on the scale and adjusts the scale until it reads properly.

At the radio factory, things are a little more complicated. The test equipment is more complex and requires very expensive equipment and highly skilled technicians to do the calibration. The radio manufacturer sends the equipment to an outside laboratory for calibration.

Once a piece of equipment is calibrated, does it ever have to be calibrated again? The answer in most cases is Yes.

Over time, equipment needs adjustment. Moving the equipment can cause it to lose its accuracy. Electrical equipment gets hot, and the heat changes values of components, which cause it to lose accuracy. Mechanical equipment has parts that wear down, and their accuracy changes. These factors and others require some equipment to be checked constantly.

How often should test equipment be calibrated? Once a year? Once a month?

The period of time between calibrations is called the **frequency of calibration.** It depends on many factors: how often the equipment is used, the kind of handling it gets, and so on. In deciding on a frequency of calibration for new equipment, it is best to consult the equipment manufacturer. Explain the kind of use the equipment will be getting and the environment it will be used in, and the manufacturer will ~~be~~ advise you on a calibration period.

For equipment that has gone through many calibrations, records can be checked. If the equipment was found to be out of calibration when it was received at the calibration laboratory, then it should be calibrated more frequently. Conversely, if it is checked at the calibration laboratory and found to be well within specifications and needing no adjustment after a number of calibrations, then perhaps it is being calibrated too often.

It is important that good records are kept on calibration. A list should be kept indicating every piece of test equipment at the factory and the calibration dates. When the equipment is returned, it should be noted if adjustments were needed or if the unit was in specification when received by the calibration laboratory. The calibrated equipment should be marked with the date it was calibrated, when it must be calibrated next, and where it was calibrated. User's manuals and operating manuals must be readily available to ensure that the equipment is properly calibrated.

Calibration is important not only because it can create agreement between supplier and customer but also because our product may be used in conjunction with other products which have their own specifications and tolerances. For example, the AM radio must tune to channels sent by transmitters made by other manufacturers. Both manufacturers must know how to measure the channel frequency. At the door factory, the door will be installed in a door frame made by carpenters using their own rulers; the manufacturer and the carpenters must have rulers that measure the same lengths.

TEST PROCEDURES, REPORTS, EQUIPMENT, AND CALIBRATION

Chapter Summary

1. The test procedure is a document that details all the information required to make a measurement or do an inspection. The test procedure should include a title page, scope, definitions, test equipment, procedure, diagrams, acceptability criteria, and references.

2. A test report contains both data and analysis. The test report may include a report summary, test data, the test procedure, and recommendations.

3. Test equipment must test in the required range of measurement with the necessary degree of accuracy, and it must perform the necessary functions.

4. In order for your measurements to agree with your customers' measurements and with other equipment that may interface or communicate with yours, it must be calibrated. Calibration is the process of checking, fixing, adjusting, or otherwise ensuring that equipment is performing to its specified accuracy.

5. Calibration is accomplished by comparing equipment to a standard. A standard is a measure that is accepted as correct by a group. The National Institute of Standards and Technology (NIST) is considered the foremost standards laboratory in the U.S.

A BEGINNER'S GUIDE TO QUALITY IN MANUFACTURING

Questions for Chapter 11

1. List some of the observations that need to be made in the production of the AM radio and the type of equipment needed to make the observation.

2. List the eight items that were suggested to be included in a test procedure.

3. Below are items to be included in a test procedure. Choose the correct part of the procedure for inclusion of each.

    a. A word that has special meaning

    b. Meter settings

    c. A drawing

    d. A department name

    e. Type of product the procedure is applicable to

    f. Model number and manufacturer of the test equipment

4. Why is it necessary to include the name of the test equipment, the manufacturer, and the model number?

TEST PROCEDURES, REPORTS, EQUIPMENT, AND CALIBRATION

5. What items are suggested for inclusion in a test report?

6. Why is it important to indicate the results of a test early in the report?

7. Why would you include histograms, control charts, and graphs in your test report?

8. For each of the following, determine the accuracy we need from the measuring device.

    a. 72" ± 0.05"

    b. 16 oz. ± 0.1 oz.

    c. 20,000 Hz ± 100 Hz

9. Why must each piece of test equipment be supplied with a specification data page or user's manual?

10. Why is it important to keep good records on calibration?

255

Chapter 11 Project

1. List all the observations you will be taking during the production of your product. Which observations will be simple and which will be complicated?

2. For each observation listed above, state the type of equipment that will be necessary to make the observation.

3. Choose one item to be observed in the production of your product. Prepare a test procedure for this observation. You may invent model numbers for the test equipment.

4. For the observation in task 3, write a mock test report for an item that has failed.

5. For the observation in task 3, write a mock test report for an item that has passed.

6. What machines and measuring devices used in the production and observations of your product will you need to have calibrated?

CHAPTER 12

A BRIEF HISTORY OF THE QUALITY MOVEMENT

12.1 Introduction

The history of quality has the drama of an epic novel. Its roots stretch back to the Industrial Revolution. It took its first steps along with the economic growth of the New World. Quality control has gone to war, reached into space, and spanned the globe in search of converts. It is no exaggeration to suggest that quality has helped shape the industrial balance of power in the world today.

On a personal level, American quality pioneers, like many heroes of an earlier day, were forced to leave their homes to find people who would share and act on their vision. W. Edwards Deming, Joseph Juran, and Armand Feigenbaum have all achieved national prominence in Japan, where product quality increasingly provided a decisive competitive edge in the international competition for customers. Faced by these foreign pressures, U.S. industry revived its interest in quality control techniques during the 1980s. As a result, SPC and vendor certification programs are now widespread among American manufacturers.

During the years since World War II, these and other theorists have substantially broadened the frontiers of quality.

Quality control theory, as we have seen, defines quality as conformance to predetermined product specifications. It provides tools such as acceptance sampling and SPC to avoid and detect these product defects during the production process.

Quality assurance, however, is a broader discipline which has grown from the combined work of Deming, Juran, Feigenbaum, and others. Quality assurance enlarges the definition of quality and looks past the assembly line to the company's management as a whole.

12.2 Quality During the Industrial Revolution

Throughout most of history, consumer products were not mass-produced in factories as we know them today, and quality was not a concern. Skilled artisans and craftspeople who had learned their trade during long apprenticeships turned out products in small numbers, often crafting each of the components by hand. Product quality was a natural outgrowth of the production system.

Quality, or the possible lack of it, became a concern with the advent of true mass-production factories in the U.S. during the 19th century. These facilities, using what is now known as the *American system of manufacturing*, featured the production of standardized articles through sequential production processes using interchangeable parts. The system was implemented by the U.S. government at both the Springfield Armory in Massachusetts and the Harpers Ferry Armory. Private firms such as Singer Company and the McCormick Harvesting Company also used the system.

Quality control efforts under the American system were based on inspections using a *gauging system*. By 1819, the government's Springfield Armory was using a gauging system which allowed inspectors to ensure that weapon components conformed to their production drawings.

The use of inspections grew in tandem with America's industrial output. The need for inspections was recognized as part of scientific management techniques developed by Frederick W. Taylor in the early 20th century.

The theoretical basis and actual procedures for inspections were formalized in 1922 by G. S. Radford in his book *The Control of Quality in Manufacturing*. Radford elaborated on the need for inspections and various methods for performing them. The book even discussed sampling techniques, although these were not based on any statistical assumptions.

12.3 Bell Laboratories and the Statistics of Quality Control

In 1924, in response to quality problems at Western Electric's Hawthorn Works, Bell Laboratories established a quality assurance department headed by Walter A. Shewhart. The men of this Bell Labs group, which included Harold Dodge, Harry Romig, G. D. Edwards, and eventually, Joseph Juran, are largely responsible for development of most basic quality control techniques.

Dr. Shewhart's 1931 book *The Economic Control of the Quality of Manufactured Product* is generally recognized as the first scientific presentation of quality control theory. In it, Shewhart developed the basis for statistical process control—a "control chart." This device, as we have seen, allows a manufacturer to identify acceptable vs. unacceptable variations in a production process and to "control" the process by tracking actual inspection findings.

Harold Dodge and Harry Romig allowed quality theory to move safely and profitably away from 100 percent inspection with their development of statistically sound acceptance sampling plans. Beginning with a discussion of sampling in 1929, their work eventually led to the publication of the Dodge-Romig "Sampling Inspection Tables" in 1944. MIL-STD-105E is a direct outgrowth of Dodge and Romig's efforts.

As of result of its development and use of these quality control techniques, Bell Telephone reaped substantial benefits in terms of rising quality and reduced costs. Nevertheless, quality control theory was largely ignored by the rest of America's industrial establishment.

12.4 Quality Control Goes to War

With the outbreak of World War II, U.S. factories were called upon as a major resource. The demand for high-quality munitions and military equipment in extremely large quantities quickly stretched America's pre-war quality control procedures to the breaking point. The country was on the horns of an industrial dilemma. On the one hand, defect rates in vital military products were high; scrap losses of over 50 percent were not uncommon. On the other hand, inefficient inspection procedures were creating a serious bottleneck. Efforts to speed inspections of critical products led to high-risk spot checking techniques.

To deal with these problems, the War Department established a committee to develop standards in the area of quality. In 1942, it created a Quality Control Section which included many of the pioneers from Bell Labs. The section's first major contribution was a new set of sampling tables for use by government inspectors. The tables were based on AQLs and included procedures for normal and tightened inspections. Publication of the sampling tables quickly led to a reduction in the inspection backlog. Through use of the tables, the number of Ordinance Department inspectors required per million dollars of acceptable material dropped by 71 percent with corresponding increases in product quality.

In addition, the Office of Production Research and Development (OPRD) of the War Production Board (WPB) implemented a series of training programs in quality control techniques in cooperation with several universities. Despite clear evidence of success in a number of applications, however, the American industrial establishment as a whole was far from receptive to training in statistical quality control techniques. Eugene L. Grant, who offered an OPRD course at Stanford University, recalls being told by one local WPB official that "if we persuaded busy employees of war plants to spend eight valuable days on such a useless venture, we were interfering with the progress of the war. Nearly all the professors ... were destined to meet this viewpoint during the years 1943 to 1945." Efforts to invite top management to attend a portion of the program met with even greater resistance.

Approximately 8,000 people in 25 states ultimately attended the WPB-sponsored quality control courses. While relatively few of them actually implemented their training, the program's graduates formed the first, relatively broad-based quality control network. A number of local societies for quality control were formed and, in 1945, 13 of these local groups joined to create what would eventually become the American Society for Quality Control (ASQC).

As World War II ended, the U.S. stood alone as the world's premier industrial power. The economies of Europe and Japan had been thoroughly ravaged by the war. America's industrial base, on the other hand, had been untouched by the fighting while being fine-tuned at unprecedented levels of capacity and output.

At the same time, the nation's managers saw before them a huge backlog in demand for consumer goods which had been restricted during the course of the war. America's factories couldn't manufacture cars, toasters, radios, and coffeepots fast enough to satisfy the legions of returning GIs who had spent years living in tents and eating K-rations.

In this atmosphere, with virtually no international competition and a seemingly endless market, plant managers were mainly concerned with meeting delivery schedules. Quality wasn't a major issue. If they could get it out the door, they could sell it.

12.5 Quality Spreads to Japan

Across the Pacific, however, the U.S. was faced with the task of helping Japan rebuild an industrial framework which could meet the basic material needs of its citizens. The occupation forces under General Douglas MacArthur saw a particular need for sufficient radios to allow rapid, official communication of news and information, thereby avoiding the spread of potentially explosive rumors among the population. As a result, the Civil Communications Section (CCS) within the Allied Command worked with the leaders of Japan's electronics firms on a variety of managerial and technical issues.

Quality control theory and techniques played an important part in the CCS courses for two reasons. The first was Japan's well-deserved pre-war reputation for the production of shoddy consumer products. The second was the fact that the CCS staff—W. S. Magil, Frank Polkinghorn, Charles Protzman, and Homer

Sarasohn—all were alumni of either Western Electric or Bell Laboratories where quality control techniques had been born in the United States.

From 1949 to 1950, CCS offered two eight-week courses on industrial management for the top executives of these Japanese firms. The courses were particularly successful and influential in shaping the future of the Japanese quality movement for several reasons. First, only top executives were allowed to attend the conferences. No substitutions or delegations of responsibility were allowed during the course of the program. Second, these top executives had only recently been named to their positions following the purging of Japan's wartime corporate management by the Allied Command. As a result, these industrial leaders were receptive to training that could help them carry out their new responsibilities. Third, the new CEOs had all been named from the ranks of their companies' operating managers. They weren't lawyers or accountants; they were engineers and technicians who understood manufacturing problems and could relate to the improvement techniques being offered.

This top-level involvement by a corporate management made up of technically-trained executives was to become the hallmark of Japan's postwar search for quality. It is epitomized by the role of the Japanese Union of Scientists and Engineers (JUSE), which was formed in 1946 to support the study and promotion of new technologies.

JUSE has always had close links with the Japanese Association of Economic Organization, or Keidanren, the nation's leading business association. Since 1948, JUSE's chairman has been either a current or former chairman of the Keidanren.

The promulgation and implementation of quality control techniques has been a primary concern for JUSE since its inception. The organization found the CCS courses so important that, when the American command discontinued them, JUSE continued to offer them itself.

In 1949, JUSE invited W. Edwards Deming to come to Japan to teach a series of courses in statistical quality control. Deming was an American statistician who had served as advisor in sampling to the Chief of Army Ordinance and had helped organize and teach the earliest courses in SPC at Stanford during the war. During the summer of 1950, Deming lectured to over 400 engineers and held conferences for top management. He repeated the process with two trips in 1951.

The impact of implementing the statistical techniques taught in Deming's courses was rapid and substantial. The Furukawa Electric Company reported a 90 percent reduction in rework on insulated wire within three months. The Tanabe

Pharmaceutical Company tripled its output of PAS (para-aminosalicylic acid) with no increase in staff or equipment. The Fuji Steel Company reported a 29 percent drop in the fuel required to produce a ton of steel.

Deming has been widely honored by the Japanese for his contributions to their economic rebirth. Each year, JUSE awards the Deming Prize to companies in several categories who have made the most substantial achievements in the field of quality. In 1960, Deming was awarded the Second Order Medal of the Sacred Treasure by the Emperor as testimony to his status as a national hero.

In 1954, Joseph Juran, another Bell Laboratories alumni, attended a series of JUSE-sponsored quality control seminars for top- and middle-management personnel. Juran's lectures focused on the need for management to address quality concerns which reached far beyond the receiving dock and assembly line. Juran's teachings were reinforced by the work of Armand Feigenbaum, the former manager of quality for General Electric, who also argued for a company-wide quality approach in his book *Total Quality Control*.

Together, the writings of Juran, Feigenbaum, and Deming have expanded the definitions of quality and created the broader discipline of quality assurance, which we will learn more about later in the chapter.

Using the teachings of these American pioneers as a foundation, the Japanese have gone on to build a quality movement that is uniquely their own. Sometimes called *Company-Wide Quality Control (CWQC)*, the Japanese theory of quality management incorporates all aspects of total quality control or quality assurance. It also stresses the substantial involvement of company employees at every level in the quality function. The level of employee involvement is the result of two separate but complementary processes: widespread training in quality control techniques for first-line foremen, and the quality circle movement.

Training for first-line foremen has been widely available and receptively received in Japan since the mid-1950s. In 1956, a 13-week course entitled "QC for First-Line Supervisors" was broadcast, initially over short-wave radio and eventually by NHK, the Japan Broadcasting Corp. During the first year alone, 100,000 copies of the transcript were sold. The radio course was rebroadcast regularly until 1962. Similarly, a weekly television series on quality control was begun in 1959. A *QC Text for Foremen* was published by JUSE in 1960 and sold 200,000 copies during its first seven years on the market.

The *formation of quality control circles* began in 1962 as an outgrowth of JUSE's publication of *Gemba-to-QC*, or *Quality Control for Foremen*. This monthly magazine was designed to be used as a text for groups of workers and a supervisor who would voluntarily join to study quality problems in their workplace. The first quality control circle was registered with JUSE in May 1962, and by 1984 the total number of circles exceeded 180,000. The circles use what are known as *the seven tools*—Pareto charts, cause and effect diagrams, stratification, check sheets, histograms, scatter diagrams, and control charts—to analyze selected problems. Although the circles are voluntary and autonomous, they serve as a link with workers in different divisions and with other layers of management in the company-wide quality control effort.

12.6 International Competition Based on Quality

The success of Japan's quality movement has had a dramatic impact on the nation's competitive position in the international marketplace. During the 1960s and 1970s, Japanese products began winning a significant portion of U.S. market share in a number of different industries. By 1979, for example, imports accounted for almost 22 percent of American auto sales. Similarly, Xerox watched its share of the copier market drop from 96 percent to less than half during the 1970s. The consumer electronics industry quickly became almost completely dominated by the Japanese and other foreign competitors who emulated their techniques.

For much of this period, U.S. industry had perceived the Japanese challenge as one of lower prices based on a cheaper labor force. By 1980, however, Americans were forced to accept the fact that they were being beaten, and beaten badly, in the arena of product quality.

In 1980, Hewlett Packard announced that in a test of 300,000 16K RAM microprocessors supplied by six suppliers—three American and three Japanese—the Japanese chips consistently scored much better. In 1981, 50 percent of Americans felt that the quality of American-made products had dropped during the preceding 5-year period. While the absolute quality of domestic products hadn't dropped, their perceived quality relative to foreign (Japanese) competition certainly had. By 1983, 40 percent of American consumers believed that Japanese cars were better than American models, three times more than a decade earlier. A similar percentage believed that Japanese consumer electronics products outperformed domestic brands.

12.7 The United States Responds

In response to the increasing level of foreign competition, many U.S. manufacturers have recognized the importance of product and service quality as a strategic element for their long-term business plans. A 1987 poll by Gallup/ASQC, for example, found that more top corporate managers saw quality as a critical issue for their company over the next 10-year period than any other topic.

To address this concern, American corporations have rediscovered the work of Deming, Juran, and Feigenbaum, along with newer proponents of quality such as Philip Crosby. These companies have implemented quality improvement programs of varying types and formats. Most of these programs featured the basic statistical quality control techniques of acceptance sampling plans, vendor certification programs, and statistical process controls.

While results have varied from corporation to corporation, there clearly have been a large number of major successes. The Ford Motor Company, for example, reports that the number of owner-reported problems on its cars fell 66 percent from 1980 to 1987. Hewlett Packard, which established more than 1,000 quality teams as part of its quality control program, saw wave soldering defects fall from 5,500 ppm to less than 100 ppm within 2 years. Xerox reports that, as a result of its vendor certification programs, defect rates on incoming components have dropped from an estimated 10,000 to 20,000 ppm in 1980 to less than 400 in 1987.

Perhaps the most dramatic symbol of improvement was reported by Hewlett Packard, which had aroused the U.S. electronic industry with its 1980 test of supplier chips. By 1987, as a result of its vendor certification programs, Hewlett Packard had sufficient confidence in its supplier quality levels and its own process controls to suspend all incoming inspection of chips.

12.8 An Introduction to Quality Assurance

Throughout this text, we have defined quality as conformance to predetermined specifications. The quality control techniques we have learned are methods of ensuring that our finished products will meet this measure of quality. Our efforts have been focused on the assembly line itself, from acceptance of incoming supplies and materials through the various steps of production, to the shipping of our final product.

Following World War II, the leading quality theorists—Juran, Feigenbaum, and Deming—moved substantially beyond this quality viewpoint and created a broader discipline which has been called *quality assurance*.

A New Definition of Quality

The development of quality assurance is largely based on a new, expanded definition of quality itself. Quality assurance looks beyond the question of whether a product meets its specifications. Quality assurance examines the establishment of the specifications themselves and asks a single, fundamental question: "Does the product satisfy the customer's needs?"

While this question seems simple, the answer may not be. Customers, in fact, have a variety of needs. Take this comparison of two automobiles as an example.

One is a boxy subcompact with an extremely small engine, no air conditioning or radio, a Spartan vinyl interior, and a hard, bouncy ride. The other is a finely crafted sedan with superior power and acceleration, excellent handling, an all-leather interior, comprehensive climate control, a Dolby stereo system, and anti-lock brakes.

Which is the quality product?

For John Jones, the choice is clear: the boxy subcompact. Why? Because Mr. Jones needs a "station car" which he will use daily to drive the three-quarters of a mile between his home and the commuter railroad. It will probably never leave this short, simple route, since it is the family's third car. They already have a station wagon which they use for most family travel, and Mr. Jones' son drives a late-model compact.

Mr. Jones' needs in a "station car" are simple. The car must start reliably so that he will always catch his train, and it must be inexpensive since his bills are already getting a little out of hand. The subcompact meets both these criteria. It has a good reputation for reliability, and it's extremely cheap. Mr. Jones doesn't want to drive fast or listen to the radio. He simply wants to get to the station.

For Mary Smith, the choice is equally clear: the luxury sedan is the quality automobile. Smith is a real estate broker who specializes in the sale of expensive homes to wealthy clients. Smith spends a considerable amount of time in her car traveling around the metropolitan area. She needs to get around quickly and comfortably. Since she often drives her clients to visit prospective new homes, she also wants to make a good impression. The luxury sedan, with its excellent reputation and considerable "snob appeal," is perfect in this regard. While the car is certainly expensive, Smith views it as a business investment and feels that it is worth the money.

As we can see, both these customers have their own sets of needs—their own specifications—and these needs are based on the uses to which they will put the product. Consequently, Juran has proposed a widely accepted, shorthand definition of quality as *"fitness for use."*

We should also note that these two customers' needs are many and varied and go far beyond the physical description of the product. Correspondingly, ANSI/ASQC Standard A3-1978 defines quality as "the totality of features and characteristics of a product or service that bear on its ability to satisfy given needs."

These various "features and characteristics" cover a wide range of areas:

Technical considerations include physical specifications of a product and, in the case of automobiles or other machines, its performance capabilities. Smith, for example, wants leather seats and "zero-to-sixty" acceleration in 6.2 seconds. Jones will accept less.

Psychological characteristics are issues of taste, beauty, styling, status, and so on. As we've seen, Smith wants her car to make a positive impression on her wealthy clients. Jones couldn't care less.

Time-oriented needs and specifications have been a major addition to the realm of quality concerns. For example, Jones' primary interest is in the reliability of his "station car": How well will it perform over time? He is also extremely concerned with the car's maintainability: How quickly and easily can he have it serviced when it breaks down? (Reliability engineering has become a major field of study in its own right which we will discuss in greater detail later in the chapter.)

Contractual issues involve product warranties, service guarantees, and other legal issues surrounding the product purchase. Jones only received what he expected and wanted with his subcompact—a 1-year/12,000 mile "drive train" warranty. Smith, on the other hand, was considerably reassured by her long-term guarantee covering any problems which might occur throughout the car.

Ethical features include courtesy, reliability, and honesty of service staff. Smith expected that the sales staff be extremely responsive to her questions regarding the car's capabilities and performance. Jones, on the other hand, purchased the car at a substantial discount from a high-volume dealership. He neither expected nor received much personal attention.

Product Quality vs. Product Cost

As we have seen, both Smith and Jones have considered the purchase price in determining which was the "quality" car for them. For Jones, price was a primary determinant in making his decision. Smith, on the other hand, felt that the sedan's "features and characteristics" sufficiently met her needs to make the price acceptable.

This critical weighing of features vs. price is essential in any evaluation of product quality.

"Quality," Armand Feigenbaum pointed out, "does not have the popular meaning of 'best' in any absolute sense. It means 'best for certain customer conditions.' These conditions are (a) the actual use and (b) the selling price of the product. Product quality cannot be thought of apart from product cost."

Total Quality Control

As the definition of quality expanded beyond simple conformance to specifications, the responsibility for quality control extended beyond the confines of the assembly line.

> Quality control enters into all phases of the industrial production process, starting with the customer's specification and the sale to him, through design engineering and assembly through shipment of the product to a customer who is satisfied with it and ending with proper installation and field service.
>
> *Armand Feigenbaum*

Total Quality Control (TQC), as outlined in Feigenbaum's 1954 book of that name, identified quality responsibilities for units of the corporation which previously had not been formally involved in quality control efforts. "Quality," said Feigenbaum, "is everybody's job."

A fundamental assumption of TQC is that improved quality cannot be achieved unless all of the quality control centers work together.

By addressing these new centers and identifying top management's responsibilities, TQC represented a coordinated, company-wide philosophy and approach to achieving quality throughout all stages of the production process. With enhancements and additional contributions by Deming, Juran, and other theorists, TQC provides a format for most corporate quality assurance programs.

The expansion of corporate responsibilities for quality can be seen in Feigenbaum's analysis of the four "jobs of quality control": new design control, incoming material control, product control, and special process studies.

New design control represents the broadest departure from the traditional assembly line-based quality control functions we have studied in this text. This quality control task deals with the actual specification of a product's appropriate characteristics and features relative to its cost. It begins with the fundamental task of identifying the product's proposed customer and reviewing the full range of the customer's needs. Then, product designers attempt to maximize customer's ultimate satisfaction through specification of the product's various features and characteristics.

A major objective of new design control is to identify and eliminate any defect-prone designs and other potential quality problems prior to actual manufacturing and product use. This requires the interaction of personnel from a broad range of corporate units and technical specialties: marketing, design engineering, environmental engineering, reliability engineering, manufacturing engineering, purchasing, shipping, and customer service.

It is important to note that *product reliability* is now recognized as a critical feature affecting overall product quality, and the specification of product reliability is an important part of new design control. Reliability is defined as the probability that an item will perform a required function under stated conditions for a stated period of time. Reliability engineers quantify a product's reliability using such measurements as Mean Time Between Failures (MTBF), Failure Rates, Mean Time to First Failure (MTFF), Mean Time Between Maintenance, b_{10} (the life during which 10 percent of the population would have failed), and others. As with AQLs, a finished product's overall reliability measures are made up of reliability measurements for all of its component parts. In calculating reliability, therefore, reliability engineers must estimate total product reliability among the various components and subsystems.

The entire concept of New Design Control is based on the assumption, which we have already seen, that quality problems become more expensive as they move along the production process. Eliminating potential defects at the design stage, therefore, can have a profound impact on our overall product quality and the costs of attaining that quality level.

Incoming material control includes acceptance sampling and vendor certification programs which we have already discussed in chapter 5. Quality assurance theory, however, has significantly expanded the quality responsibilities of the corporate purchasing department and changed the way many corporations structure their supplier relations programs.

Traditionally, procurement departments viewed suppliers with suspicion and based purchasing decisions primarily on bid prices for relatively short-term contracts. As the end of the contract approached, the company would again seek bids and award the next short-term contract to whichever vendor proposed the lowest price. This approach results in generally low quality levels and limits vendor interest in improvement programs, since vendors never know if they will win the next contract.

This approach can also substantially increase a company's total cost for materials and components. Total cost includes not only the original purchase price of a component but also subsequent costs for inspection, scrap, and rework. The vendor with the lowest initial purchase price, therefore, may have the highest total cost as a result of the additional costs incurred from poor quality. In the words of W. Edwards Deming, "He that has a rule to give his business to the lowest bidder deserves to get rooked."

Consequently, quality-conscious manufacturers are now looking beyond a supplier's initial bid price for materials and components; they make purchasing decisions on vendor quality ratings and the resulting total price.

In an effort to increase vendor quality, manufacturers are establishing long-term "teamwork" relationships with suppliers who have been receptive to this approach. These manufacturers require that vendors utilize a full range of quality control tools in their facilities. Frequently, manufacturers will provide considerable technical assistance and training to help in the implementation of these quality control programs. Manufacturers will also involve vendors in the earliest stages of their own new product development to ensure the highest quality design for component parts and materials.

In return, manufacturers have moved away from annual purchasing and now offer certified vendors multi-year agreements or, in some cases, "life of the part" contracts. The intimate knowledge of a supplier's operations which results from this teamwork approach has allowed some firms to suspend the bidding process entirely for certain critical components. Instead, manufacturers and certified vendors simply negotiate an agreement based on a mutually acceptable "target price." This target price is generally subject to revision in the event that the supplier can show cost increases for its own materials or operations. On the other hand, manufacturers may look for price reductions from vendors as a result of savings generated through continuing improvements in the vendor's quality programs.

These philosophical and operating changes in supplier relations have substantially reduced the total number of vendors for many manufacturers. During the 1980s, many major companies reduced their supplier base by approximately one-third.

Product control includes all of the statistical controls and sample inspection programs which we have discussed in relation to the manufacturing process. TQC programs, however, extend the quality control function at the tail end of the production process, carrying it out through packaging, product delivery, installation, and ongoing field service.

It is clear that appropriate planning and implementation of quality controls during these phases of the product's life can have a significant impact on customer satisfaction. Juran notes that one department store found that more customer complaints were caused by store activities in packaging, storing, and delivering the product than were caused by the original manufacturer.

Customer service functions have also become a vital source of information on actual customer needs and the product's ability to satisfy those needs. Careful analysis of customer complaints, field service information, and warranty costs can provide valuable feedback on quality problems which originated anywhere in the production process, from initial product development through installation.

Internal vs. External Customers

TQC programs, with their aim of satisfying customers, have also emphasized the concept of the *internal customer*. This means that an assembly worker at one station in the manufacturing process is the customer of the worker at the preceding station. If the first worker doesn't process the component or material correctly, the second worker won't be able to produce a defect-free product. Similarly, the first assembly worker is a customer of the manufacturing engineer who has created a production drawing and process plan for the work station. If the drawing is wrong or the process plan is inaccurate, the assembly worker won't be able to turn out the component which the second assembly worker needs.

If employees at each step in the process ensure that they are satisfying their internal customers, rather than simply "throwing their work over the wall" to the next worker, the chances of obtaining defect-free products are greatly improved.

Big Q vs. Little Q

As we have seen, the expanded definition of quality considers all the features and characteristics associated with a product which affect the customer's satisfaction. Some of these features may have nothing to do with the product itself. Our fictitious Ms. Smith, for example, was concerned with getting prompt and courteous service at her automobile dealership. This further extends responsibility for quality and quality control efforts to corporate support areas which may be totally unrelated to actual production. The term "Big Q" has been used to designate efforts to improve service quality in these corporate support areas in addition to upgrading product quality. Examples are standards for how quickly phones are answered or calls returned, and the accuracy and clarity of invoices.

12.9 Management's Role

"Quality is everybody's job, but quality must be led by management."

This comment by W. Edwards Deming speaks for each of the quality assurance theorists in laying the responsibility for corporate quality clearly on the shoulders of top management. It is generally accepted that quality improvement programs succeed only if they have the enthusiastic support and ongoing involvement of senior corporate executives. As we have seen, early and continuous involvement by top management in Japan's quality movement served as a foundation for that country's dramatic achievements.

12.10 Continuous Improvement and Zero Defects

Among the prescriptions for management proposed by Deming and others is the need to continuously strive for improvements in the system of production and the quality level of finished products.

Feigenbaum's fourth "job of quality control," for example, is "special process studies," which he defined as "investigations and tests to locate the causes of defective products and to determine the possibility of improving quality characteristics."

As we have seen in our discussion of statistical process controls, once the process is in control, additional improvements in quality levels can only come through efforts to improve the capabilities of the process itself.

The objective of continuous improvement has been incorporated into the Japanese quality movement and is viewed as another foundation for that country's successes.

The concept of continuous improvement has been pressed to its logical conclusion through a movement called *zero defects* which developed at the Martin Company in the early 1960s and which was popularized by Philip Crosby, a former Martin employee, in his 1979 book *Quality Is Free*.

The zero defects program grew out of the Martin Company's experiences in the production of Pershing missiles for the U.S. Army. In 1961, as a result of extensive inspection and testing, the company delivered a missile with no defects. Later that year, the company committed to and did deliver a second missile both ahead of schedule and with no defects. The zero defects program as articulated at Martin emphasized employee motivation and strived to promote "a constant, conscious desire to do the job (any job) right the first time."

Although our goal is to do the job right the first time, zero defects, which maintains that the only AQL is no defects at all, continues to be controversial. Juran, for example, counters that "the concept has value as a long-range objective, since it implies the need for never-ending improvement …. In contrast, if we decree defect-free product as a short-range objective, such a goal is in the great majority of cases not attainable. In such cases, the risk is that the decree will be counterproductive by shutting off efforts to reach attainable goals."

Chapter Summary

1. Inspections were the first quality control techniques to be used in the American system of mass production that developed in the nineteenth century.

2. Statistical quality control techniques were introduced by Dr. Walter Shewhart and the pioneers of Bell Laboratories' Quality Assurance Department.

3. During World War II, training in statistical quality control tools was offered to over 8,000 engineers and managers by the War Production Board and various universities. Acceptance sampling plans were used to improve inspection procedures.

4. Following World War II, American interest in quality control lagged as manufacturers were faced with huge unmet demands for consumer goods, coupled with little foreign competition.

5. In Japan, quality control techniques were first introduced in management courses offered by the Civil Communications Section (CCS) of the Allied Command. The courses were partly a response to Japan's pre-war reputation for the manufacture of low-quality consumer goods.

6. A hallmark of the Japanese quality movement has been the enthusiastic support and ongoing involvement of the nation's top corporate management. This is epitomized by the role of JUSE, the organization which invited W. Edwards Deming and Joseph Juran to teach during the early 1950s.

7. Another characteristic of Japan's quality efforts has been the broadbased involvement of employees at all levels of the corporation. This can be seen in the widespread availability of training in quality control techniques for first-line supervisors and development of hourly production workers. It can also be seen in quality control circle movement.

8. During the 1970s, the success of Japan's quality movement has allowed it to win substantial U.S. market shares in a number of industries. In response to this competitive threat, a large number of American companies have renewed their interest in quality theory, implemented quality control programs, and achieved substantial improvements in the quality level of their products.

9. Since World War II, the broader discipline of quality assurance has developed.

10. Quality assurance's new definition of quality goes beyond conformance to predetermined specification. The new definition of quality is based on the needs of the customer.

11. Quality is now defined as "the totality of features and characteristics of a product or service that bear on its ability to satisfy given needs."

12. These "features and characteristics" include time-based parameters such as reliability, psychological features such as beauty and styling, and service characteristics such as courtesy and promptness.

13. The expanded definition of quality gives quality control responsibilities to new areas of the corporation, e.g., product development or marketing. These company-wide quality control programs have been called Total Quality Control.

14. The primary responsibility for improving quality throughout the company rests with top management.

Questions for Chapter 12

1. How did quality control theory originally define "quality"?

2. Why did War Production Board officials resist taking quality control training?

3. What were the reasons for CCS training becoming influential in shaping the Japanese quality movement?

4. Who are three architects in the definition of quality and the creation of quality assurance?

5. What are the "seven tools" used by quality control circles to analyze problems?

6. What are the basic statistical quality control techniques featured by quality improvement programs?

7. What is the new definition of quality on which quality assurance is based?

8. What are the four "jobs of quality control"? Summarize the major tasks of each of these.

9. Explain why contracting with the lowest bidder might result in the highest total cost.

Chapter 12 Project

1. Determine the customers' needs that your product satisfies. Create a profile of a customer who would have needs that your product would satisfy and another profile of a customer who would have needs that your product would not satisfy. How would you change your product to meet a need that is not currently being met?

2. For each of the features and characteristics of your product, give specific examples of how it satisfies given needs.

CHAPTER 13

PEOPLE OF QUALITY

13.1 Introduction

Quality products are manufactured by people. It is these people—all the people making up a company—who can perform the full cycle of tasks that lead to ever higher-levels of product quality.

Over the years, as quality theory has developed, the responsibility for quality control has shifted among individuals and organizations within the company. The application of Taylor's principles of scientific management to mass production manufacturing assigned a primary role to inspectors. These individuals checked products to see if they matched specifications and separated those that didn't conform. Following World War II, efforts to prevent product defects prior to processing led to the establishment of an entirely new group of specialists, the quality engineering department. Further refinements in quality theory expanded the range of quality-related tasks to include reliability engineers, quality assurance staff, trainers, and others.

The gradual development of these various disciplines and their evolution into a common, if not consistently uniform, organization structure has "professionalized" quality and established it as a career path in its own right.

However, while quality professionals perform vital functions in a company's quest for product quality, it is only through the involvement of other staff—product designers, manufacturing engineers, first-line production supervisors, and hourly production workers—that substantial improvements in quality can be achieved and maintained.

The full dedication of a company's workforce to quality can only be achieved if there is an equal commitment on the part of top management. As we have seen, the early involvement of Japanese executives in quality improvement efforts was a cornerstone for that country's accomplishments in this area.

Only top management can solve systemic failures which lead to the majority of quality problems. Only top management can create a state of control which will allow workers to identify and correct deficiencies in manufacturing processes and products.

In order for these employees to improve and maintain the quality of their product, however, they must be in a state of control. They must know what they are supposed to do; they must know what they are doing; and they must be able to regulate the process of their work. Only management can change the system so that employees will have control.

13.2 The Evolution of the Quality Professional

The quality manager found today in corporations, divisions, and manufacturing plants throughout the U.S. is the latest link in an evolutionary chain forged over the course of a century.

As we learned in chapter 12, the first quality control efforts to be used in mass production manufacturing were based on product inspections. As early as the 1820s, individuals were being assigned at the Springfield Armory to measure newly-manufactured, interchangeable musket parts against a series of gauges which had been developed from a model musket. The role of inspection was reinforced with the advent of Frederick W. Taylor's principles of scientific management. Groups of individual inspectors gradually grew to become an inspection department headed by a chief inspector.

In time, the inspection department also came to include some additional support functions such as testing laboratories and inspector training.

Based on the experience of manufacturers during World War II, many companies soon undertook a series of separate tasks aimed at preventing defects in advance through statistical controls rather than finding them after the fact through inspection. Organizationally, this function was embodied in a newly-created quality engineering department. The responsibility of this department was the assessment of processing capabilities, the development of statistical process controls, the analysis of data on process and product quality levels, and the planning of specific quality improvement projects.

In time, a third leg was added to the quality management structure. Many companies established a quality assurance department with responsibility for assuring that the firm's quality improvement goals were being fully achieved. In part, the establishment of a quality assurance organization represented a recognition that quality itself means more than simple conformance to specifications and that quality concerns extend beyond the realm of the manufacturing process itself. Quality assurance assumed responsibility for ensuring that quality considerations were identified and addressed in all phases of the company's operation, from initial market research through new product design, procurement, and manufacturing to final delivery and follow-up customer service. Quality assurance develops company-wide plans for quality improvements, audits actual performance against planned goals, and monitors the costs of quality.

Actual organizational structures and the nominal assignment of responsibilities for quality functions vary from company to company. Nevertheless, this basic triad of quality responsibilities—inspection, quality engineering, and assurance—forms the basis of most quality programs.

The creation of these organizational structures for accommodating the quality function has, in turn, led to the emergence of comparatively new positions on the corporate scene—professional quality specialists. A variety of career paths extend from entry-level inspector jobs through various quality engineering titles up to quality manager, quality director, and vice president of quality.

In many cases, quality specialists enter the field with education and experience in related technical fields. Increasingly, educational programs in industrial engineering offer, or even require, course work in quality control. Additionally, university-based education in engineering may be supplemented by specialized courses in quality control techniques which are available through a variety of sources.

The American Society for Quality Control (ASQC) offers a wide range of courses on aspects of quality control theory and techniques. ASQC also offers a series of examinations by which individuals can obtain certification as quality or reliability engineers.

Alternately, individuals interested in careers in quality can seek specialized university degrees in quality. Various universities are currently offering associate, bachelor, and master's degree programs in quality.

13.3 Quality is Everybody's Job

Unfortunately, the existence of a growing cadre of trained quality professionals does not guarantee an ever-increasing level of product quality.

Inspectors only find defects, they do not prevent them.

Quality engineers can develop tools for controlling a manufacturing process, but they don't operate the production machinery themselves.

Quality assurance staff can talk about the importance of building in quality during the design stage. However, if no one listens to them, it won't help.

Quality control specialists can only ensure the manufacture of quality products when everybody in the company is willing to "specialize in quality."

13.4 Management's Role

To win a quality commitment from their colleagues, quality specialists must first win the support of their company's top management. There are two reasons why this executive-level vote of confidence is absolutely necessary.

First, without a clear show of top-level commitment to quality as a primary corporate goal, other company staff will be reluctant to accept it as a mandate in their own areas of concern. They will question whether the firm's leadership will support and reward the efforts needed to implement quality improvement projects. They may also remain skeptical as to whether quality concerns actually supersede contradictory corporate mandates such as production quotas and cost-based guidelines for purchasing equipment, components, and raw materials.

Secondly, top management is the only group which can actually take steps to eliminate most of the systemic causes of defects inherent in the manufacturing process itself. Only top management can order a product redesign to eliminate quality problems which have been identified at other points in the process. Only top management can implement vendor certification programs, purchase higher quality equipment, restructure the manufacturing process, eliminate production quotas, and increase the levels of employee training and communication. Only top management can decide to stop sending out defective finished products.

Money Talks

The most effective way to win top management support for any quality improvement program is to demonstrate that it will save money rather than increase costs. As we saw in chapter 1, each of our manufacturers was able to determine the costs of poor quality level. By implementing quality improvements, they were able to reduce scrap and rework costs and increase their total usable production. As a result, their unit costs of production fell and their profits rose.

In 1951, Joseph Juran presented a framework for assessing the costs incurred by a company as a result of poor quality. He divided these costs into four categories:

Internal failure costs result from defects found while the product is still in the manufacturing facility. These include scrap costs, rework, 100 percent inspections on lots containing excessive defects, downgrading the selling price on defective products, and so on.

External failure costs result from defects in products shipped to a customer. These include warranty charges, processing of returns and complaints, and others.

Appraisal costs result from efforts to determine whether materials, components, and products conform to specifications. These costs include incoming inspections, final inspections, and quality audits.

Prevention costs are associated with efforts to avoid quality problems before they occur. These include quality planning, new design control, process controls, training, and supplier quality evaluations.

The total cost of quality obtained through this type of analysis can have a striking impact on top management. Costs of quality typically range between 20–40 percent of gross sales. This type of analysis enables quality specialists to communicate in the language of corporate management—dollars and cents.

Just as important, the structure of the analysis allows the quality manager to demonstrate specific areas where substantial savings are possible through implementation of a quality improvement program.

Costs associated with both internal and external failures are avoidable, since these costs decrease as the number of product defects decrease. These avoidable costs will almost always represent the bulk of a company's total cost of quality. Appraisal costs may also offer opportunities for savings if current inspection and testing programs are badly planned and implemented.

To generate savings in these areas, top management must support offsetting, but significantly smaller, expenditures in the area of defect prevention. These costs are usually minimal prior to the start of quality improvement efforts, and each additional dollar of prevention expense generally leads to substantially greater savings from declining failure costs.

A full "cost of quality analysis" requires the active involvement and complete support of the firm's accounting department. However, prior to initiating a quality improvement program, few accounting systems will maintain information on all the components of quality costs. Moreover, even fewer accounting departments will support a move to dramatically expand their accounting framework.

As a first step, quality specialists may be able to estimate the costs of quality by using information gathered from a wide range of sources. The accounting department may be able to provide information on such items as scrap costs, salaries of inspection staff, and warranty claims from the existing accounting structure. Additional costs may be estimated based on information obtained through interviews, sample inspections, and other procedures. For example, the costs of rework may be roughly calculated, based on salaries and estimates of time devoted to this function by hourly employees.

Quality managers should be prepared to deal with initial skepticism regarding their cost of quality analysis. The basis for all estimates, even rough approximations, should be carefully documented. Moreover, the analysis as a whole should err toward the conservative to avoid being dismissed as a series of exaggerated claims. The true level of quality costs will generally allow even the most conservative estimates to present possibilities for dramatic savings.

One Step at a Time

Top management may be reluctant to completely revamp the corporate culture, however, even when presented with potential benefits for the bottom line. The quality department staff may be able to overcome this problem by suggesting that the quality program be initiated with a single, narrowly-identified improvement project. By winning with this flagship effort, the quality department can clearly demonstrate the viability of its approach, and management can taste the first financial rewards of improved quality.

Using both the cost of quality study and the Pareto analysis tools which we have discussed previously, a project should be selected based on the following criteria:

- It should have limited implementation costs in terms of required resources and organizational dislocation.

- It should have a high probability of success.

- It should offer a substantial potential payoff in both reduced costs and higher profits.

- It should have at least some support from the operational managers and line staff who will be required to implement it.

Based on an initial success with a single project, additional commitments in terms of resources and organizational support will be easier to achieve for future improvement efforts.

It is also important that quality managers seek to build on management's initial acceptance of a quality cost analysis by expanding the firm's accounting structure to incorporate these quality cost components. This will allow data for an ongoing analysis of relative costs and savings from subsequent improvement projects. This continuing effort to document a positive impact on profits will be important in maintaining top management support for the quality program as a whole.

Quality Councils

One particularly effective mechanism by which top management can begin implementing a quality improvement program is to establish a company-wide quality council. This group, which should consist of top-level managers from each of the firm's operating and support areas, has responsibility for establishing the company's quality policies and the goals it wishes to achieve. The council will select both the initial improvement project and subsequent improvement efforts. It will also assume responsibility for monitoring the firm's general quality performance and the results of all specific improvement projects.

The combined membership of the council, if selected appropriately, will have the authority to allocate resources and make other policy and procedural changes required to successfully implement specific improvement projects and the quality program as a whole.

It is important that upper management members of the council actively participate in its functioning, rather than delegate the responsibility to lower level staff. This personal participation sends a message of managerial commitment to quality and ensures that the deliberations and decisions of the council are meaningful.

Depending on the size of the company in question, the quality council may utilize a series of divisional quality councils which focus their attention on quality policies, issues, and goals within specific responsibility areas, such as manufacturing or sales. These sub-councils should be chaired by a member of the company-wide quality council.

Improvement Teams

Another official way of upgrading quality is through quality improvement projects. Quality improvement projects are selected for implementation by the quality council. They should be managed by separate improvement teams consisting of representatives from the areas involved in the problem to be corrected.

As we have seen, quality problems often have roots far from the point where they first reach our attention. The radio manufacturer, for example, found a number of problems with defective components following auto-insertion and soldering of the Printed Circuit Boards (PCBs).

One defect resulted from design problems with the PCB itself. Another grew out of a weakness in one of the purchased components. If the manufacturer's quality improvement team had only consisted of staff from the manufacturing department, which had responsibility for the auto-insertion and soldering process, it might never have uncovered the causes of these problems or identified non-manufacturing solutions to them.

The improvement team should have representatives of all organizational units which may be able to identify or offer solutions to problems resulting in product defects. The team members should also have ranks appropriate to the problem they are addressing.

13.5 Enlisting the Troops

Once management has declared war in the fight for improved quality, it will be easier to gather the rest of the army—production workers, first-line supervisors, secretaries, sales representatives, buyers, product designers, engineers, and others.

Unfortunately, many managements wage only a war of words in the fight for quality. They adopt empty slogans, announce impossible improvement targets, focus attention on employee failures, and refuse to address systemic problems which only management can correct. In these cases, it is likely that the call to arms will fall upon deaf ears. Even when it doesn't, the effort is still doomed to defeat, and the firm's employees will feel even more demoralized.

The true message of quality is one which most employees want to hear because it recognizes the importance of their labors and offers them a well-deserved pride in their product. An actual management commitment to quality acknowledges that as much as 80 percent of all defects result from systemic problems which are beyond an individual worker's control. Consequently, managerial support for quality improvement requires the elimination of these obstacles to employee performance and represents a vote of confidence in the worker.

The involvement of individual workers in a company-wide quality improvement program can require a substantial change in the way management thinks about itself and the people who work for it.

It means a move toward two-way communication between supervisors and line workers in companies where employees were trained to simply do what they were told.

PEOPLE OF QUALITY

Workers know, far better than management, where the system is failing and how it leads to product defects. To harness this fundamental knowledge of how the company can improve its performance, management must ensure that workers feel comfortable in openly identifying and discussing product defects and problems in the process. Only when management creates an atmosphere which is free of criticism and blame can this level of open communication flourish.

QC Circles

As we saw in chapter 12, open communication regarding quality has been aided in many Japanese companies through the spontaneous growth of quality control circles, small groups of workers who come together voluntarily with their supervisor to address quality problems in their work area.

While there have been attempts to establish quality control circles in American companies, these efforts have usually grown out of official management-led quality improvement programs rather than through separate employee initiatives. Consequently, their growth has been limited. Moreover, the focus in some U.S. applications has been on the circles' role as a motivational tool rather than as a means of identifying and solving specific quality problems. Nonetheless, quality control circles, when coupled with serious managerial efforts to address systemic, process-related quality issues, have served as a useful tool for encouraging open communication.

Workers' Contribution to Quality

Communication is also fundamental to the workers' contribution to product and process quality. Employees can only be held accountable for their performance when:

1. They know what they are supposed to do

2. They know how well they are doing

3. They are able to correct their performance

For employees to contribute to the quality level of their product, they must be in a state of control.

Production workers must clearly understand the target specifications and acceptable tolerances for processing their material, component, subassembly, or finished product. As we have previously indicated, each work station should have well-documented procedures which include production drawings showing the required specifications for the process' finished product. These procedures and drawings should allow employees to fully understand their duties and the definition of an acceptable product. Management policies should also state unambiguously that quality targets, not production quotas, determine the acceptability of product.

Production workers must also be able to tell whether their product is meeting these target specifications. In some cases, workers may do their own sample inspections based on statistical process control requirements. In these cases, the employee must have clear instructions on when and how inspections are to be conducted. They must have the correct equipment for taking measurements and understand how to use it. They must also understand how to relate their sample measurements to the specifications. In these cases, when the process is being monitored using process control charts, the worker must understand when the chart indicates an unacceptable trend.

In cases where sample measurements may be taken by quality control inspectors, production workers should be informed as quickly as possible of the identification of unacceptable products.

Employees must also be able to correct their performance. They must have authorization to halt production in response to unacceptable trends in control chart readings. They must understand how to adjust their machinery and processing procedures to correct various product defects. Finally, there must be clear guidelines on the circumstances under which employees should seek additional direction from their supervisors.

13.6 Quality Means People

Quality improvement requires respect for the natural pride employees take in their work and a recognition of the contributions they can make toward improving company performance. It requires appropriate levels of training for all staff in both their specific production tasks and relevant quality control skills. By equipping all employees to specialize in quality, we are multiplying our chances of eventually achieving the goal of zero defects.

PEOPLE OF QUALITY

Chapter Summary

1. Inspectors were the first quality specialists.

2. Quality control engineering departments developed following World War II to implement statistical controls aimed at preventing defects before they occurred.

3. Quality assurance departments developed in recognition that quality means more than just conformance to specifications and that quality concerns extend beyond the assembly line. Quality assurance seeks to guarantee that the company's quality goals are being met and that quality issues are addressed in all aspects of company activity.

4. These organizational developments have professionalized the quality function and made it a career path in its own right.

5. Quality specialists, alone, cannot guarantee quality products.

6. Top management support and participation is essential to any quality improvement program.

7. An analysis of the costs of quality is an effective way of winning executive management support for quality.

8. Internal failure costs result from defects which are found before the product leaves the factory.

9. External failure costs result from defects in products shipped to customers.

10. Appraisal costs are the expenses of identifying product defects.

11. Prevention costs are the expenses of efforts to avoid defects before they occur.

12. Proposing and successfully implementing an initial, narrowly-defined quality improvement project is a good way to win support for a general quality improvement program.

13. Establishing a quality council consisting of senior executives from each of the company's operating and support departments is a good way for top management to support and participate in a quality improvement program.

14. Quality improvement projects should be managed by an improvement team consisting of representatives from areas which may be able to identify and offer solutions to the quality problems being addressed.

15. Workers can only contribute toward improved quality when there is an atmosphere of open communication and when they are in a state of "control." "Control" means that they know what they are supposed to do, they know how they are doing, and they are able to correct their performance.

PEOPLE OF QUALITY

Questions for Chapter 13

1. Initially, who had the responsibility for quality control? Following World War II, where had this responsibility shifted? To which groups does quality theory now assign responsibility? In addition to the quality professionals, list other staff members who are vital in achieving and maintaining substantial improvements in quality.

2. Define a state of "control" for line workers.

3. What is the process that aims at preventing defects in advance of final inspection? Which department embodies this responsibility? How does this department perform its responsibility?

4. What are the responsibilities of the quality assurance department?

5. What is the basic triad of quality responsibilities?

6. Give the two reasons why quality specialists must win the support of a company's top management.

7. Name and explain the four categories of assessing the cost of poor quality.

8. Which sources could be used by the quality specialists to estimate the costs of quality?

9. What criteria should be used for choosing the first project to improve quality?

10. Why haven't quality control circles been as successful in the U.S. as they have been in Japan?

Chapter 13 Project

Construct a quality council and an improvement team for your organization. Which members of your organization will you include in each group?

INDEX

Acceptable quality level (AQL)
   AM radio manufacturer, 86
   definition, 81
   for production processes, 133
Acceptance rate, 12-13
Acceptance sampling plan. *See also*
   Probability of acceptance
     calculations
   attribute sampling defined, 89
   consumer's risk in, 186-187
   double sampling plan, 102-105
   MIL-STD-105E, 89-113
   multiple sampling plan, 105-109
   normal inspection, 90-95
   producer's risk in, 186
   reduced inspection, 98-102
   rejects, 112
   sample size, 89
   single sampling plan, 90-102
   tightened inspection, 95-98, 190-192
   true quality level versus measured quality level in, 177-178
American National Standards Institute (ANSI), data processing symbols, 31-33
American Society for Quality Control (ASQC), 260, 279
American system of manufacturing, 258
AM radio manufacturing process
   acceptable quality level at, 86
   facility layout for, 57
   field return analysis at, 215-219
   final inspection for, 204
   incoming inspection for, 83-84, 87-88, 94, 112-113
   Pareto analysis at, 230-231
   Statistical Process Control (SPC) at, 126-128, 165-168
ANSI/ASQC Standard A3-1978, 265
Appraisal costs, 281
Attributes
   control charts for data, 165-168
   measuring quality level by, 153-155
Average quality level, and inspection records, 112-113

Bakery production process, 30-31
   facility layout for, 47-50
   final inspection, 205-206
   flowcharting in, 34, 36
   incoming inspection, 111
   quality control measures at, 71-74
   and Statistical Process Control (SPC), 156-165
Bell Laboratories, 261
   and statistics of quality control, 258-259
Big Q, versus Little Q, 270
Bill of materials, 8-9
Binomial distribution, for probability of acceptance calculations, 182-183
Burn-in process, 217-219

Calibration
   frequency of, 251-252
   standard in, 250-251

Central tendency measures
    and normal distribution curves, 134-144
    population mean, 134-135
    standard deviation, 135-144
Civil Communications Section (CCS), 260-261
Classes of defects, 109-111
    critical defects, 110
    major defects, 110
    minor defects, 110-111
Closet door manufacturing process, 31
    corrective action and savings at, 234-236
    facility layout for, 50-54
    final inspection, 204-205
    flowcharting, 33-35
    incoming inspection for, 93, 96, 98-109
    operating characteristic curves for, 187-190
    quality control procedures at, 62-64, 66-71
    and Statistical Process Control (SPC), 128-153
Communication, need for, in quality improvement program, 285-286
Company-Wide Quality Control (CWQC), 262
Complaint hotlines, and customer satisfaction, 221
Component failures/malfunctions, as source of field returns, 213
Confidence levels, 184-186
Consumer Reports, 221
Consumer's risk, in acceptance sampling plans, 186-187
Continuous improvement, 237, 271
Control charts, 156-60, 258-259, 263
    $1s_m$ control level, 163-164
    $2s_m$ control levels, 162-163
    $3s_m$ control limits, 160-162
    non-random distributions and interpreting results, 164-165
    standard deviation of the sample mean, 159
Control of Quality in Manufacturing, The (Radford), 258
Corrective action
    cost-effectiveness of, 233-236
    identifying, 232-233
    quality control and production costs, 11-15
Costs per unit, 10, 12
Critical defects, 110
Crosby, Philip, 264, 271
Cumulative probability, in probability of acceptance calculations, 184
Customer
    abuse by, as source of field returns, 214
    complaints from, and field returns, 215-219
    external versus internal, 270
    focus groups, 221
    internal versus external, 270
    product specifications by, 2, 3
    surveys of, and product quality, 220-221

Data processing symbols, 32-33
Decision symbol, for flowcharting, 32
Defects per hundred units, 83-84
Deming, W. Edwards, 257, 261, 262, 264, 267, 269, 271
Deming Prize, 262
Device Under Test (DUT), 245, 246, 247
Documentation
    of production process, 25
    and test equipment, 250
Dodge, Harold, 259
Dodge-Romig "Sampling Inspection Tables," 259
Double sampling plan, 102-105
Drawings
    pre-production, 24
    production, 24

Economic Control of Quality of Manufactured Product (Shewhart), 258
Edwards, G. D., 258
Environmental stress, as source of field returns, 214-215
Equipment
    calculating production needs for, 27-28
    for quality control program, 75
Expected results, probability calculations for, 178-182
External failure costs, 281

Facility/facility layout
  for AM radio manufacturing process, 57
  for bakery production process, 47-50, 76
  for closet door manufacturing process, 50-54
  fixed position facilities in, 45
  process flow incompatibilities in, 46
  process layouts in, 45
  product layouts in, 45-46
  for quality control program, 75
Facility components
  guidelines for arranging, 44-45
  for packaging, 44
  for production processing, 44
  for receiving, 43
  for shipping, 44
Federal Communications Commission (FCC), 5
Feigenbaum, Armand, 257, 262, 264, 267, 271
Field data and quality control, 213
  competitive analysis in, 222
  field returns and customer complaints in, 215-219
  market research organizations in, 221
  new defectives, 217-219
  rate of return, 216-217
  reasons for field returns in, 213-215
  sales and profits in, 222
  soliciting customer input, 219-221
Field failures, 213
Field returns
  analysis of, 215
  and customer complaints, 215-219
  reasons for, 213-215
Final assembly, 22-23
Final inspection, 71
  for AM radio manufacturing process, 200-204
  for bakery production process, 205-206
  for closet door manufacturing process, 204-205
  and fitness for use decision, 206-207
  need for, 199-200
First-line foremen, training for, 262
First piece inspection, and process control, 168-169
Fitness for use decision, 206-207

Fixed costs, 10
Fixed position facilities, 45
Flowcharting
  of bakery production process, 34, 36, 72-73
  of closet door manufacturing process, 33-34, 35, 67-69
  of manufacturing process, 31-36
Flowline symbol, for flowcharting, 32-33
Ford Motor Company, 264
Frequency distribution, 130-131, 145, 150
Functional specifications, 3

Gauging system, 258
Gemba-to-QC, 262
Government, role in regulating manufacturers, 4-5
Grant, Eugene L., 259

Hewlett Packard, 263, 264
Histogram, 131-132
  of door panel widths, 131, 147, 151
  and normal distribution curve, 133, 137

Improvement teams, 283-284
Incoming inspection, 62-64, 81-82
  acceptable quality level in, 86-88
  for AM radio manufacturing process, 83-84, 87-88, 94, 112-113
  for bakery production process, 111
  classes of defects in, 109-111
  for closet door manufacturing process, 62-64
  inspection records and average quality level in, 112-113
  measuring quality in, 82-85
  MIL-STD-105E, 89
  100 percent inspection in, 111
  rejects in, 112
  sample inspections in, 88-94
  sampling plans in, 95-99, 102-109
  and supplier certification instead of, 114-115
Incoming material control, 268-269
Industrial Revolution, quality control during, 258

Industry standards, 4
Inspection plans, *See* Sampling plans
Inspection points
    in final inspection, 71, 199-207
    in incoming inspection, 62-64
    process control points as, 64-71
Inspection records
    and average quality level, 112-113
    and product quality records, 202-204
Internal failure costs, 281
Inventory
    just-in-time (JIT) philosophy for, 23, 29
    minimizing storage of incoming and finished goods, 28-29

Japan
    quality circles in, 285
    quality control in, 260-263
Japanese Association of Economic Organization, 261
Japanese Union of Scientists and Engineers (JUSE), 261
Job shops, 25
Juran, Joseph, 257, 258, 262, 264, 267, 271, 280
Just-in-time (JIT) philosophy, 23, 29

Keidanren, 261

Little Q, versus Big Q, 270

Magil, W. S., 260
Major defects, 110, 111
Make versus buy decision, 24-25
Management
    role of, in quality movement, 270-271
    support of, for quality improvement program, 280-284
Manual operation symbol, for flowcharting, 32
Manufacturing defects, as source of field returns, 214
Manufacturing feasibility study, 24-25
    documentation of, 25
    and pilot run, 24
    and preproduction drawings, 24
    and production drawings, 24
Manufacturing process
    American system of, 258
    basic steps in, 22-23
    in-control, 129, 155
    controlling variations in, 128-129, 155
    flowcharting in, 31-36, 67-69, 72-73
    increasing capabilities in, 144-153
    and inspection points, 62-71
    manufacturer's product specifications in, 2-3
    measuring capabilities in, 129-132
    as out-of-control, 129, 155-156
    primary processing in, 21
    secondary processing in, 21
Manufacturing process planning
    balancing production line in, 26-28
    implementing process in, 29-30
    laying out overall process in, 25-26
    minimizing inventory storage in, 28-29
    sequence of processing steps in, 26
    specifying steps in, 23-25
Manufacturing process steps
    final assembly, 22-23
    packaging, 23
    processing, 22
    receiving, 22
    shipping, 23
    subassembly, 22
Martin Company, 271
MIL-STD-105E, 177, 259
    accepting/rejecting shipment, 93-94
    classification of defects, 109-111
    inspection levels in, 90-91
    inspection sampling plans, 95-109
    for rejects, 112
    scope of, 245
    selecting sample size, 89-93
    title page of, 244
Minor defects, 110-111
Multiple sampling plans, 105-109
    advantages/disadvantages of, 109

National Bureau of Standards, 148
National Institute of Standards and Technology (NIST), 148
    calibration services by, 250-251

INDEX

Net savings, for quality solution, 233-236
New design control, 267-268
Non-random distributions, on control chart, 164-165
Normal distribution and central tendency, 133-153
Normal inspection plan, 93-95
Normalized distribution and central tendency, 133-153
  normalized values, 138-142
Normalized value, and central tendency measurement, 138-139, 142

Office of Production Research and Development (OPRD), 259
100 percent inspection, 111
  for AM radio manufacturing process, 200-204
  for bakery production process, 206
  for closet door manufacturing process, 205
Operating characteristic curves, in probability of acceptance calculations, 187-190
Operating manuals, 252

Packaging, 23
  facility workstation for, 44
  inspection and, 205
Pareto analysis, 229-231
Parts per million (ppm), 84-85
Percent defective, 82-83
  advantages of, 84
Personnel, 277-278
  and evolution of quality professional, 278-279
  importance of feedback from, 29-30
  involvement of, in quality improvement programs, 75, 284-286
  team work among, 279-280
Pilot run, 24
  monitoring, 29
Polkinghorn, Frank, 260
Population mean, in Statistical Process Control (SPC), 134-135
Population variance, and central tendency measurement, 136
Powers, JD, Inc., 221

Pre-production drawings, and manufacturing feasibility, 24
Prevention costs, 281
Probability of acceptance calculations. *See also* acceptance sampling plan
  binomial distribution, 182-183
  consumer's risk, 186-187
  cumulative probability, 184
  and expectations, 178-182
  levels of confidence in, 184-186
  operating characteristic curves, 187-190
  producer's risk, 186
  tightened inspection plan, 190-192
Problem analysis
  cost-effectiveness of corrective action in, 233-236
  finding source of problem in, 232
  identifying corrective action in, 232-233
  Pareto analysis, in, 229-231
  troubleshooting versus quality improvement in, 228-229
Process control points, 64
  action step in, 65-66
  for closet door manufacturing process, 66-71
  decision step in, 65-66
Process control sites, 125-128
Process layouts, 45
Process symbol, for flowcharting, 32
Producer's risk, in acceptance sampling plans, 186
Product control, 269-270
Product cost, versus product quality, 266-267
Product dissatisfaction, as source of field returns, 215
Product infant mortality, 217
Product inspections, and quality control, 59-61
Production costs
  for costs per unit, 12
  effect of quality control on, 11-14
  for fixed costs, 10
  for scrap costs, 11-12
  for total cost, 10-11
  for variable costs, 8-9
Production drawings, 24
Production line, balancing, 26-28
Production line manufacturers, 26
Production requirements, 27-28, 47

Product knowledge, as source of field returns, 215
Product layouts, 45-46
Product processing (manufacturing), facility workstation for, 44
Product quality, versus product cost, 266-267
Product quality audits
   for AM radio manufacturing process, 202-204
   for closet door manufacturing process, 205
   for bakery, 206
Product reliability, 268
Product requirements, 3-5
Product specifications
   of customers', 2
   in final inspections, 201-202
   functional, 3
   of manufacturer's, 2-3
   and tolerances, 5-7
Profit
   effect of quality control on, 14-15
   as indication of changing quality levels, 222
Protzman, Charles, 260
Purchasing department, responsibility of, 9

"QC for First-Line Supervisors," 262
QC Text for Foremen, 262
Quality assurance, 257
   Big Q versus Little Q, 270
   internal versus external customers, 270
   new definition of quality, 264-266
   product quality versus product cost, 266-267
   Total Quality Control (TQC), 267-270
Quality control
   basis resources for, 74-75
   effect of, on production costs, 11-14
   effect of, on selling price and profit, 14-15
   inspection points in, 62-71, 81-115
   inspections for, 88-115
   mathematics of, 177-192
   measurements, 81-88
   and product inspections, 59-61
   and statistical process control, 125-169
   use of field data for, 213-222

Quality control circles, 285
   formation of, 262-263
Quality Control for Foremen, 262
Quality control program
   equipment in, 75
   facilities in, 75
   staff in, 75
Quality costs, 280-282
Quality councils, 283
Quality improvement, versus troubleshooting, 228-229
Quality improvement loop, 227
   action, 236
   analysis, 228-236
   observation, 227-228
   repeating the cycle, 237
Quality improvement program
   improvement teams in, 283-284
   initiation of, 282-283
   involvement of personnel in, 284-286
   management support for, 270-271, 280-284
   need for communication in, 285-286
   quality councils in, 283
Quality Is Free (Crosby), 271
Quality level, true versus measured, 177-178
Quality measurements
   defects per hundred units, 83-84
   parts per million (ppm), 84-85
   percent defective, 82-83
Quality movement, 257
   Bell laboratories and statistics of quality control, 258-259
   continuous improvement and zero defects, 271
   during Industrial Revolution, 258
   international competition, 263
   in Japan, 260-263
   management's role in, 270-271
   quality assurance in, 264-270
   United States responds, 263-264
   during World War II, 259-260
Quality professional, evolution of, 278-279

Radford, G. S., 258
Range of variation, in measuring process capability, 130
Rate of return, calculating, 216-217

INDEX

Receiving, 22
    facility workstation for, 43
Record-keeping
    and calibration, 252
    and quality control, 109, 112-113
Reduced inspection plan, 98-102
Rejects, and quality control, 112
Reliability engineering, 219, 268
Romig, Harry, 258, 259

Safety, inspection requirements for, 110-111
Sales, as indication of changing quality levels, 222
Sales staff, and field data on product quality, 220
Sample size, selecting, 89-93
Sampling and inspection by attributes, 89
Sampling plans
    double, 102-105
    MIL-STD-105E, 89-113
    multiple, 105-109
    normal, 90-95
    reduced, 98-102
    single, 90-102
    tightened, 95-98, 190-192
Sarasohn, Homer, 260-261
Scientific management, principles of, 277, 278
Scrap costs, 11-12
Selling price, effect of quality control on, 14-15
Seven tools, of quality control circle, 263
Shewhart, Walter A., 258
Shipping/shipments, 23
    accepting/rejecting, 93-94
    facility workstation for, 44
Single sampling plan, 90-102
Springfield Armory, 258, 278
Staff. *See* Personnel
Standard deviation
    and acceptable quality level, 137-144
    in Statistical Process Control (SPC), 135-144
Statistical Process Control (SPC)
    and acceptable quality level, 133
    for AM radio manufacturing process, 126-128, 165-168
    for bakery production process, 156-165
    for closet door manufacturing process, 134-153
    control charts in, 156-168
    controlling variation in, 155-156
    first piece inspection in, 168-169
    histogram, 131-132, 134, 137, 147, 151
    mean, 134-135
    measures of central tendency in, 134-144
    measuring process capabilities in, 129-130
    measuring quality level by attribute in, 153-155
    normal distribution curves in, 133-153
    population variance, 13
    process control sites in, 125-128
    range, 130
    standard deviation, 135-144
    variations in manufacturing process in, 128-129
Subassembly, 22
Supplier certification, 114-115, 264
Supplier's risk, in acceptance sampling plan, 178

Taylor, Frederick W., 258, 277, 278
Test equipment, 248-252
    accuracy, 249-250
    calibration of, 250-252
    for quality control program, 75
    range, 248-249
    specification data page, 249
    user's manual, 249
Test procedures, 243
    acceptability criteria in, 247
    definitions in, 246
    diagrams in, 246-247
    procedure in, 246
    references in, 247
    scope in, 245-246
    test equipment in, 246
    title page in, 244
Test reports, 247
    recommendations in, 248
    report summary in, 247
    test data in, 247-248
    test procedure in, 248

Tightened inspection plan, 95-98
   and probability of acceptance
     calculations, 190-192
Tolerances
   definition of, 6
   and product specifications, 5-7
Total cost, 10-11
Total Quality Control (Feigenbaum), 262
Total Quality Control (TQC), 267-270
   in incoming material control, 268
   in new design control, 267-268
   in product control, 269
   in special process studies, 270
Troubleshooting, versus quality
   improvement, 228-229

Underwriters Laboratories (UL)
   standards, 4
United States
   Industrial Revolution, 256
   quality circles in, 285
   quality control in, 263-264
   World War II, 259-260

User's manual, 249, 252

Variable costs, 8-9, 11
Variable measurements, 153-154
Vendor certification programs, 114-115, 264
Visual inspection
   for AM radio manufacturing
     process, 201-202
   for bakery production process, 206
   concerns in, 201-202

War Production Board (WPB), 259
Western Electric, 261
World War II, quality control during, 259-260

Xerox, 263, 264

Zero defects, 227, 271